IFS ICAEW

Self-Assessment for Income Tax

N. A. BARR

S. R. JAMES

A. R. PREST

Heinemann Educational Books · London

ISBN 435 84060 6

First published 1977

Published for The Institute of Chartered Accountants in England and Wales
and The Institute for Fiscal Studies
by Heinemann Educational Books Ltd., 48 Charles Street, London W1

Printed in Great Britain by George Berridge & Co. Ltd., London & Thetford

Contents

List of Tables and Figures

Figures

Preface

Our first thanks are due to the Institute for Fiscal Studies and the Institute of Chartered Accountants which jointly financed this study and provided assistance when needed but did not interfere in the slightest degree with the detailed progress of the study. No academic worker could wish for more liberal treatment than that which we received from our sponsoring bodies.

Our Advisory Committee was appointed jointly by the two Institutes. It consisted of the following members:

David Brewer, Finlay Robertson
Anthony Christopher, Joint General Secretary, Inland Revenue Staff Federation
Sir Arthur Cockfield, Chairman, Price Commission
Professor Harold Edey, London School of Economics
Halmer Hudson, Robson Rhodes & Co.
Roy Jennings, Arthur Andersen & Co.
Professor S. J. Prais, National Institute of Economic and Social Research
I. P. A. Stitt, Arthur Andersen & Co.

The Committee was extremely generous in the time it gave to helping us with the general direction of the enquiry, commenting on drafts of various chapters and generally giving sagacious advice to authors who had (and no doubt, still have) a very great deal to learn about the UK income tax system.

Next we must single out a number of officials at the Inland Revenue who showed the greatest interest in our work, spent a great deal of time reading it and discussing it with us and throughout gave us the most patient hearing even if they disagreed with our thoughts and proposals. The number of propositions which are either wrong or wrong-headed or both would have been far greater were it not for this quite indispensable source of advice and assistance.

We should also acknowledge in similar vein the very considerable help given to us by officials connected with income tax administration in Washington D.C., Ottawa and Stockholm. Their openness and patience both in verbal discussion and written assistance far exceeded what we had any right to expect. Without their help, the descriptive material in Chapter III simply could not have been written with any pretence of authenticity.

Then we had a great deal of help on particular points from a large number of other individuals and organisations both in this country and overseas. There are so many of these that it would be impossible to name them individually but our thanks to them collectively are genuine enough all the same.

We must also acknowledge our indebtedness to the J. Walter Thompson Company Ltd. for advice on the design of the proposed tax return form in Chapter VI, Appendix 1. We also gratefully acknowledge the permission of the Board of Inland Revenue to quote from the Tax Return Guide; and that from *The Evening Standard* and *Punch* to reproduce the cartoons on p. 41 and p. 45. And not least we acknowledge secretarial and typing assistance at the London School of Economics from Mrs. M. A. Romaine, Miss A. Kowczyk, Miss E. Fennelly and Mrs. B. A. Silver.

Finally, although particular authors were largely responsible for particular chapters we have all vigorously criticised one another's drafts and fully accept joint responsibility for the work as a whole. No one else but us should be blamed for its faults.

N. A. BARR, London School of Economics
S. R. JAMES, University of Exeter
A. R. PREST, London School of Economics

October 1976

Glossary of Terms

Fuller definitions are given at the appropriate points in the text. References to specific forms all appear under the general heading FORMS. A list of Inland Revenue forms and explanatory literature appears in Appendix II–1.

AGE ALLOWANCE: A personal allowance granted to elderly people with modest incomes.
ALLOWANCES: Income regarded as tax-free irrespective of its source or of how it is spent. See also *Exemptions* and *Tax-Credits*.
ASSESSMENT: The detailed calculation of tax liabilities.
A-TAX: Income tax payable in Sweden on employment income (broadly equivalent to tax liability in the UK on income taxed under Schedule E, q.v.). See also *B-Tax*.
AUDIT: The detailed examination of books and accounts to establish the degree of accuracy of the information about income, numbers of dependants, etc. appearing on a tax return. See *Verification*.
AVERAGE RATE OF TAX: The amount paid in tax as a percentage of income received during a given period.
AVOIDANCE: The manipulation of one's affairs, within the law, to reduce one's tax liability.
BASIC RATE OF TAX: The rate of tax applying in the UK to the first £5,000 (1976/77) of taxable income.
B-TAX: Income tax payable in Sweden on non-employment income (broadly equivalent to tax liability in the UK on income taxed under Schedule D, q.v.). See also *A-Tax*.
BMF (Business Master File): The master file of all corporate tax returns in the USA.
CHECKING RETURNS: The examination of tax returns to ensure consistency, e.g. that the arithmetic is correct.
CITS (Community Income Tax Service): Assistance to taxpayers organised by the Government of Manitoba.
CODE: A means of summarising the amount of allowances and deductions due to a taxpayer, so as to determine his taxable income.
CODING-IN: The UK method of adjusting a taxpayer's code to recover outstanding tax liability.

CODING-OUT: The UK method of adjusting a taxpayer's code to deal with the tax liability on small amounts of income from sources other than employment.
CUMULATION: A system of withholding tax from income at source in such a way that the amount of tax withheld in any week (month) during the tax year is based on that week's (month's) addition, positive or negative, to the cumulated total of taxable income (i.e. cumulated gross income less cumulated allowances and deductions) since the beginning of the tax year. See also *Non-Cumulation.*
CURRENT YEAR BASIS OF ASSESSMENT: The assessment to tax in any one year if based on the income received in that year. See also *Preceding Year Basis of Assessment.*
DEDUCTIONS: Income that is free of tax provided it is spent on certain types of expenditure, e.g. the deduction for qualifying life assurance premia.
DIF COEFFICIENTS: Probabilities of error in tax returns revealed through discriminant function analysis.
DIRECT COLLECTION ASSESSMENT: The technique of assessing and collecting tax four times a year on some incomes that are assessed on a current year basis under Schedule E (q.v.) but not covered by PAYE (q.v.).
EMERGENCY CODE: The code applied by a UK employer to an employee for whom no code (q.v.) has been received from the tax office. The value of the code is the same as the single person's allowance and is operated on a non-cumulative basis (q.v.).
EVASION: The illegal manipulation of one's affairs to reduce one's tax liability.
EXEMPTIONS: Synonymous with *Allowances.*

FORMS

FORM P45: A form issued by employers in the UK to employees leaving their employment during the tax year. The form gives details of cumulative earnings, tax withheld and National Insurance contributions withheld for the tax year and the employee's code (q.v.).
FORM P60: A form issued by employers in the UK to employees in their employment at the end of the tax year. The form gives details of cumulative earnings, tax withheld, and National Insurance contributions withheld for the tax year and the employee's code (q.v.).
FORM T4: A form issued by employers in Canada to each person employed by them at any time during the tax year. The form gives details of earnings in that employment, tax and Social Insurance contributions withheld and the employee's Social Insurance number.
FORM T5: A form issued by payers of interest in Canada to each person who has received interest from them during the tax year. The form shows total interest paid.

FORM T600: A form issued by payers of dividends in Canada to each person who has received a dividend payment from them during the tax year. The form shows total dividend payments.

FORM W2: A form issued by employers in the USA to each person employed by them at any time during the tax year. The form gives details of earnings in that employment, tax and Social Security contributions withheld and the employee's Social Security number.

FORM 1099: A form issued in the USA by all payers of interest, dividends and fees to each person who has received them during the tax year. The form shows total income paid.

GROSS INCOME: The total income of a taxpayer before subtracting his allowances and deductions to arrive at his taxable income.

HIGHER RATE TAX: The rates of tax levied in the UK on taxable income in excess of £5,000 (1976/77).

HRB (H & R BLOCK): The largest firm of tax preparers (q.v.) in the USA.

IDRS (Integrated Data Retrieval System): The method by which the US tax authorities can immediately retrieve information from disc storage about cases where money is still owed by the taxpayer.

IMF (Individual Master File): The master file of all individual tax returns in the USA.

INFORMATION RETURN: A form issued in the USA and Canada to recipients of non-employment income by the payers of such income. These forms give details of the income paid (e.g. Forms T5, T600, and 1099, q.v.).

IRS (Internal Revenue Service): Agency responsible for the assessment and collection of income tax in the USA.

IR (Inland Revenue): Board responsible for the assessment and collection of income tax in the UK.

INVESTMENT INCOME: Interest, dividends and rent.

INVESTMENT INCOME SURCHARGE: The UK levy imposed on investment income in addition to the rates of tax applying to earned income.

MARGINAL RATE OF TAX: The rate of tax applicable to a small increase in an individual's income.

NON-CUMULATION: A system of withholding tax from income at source in such a way that the amount of tax withheld in any week (month) during the tax year is calculated on the basis of income of that period less 1/52 (or 1/12 if monthly) of annual allowances and deductions but without reference to the income received or tax paid in preceding periods. See also *Cumulation*.

PAYE (Pay-As-You-Earn): The mechanism for withholding tax from wages and salaries. In the UK this is done on a cumulative basis (q.v.) and in nearly every other country on a non-cumulative basis (q.v.).

PRECEDING YEAR BASIS OF ASSESSMENT: The assessment to tax in any one year if based on the income received in the preceding year. See also *Current Year Basis of Assessment.*

PRIME RATE OF INTEREST: The interest charged in the USA for loans to major companies—analogous to the Bank of England Minimum Lending Rate in the UK in being a key to other rates.

PROGRESSIVE TAX: A situation where the marginal tax rate (q.v.) exceeds the average tax rate (q.v.) with the result that a higher proportion of income is absorbed in tax at higher income than at lower income levels.

SCHEDULES: UK income tax is assessed under six schedules as follows:

- Schedule A: Income from property.
- Schedule B: Income from commercial woodlands.
- Schedule C: Interest and annuities payable out of public revenue.
- Schedule D: Income from trades, professions, business, property and other annual profits.
- Schedule E: Income from employment.
- Schedule F: Dividends subject to higher rates of tax.

SELF-ASSESSMENT: The taxpayer has the responsibility for calculating his total income, his tax-free income and his taxable income and (often) the amount of tax due. The tax authorities carry out an arithmetical check on all returns but examine only a sample intensively.

TCMP (Taxpayer Compliance Measurement Program): The US system of selecting a sample of tax returns for detailed study of taxpayer compliance in order to estimate the effectiveness of enforcement activities.

TAX-CREDITS: A system of making payments to people whether by way of tax reductions or actual cash payments in respect of dependants etc. This contrasts with the alternative of making certain amounts of income tax-free. See *Allowances.*

TAX PREPARER: Someone assisting a taxpayer to complete his return.

TAX RETURN: A statement to the authorities of sources and totals of income during a given period.

TAXABLE INCOME: Gross income (q.v.) less allowances and deductions, as relevant.

VERIFICATION: Synonymous with *Audit.*

VITA (Volunteer Income Tax Assistance Program): A US system of helping elderly people to complete their tax returns.

Chapter I

Introduction, Summary and Conclusions

The Glossary of Terms should be consulted for the exact meaning of technical expressions.

1 Background to the Study

The costs of income tax administration in this country, as in others, have risen steadily over the years as such taxes have become more complicated in operation and more widespread in coverage. These are true economic costs in the sense that funds not devoted to income tax administration could be used for more public expenditure (e.g. to build roads or hospitals or to teach the young) or, alternatively, to increase people's command over goods and services by reducing taxes. So tax administration costs have long been a matter of legitimate concern to policy makers as well as to specialists in matters of taxation. More recently, the debate has reached a wider public. The present position might best be summarised by quoting *in extenso* from a newspaper article[1] where the UK present position was placed in historical and international perspective:

> 'The large increases in staff and administration costs in the Board of Inland Revenue are a cause for concern the Commons Public Accounts Committee says in a report published today.
>
> The board had told the committee that the cost of collecting taxes during 1974–75 was about £200m, most of it staff salaries.
>
> Its staff had increased by more than 7,000 last year . . . to nearly 81,600. Without changes in tax allowances, an increase to 90,000 was expected by March next year.

---

[1] 'MP's criticise large increases in Inland Revenue costs for administration and staffing' *The Times*, 6 August 1976. See also *Fifth Report from the Committee of Public Accounts*, Session 1975/76, HC 556, HMSO, 1976.

The cost of administering individual taxes averaged $1\frac{3}{4}$ per cent of the net revenue collected.

That proportionate cost was high compared with other countries, and in particular was about double the figure in the United States, where staff numbers were thought to be comparable with those in Britain.

That was partly because of the United States' simple system of tax allowances and partly because of its more extensive use of computers. Britain placed more emphasis on equity between taxpayers using a complex system of individual reliefs and allowances, and made greater efforts to collect all tax payable.'

As Section 2 of this chapter will make clear, any discussion of reductions in publicly incurred costs of Inland Revenue taxation leads naturally to a consideration of self-assessment for income tax as this is by far the most important of that department's responsibilities. Hence the first root of this study.

A second reason for investigating self-assessment for income tax arose out of the debate on tax-credits in the early 1970s.[2] It would appear that one reason why these proposals were not adopted was the lack of a lower marginal rate band for those with lower incomes. The fact that administrative considerations necessitated a single marginal tax rate covering most incomes was certainly one of the most criticised features of the scheme[3] in public discussion. The administrative argument for a single marginal rate arose out of the need to withhold tax accurately from the vast bulk of taxpayers even when they had one source of income only, let alone those cases where there were multiple sources.

The chain of reasoning in this aspect of the debate on tax-credits may be summed up thus:

(1) the existence of a reduced-rate band for those with low incomes would result in many end-year adjustments in so far as amounts of tax withheld each week would not add up exactly to the total of tax due for the year as a whole; but

(2) present administrative arrangements could not cope easily with many end-year adjustments; therefore

(3) the tax-credit scheme could not easily incorporate a reduced rate band.

We are not concerned now with any other arguments for rising marginal tax rates in this context—we concentrate simply on the administrative issue. And here it can be seen immediately that a logical response to the chain of reasoning above is to consider ways of administering income tax in this country so as to make it easier to cope with end-year adjustments. The need to withhold with complete accuracy during the year would then be less; and it would be possible to have a reduced-rate band (or, for that matter, any pattern of rising marginal tax rates) within a framework such as the tax-credit pro-

---

[2] *Proposals for a Tax-Credit System,* Cmnd 5116, HMSO October 1972.

[3] See, for instance, N. Kaldor, 'A Critique of the Green Paper Proposals' in *Select Committee on Tax-Credit,* Volume II, HC.341–II, HMSO June 1973, p. 211 ff.

posals. This, again, brought us immediately to the consideration of self-assessment for income tax.

A third strand is to be found in the discussion of local government finance culminating in the Report of the (Layfield) Committee of Enquiry.[4] This particular debate on the merits or otherwise of local income taxes came too late to be an origin of our own study but obviously reinforces its relevance. The link between local income taxation and self-assessment is via the costs of administration. The Inland Revenue estimated that a tax of the sort outlined by the Committee of Enquiry would require some 12,000 additional civil servants.[5] In contrast, it can plausibly be shown that if there were a national system of self-assessment the cost of a local or regional income tax over and above that of the national tax would be very low. Such schemes operate cheaply and well in, amongst other countries, the USA, Canada and Sweden.

For all these three reasons—the costs of public administration, the flexibility of the structure of marginal tax rates, and the feasibility of a local or regional income tax—we feel that a study of self-assessment for income tax has very considerable relevance in the UK today.

2 Self-Assessment: Meaning and Implications

Contrary to commonly held beliefs, the principle of self-assessment is in no way a radical departure from current tax practice in the UK. For example, Value Added Tax is organised on a basis of self-assessment; the recent Wealth Tax proposals[6] generated considerable controversy both in the Select Committee and outside Parliament,[7] but one of the few aspects of the tax on which there was no disagreement was that liability would be self-assessed; estate duty during its last years was self-assessed in practice inasmuch as probate was granted on the strength of payment of duty as assessed by the executor; and Capital Transfer Tax contains significant elements of self-assessment.

When applied in such a wide variety of contexts the term 'self-assessment' may clearly have significantly different meanings for different taxes. To grasp the meaning in the personal income tax case it is best to think of the administration of the tax as having two broad functions. *Primary* functions are those that are logically essential to the operation of income tax: they are (a) the calculation of total income, (b) the calculation of total tax-free income, (c) the calculation of total taxable income and (d) the calculation of tax due. *Secondary* functions are those that are not *logically* necessary for the operation of an income tax, but which are needed in practice as an aid to the primary functions: they are (a) withholding of tax at source on some kinds of income, (b) official assistance to taxpayers, and (c) checking and verification by the tax authorities of returns prepared by the taxpayer.

---

[4] *Local Government Finance,* Cmnd 6453, HMSO May 1976.
[5] *Ibid.,* Chapter 11, paragraph 25.
[6] *Wealth Tax,* Cmnd 5704, HMSO August 1974.
[7] *Select Committee on a Wealth Tax,* Session 1974/75, Volume I, *Report and Proceedings of the Committee,* HC 696–I, HMSO, November 1975.

We therefore define self-assessment for personal income tax as having two separate features:

(1) the taxpayer, and not the tax administrator, is responsible for the first three primary functions, the fourth being optional; and

(2) verification activities (or audit) are carried out by the tax administration only on a sample of tax returns though it is likely to be necessary to carry out an arithmetical check of all returns.

Though not an integral part of self-assessment there are a number of closely related issues, all of which will be discussed in some detail in succeeding chapters. The most important are:

(1) The prior or simultaneous simplification of tax allowances: this would make it easier for the taxpayer to understand and comply with the requirements of a new system;

(2) Non-cumulative withholding on wages and salaries: the main reason for withholding tax cumulatively, as in the UK, is that it makes end-year adjustments infrequent. But once all taxpayers file an annual return assessing their own liability end-year adjustments become normal and natural; and so there is little cost on that score and large gains in other directions (to be specified later) from a switch to the non-cumulative withholding generally found in other countries;

(3) Current year payment of tax under Schedule D: if a taxpayer is responsible for his own tax affairs it is reasonable to ask him to make an estimate of his income for the current year and to make interim payments of tax on account. It should be noted that there is little to be gained here by way of administrative savings—the main argument is one of equity between Schedule D and Schedule E taxpayers in so far as tax payments tend to be delayed much more in the former case than in the latter;

(4) Flexible marginal tax structures: once it is no longer necessary to avoid at all costs large numbers of end-year adjustments it becomes possible to have a variety of structures of rising marginal tax rates if one wants to do so. This is true whether one moves to a tax-credit arrangement or not.

A caveat must be entered at this point. We contend that self-assessment offers scope for reducing *public* costs of tax administration; but this will be at the expense of increasing *private* costs to an unknown extent, because of the additional cost to the taxpayer both in the expenditure of his own time and effort and in paying for expert advice. It is not possible to say for certain that there will be a decline in the *total* resources, public plus both kinds of private, devoted to tax administration. Nevertheless, the excess of the resources saved in the public sector over those newly employed in giving private tax advice would be available for other purposes, whether of a public or private character.

3 The Factual Background

Considerable effort was put into investigating the income tax systems of other countries. Detailed studies were made of the USA, Canada, Australia, Japan, and Sweden, while aspects of the systems in Ireland, New Zealand, South Africa and other countries were also examined. Once the initial studies had been completed visits were made to the USA, Canada, and Sweden to discuss their systems, both with tax officials and other observers.

This comparative part of the study is contained in the next two chapters, Chapters II and III. Chapter II outlines the current UK income tax system and its administration, highlighting and emphasising those aspects (such as the cumulative withholding system, taxation in arrears of Schedule D, tax administration practices, official and unofficial assistance to taxpayers) which would be most affected by a change to self-assessment. It also outlines two major ways in which it has been suggested that the system might be changed: the introduction of tax-credits and the grafting of a local income tax on to the national system. This is also a discussion of the ways in which self-assessment operates with other taxes in the UK. An Appendix lists the main UK income tax forms, guides, pamphlets etc. Chapter III describes in detail the systems in the USA and Canada, with some discussion also of Sweden; and again concentrates most on those features that are relevant to the operation of self-assessment, especially the completion of tax returns, assistance to taxpayers and enforcement procedures at the checking and auditing stages. Appendices deal successively with the problems encountered in introducing self-assessment abroad; lessons to be learned from the format of tax returns and explanatory literature in other countries; and miscellaneous aspects of tax administration overseas.

We must make clear the limited nature of the topics covered in these two chapters. We confine our attention to personal income tax (including capital gains tax), with no discussion of corporation tax. Furthermore, we treat in detail only those topics that are directly related to the operation of self-assessment. Such important issues as tax evasion in this country, the relative treatment of married couples and single persons or of employment and investment income, and the structure of marginal tax rates are touched on only briefly as self-assessment is compatible with a wide variety of answers to these questions. In other words, discussion of them is not directly germane to the issues of self-assessment *per se*.

However, specialised as these two chapters are, their contents will nevertheless be familiar to people with expert knowledge in these fields. Such readers may therefore wish to skim through one or both of these chapters quickly, in preparation for the discussion of the central issues which follows.

4 The Pros and Cons of Self-Assessment for Personal Income Tax

The pros and cons of self-assessment, as defined earlier, are discussed in some detail in Chapter IV, a major distinction being drawn between the arguments applying to earnings and to profits. The case for self-assessment can be summarised under three main headings:

(1) Productivity and cheapness: there would be net savings, other things equal, of tax administration in the public sector mainly because the Inland Revenue would no longer have to bear the burden of issuing withholding codes for employees, and would no longer have to move taxpayer files during the year to maintain the continuity of cumulative withholding records. The potential scope for such public sector savings is highlighted by the contrast between income tax administration employment in the UK and other countries; for instance, roughly the same number of people are employed in both the UK and the USA, but *four* times as many returns are dealt with in the latter.[8] Local or regional income taxation is also much easier and cheaper to introduuce under self-assessment.

(2) Flexibility of the income tax structure as an aid to other policy objectives: for example, self-assessment makes possible any desired structure of marginal tax rates. It also facilitates a current year basis for the taxation of non-wage income with attendant equity implications; and in addition, the taxation of short-term National Insurance benefits would be possible, with all that this implies for both incentives and equity.

(3) Greater taxpayer understanding: it can be plausibly asserted that self-assessment will force the taxpayer into a better understanding of the tax system as it applies to him; this is likely to be enhanced by the efforts that the tax authorities will have to make under self-assessment to educate the taxpaying public. This aspect has not only economic effects, narrowly defined, but also implications for citizenship and democracy.

Against these arguments it is possible to list others which some may regard as being against self-assessment:

(1) Costs: the cost argument may run the other way to the extent that self-assessment involves high initial costs in replacing a well-established system by a new one, or increases costs in the *private* sector, or entails new costs associated with end-year adjustments and a peak load of activity both for the tax authorities and for private advisers.

(2) Decline in the standard of tax administration: it is asserted by some that self-assessment will result in a lower proportion of total tax liability being actually collected, and an increase in the variance of tax actually paid by taxpayers in identical circumstances.

(3) The philosophy of taxation: one argument here is that if computation by self-assessment is less exact than the current system then it will produce 'rough justice' rather than exact justice. Whether or not one accepts this proposition depends largely on whether or not one believes exact justice to be a realistic possibility or merely a philosophical mirage. A second and rather different argument under this heading is that self-assessment is inferior to the present system because it requires more obtrusive verification.

---

[8] See Table IV–1 for more details. In Canada the number of employees is only about 20 per cent of that in the UK but 50 per cent as many returns are processed; in Sweden the corresponding percentages are 11 per cent and 25 per cent.

In addition to the exposition of these and related arguments at length, Chapter IV also shows how elements of self-assessment feature much more in the tax systems of other countries than in the UK and also describes an experiment in self-coding in the UK.

5 Outline of Proposals for Self-Assessment in the UK

The last two chapters, Chapters V and VI, lay out our proposals for a system of self-assessment for the UK. The gist is as follows:

(1) Simplification of allowances, extensive computerisation, non-cumulative withholding and self-coding are all necessary and desirable.

(2) Self-assessment, as defined earlier, should be introduced in stages; first, for those currently assessed under Schedule D (and A, B, C and F); the system would then be extended to capital gains, and finally to Schedule E income. As in Chapter IV, emphasis is laid on the differing arguments applying to earnings from employment and profits and on consequential differences in their treatment.

(3) Tax-credits could easily be fitted into this system, if so desired.

(4) Schedule D type income would be subject to taxation on a current basis, with estimated tax payments payable in instalments during the year.

(5) Every taxpayer (except those below any tax threshold) should complete an annual return in which he calculates his net tax liability. When tax is underpaid, he should send a remittance with the return.

(6) Extensive public sector assistance would be offered to taxpayers initially. It is to be expected that private sector assistance would grow over time and develop new forms.

(7) There would be a computer check of the arithmetical and internal consistency of all returns; verification would be restricted to a sample of returns.

(8) A new type of tax return form would be needed; a specimen design is given in the Appendix to Chapter VI.

6 Overall Conclusions

It can be inferred from the paragraphs above that, on balance, we favour a changeover to a system of self-assessment for personal income tax in the UK.

One can examine the arguments for and against such a change a hundred times but no one can get away from the central indisputable fact that the US income tax administration processes four times as many tax returns per employee as the British. Various explanations can be given of this productivity gap (see Ch. IV p. 150) but none of them are sufficiently persuasive to enable one to rest content with the *status quo.* One must not make the vulgar error of imagining that all the resources released from these public sector activities would be available for unrelated purposes, in that a self-assessment régime must be expected to generate more tax advisory services in the private sector. Nevertheless, some resources would be freed all the same. Those who attach importance to denationalisation as a principle would no doubt give an even bigger welcome to the outcome.

As already explained, and as shown later in much more detail, there are many other issues of equity, flexibility of the tax structure and tax administration which have to be weighed in the balance. One point should perhaps be singled out as it is a source of much confusion and misunderstanding: the allegation that those countries which rely more on self-assessment than ourselves fail to collect large sums of revenue due from taxpayers. The evidence that this happens elsewhere is in fact flimsy; and there is certainly no reason whatever why it need happen here. As shown later, most recipients of employment income would be in the position of having over-paid tax at any given time during the fiscal year; the degree of surveillance of Schedule D incomes would be at least comparable to that exercised at present; and the danger of the revenue loss which occurs in some countries because of payment of dividends and interest on a gross basis would simply not arise, given our tradition of deduction of tax at source.

So it seems clear to us that the balance of the argument is in favour of the self-assessment principle. But this does not mean that we believe that any such reforms could be made quickly. This is for two quite different reasons. The first is that an investigation by a small academic team with very limited resources cannot pretend to do more than open up lines of enquiry and form preliminary judgements of statistical orders of magnitude. Much more detailed investigation into all aspects of such a far-reaching change is needed before embarking on it. At the same time, a reservation must be made about such an enquiry. Inevitably, the Inland Revenue would be the leading, if not the sole, investigator. Yet, to put it bluntly, some of its officials might sooner or later lose their jobs or find their prospects of promotion diminished as a result of the findings. It is perhaps over-sanguine to imagine that complete objectivity would necessarily prevail in such circumstances.

The second reason for taking time is that a large number of preparations would have to be made before any changeover took place. This is partly at the more technical level sketched out in later chapters. But it is also a matter of preliminary education of taxpayers about a forthcoming change of system. Nor must one assume that Ministers would necessarily understand or accept that the balance of the argument was in favour of the switchover without a good deal of advance discussion and controversy.

So our overall position is that on the basis of our enquiry we think there is unquestionably a *prima facie* case for a change of system. But we should certainly not pretend that this could come about without a considerable period of further investigation and prior discussion. Nor could the actual process of implementation be an overnight affair. This in turn implies that it would be highly desirable to have a large measure of bipartisan support for such a major change. The UK tax system has suffered more than enough in recent years from policy *bouleversements* which were at best ill-considered and at worst irresponsible.

Chapter II

Income Tax Administration in the UK

In this chapter we make a close examination of what Gladstone once referred to as an 'engine of public extravagance': the income tax and its administration in the United Kingdom. In many ways the British system is unique, in particular in its methods of assessment, the main area of interest to us here. We shall look first at some historical features of the British system. Then, in Section 2 we shall discuss the tax structure in being in 1976/77; the administration of the income tax is discussed in Section 3; sources of assistance to taxpayers in Section 4; various proposals for reform in Section 5; and some aspects of other taxes are examined in Section 6.

1 Historical Features of the UK Income Tax System

The basic characteristic of tax administration in the United Kingdom is that the Inland Revenue rather than the taxpayer has the responsibility for raising assessments to income tax. This works so that most taxpayers with incomes from sources other than employment complete a tax return annually and are then assessed to tax. However, for most wage and salary earners an annual assessment is not necessary. This is because, as we shall see, the sophisticated Pay-As-You-Earn machinery which works on a cumulative basis over the tax year withholds tax from wages, salaries and some other small incomes extremely accurately. Provided that an individual does not have further financial interests such as a part-time business there is no need to make a formal assessment of his tax liability; he will normally receive a tax return only once every three years and this period is being extended to five years. We may say, therefore, that the British system is a combination of official assessment for those with complicated financial circumstances and non-assessment for straightforward cases. To help us understand the peculiar characteristics of the UK system we shall briefly describe the development of three aspects: the system of schedules, the degree of complexity and withholding at source.

The System of Schedules

The system of taxing under different schedules came in response to a requirement for individual privacy. Taxing by schedules meant that officials would know only a taxpayer's income from different sources, and not his total income. The British traditionally take their privacy very seriously. At the very start, on the introduction of income tax in 1799 one rather forceful expression of the desire for privacy was heard from the Navy:

'It is a vile, Jacobin, jumped up Jack-in-office piece of impertinence—is a true Briton to have no privacy? Are the fruits of his labour and toil to be picked over, farthing by farthing, by the pimply minions of Bureaucracy?'[1]

In fact in 1799 the disclosure of income was not even compulsory. Virtually all that was required was a signed statement declaring the amount that the taxpayer intended to pay, and certifying that this sum was not less than one-tenth of his total income less deductions. But there was well-founded suspicion that a significant number of gentlemen were being somewhat modest about their incomes. As a result, on the resumption of the war with France in 1803 two powerful and lasting refinements were introduced: the first was a wide-ranging scheme for withholding tax at source, and the second the abolition of the general return of income and its replacement by returns of income from particular sources so that the tax was broken up into five schedules—A, B, C, D and E. This system remains today in modified form, the most important schedules being Schedule E covering incomes from employment, and Schedule D covering a range of incomes but mainly profits, interest and dividends. Currently, the need for privacy is acknowledged in several ways, perhaps the most important being the codes of the Pay-As-You-Earn system discussed below. Whatever other changes take place, the need for privacy will have to be accommodated in the future particularly with widespread fears of the use of computers; such necessary safeguards will do nothing to modify the complexity of the tax system.

The Degree of Complexity

British income tax administration has never been simple. Originally, in 1799, an individual's annual income was exempt from the tax if below £60. Income between £60 and £200 was subject to a graduated scale of tax rates starting at 2d in the pound (or 0.833 per cent) and income in excess of £200 was subject to a rate of 10 per cent. There was an allowance for children and deductions against gross income for interest on debts, amounts payable to children or other relatives, annuities and life assurance. Payments of the existing assessed taxes, such as the window tax and the inhabited house duty, were also deductible in assessing income tax liability. Already in 1799, there were complaints that the income tax returns were difficult to complete.

---

[1] B. E. V. Sabine, *A History of Income Tax* (George Allen & Unwin, London, 1966) p. 31.

Despite these complications the original income tax was very rough and ready by modern standards. It could afford to be. Tax rates were very low and were levied on a relatively small proportion of the population. As the desire and the need for revenue increased over the years the tax system had to become increasingly complex. With marginal rates of tax on investment income as high as 98 per cent in 1976/77 broad rudimentary principles will no longer serve and more sophisticated rules are required. In addition evasion and avoidance, and attempts by the authorities to prevent such evasion and avoidance, become more remunerative at higher rates of tax and so lead to more complicated tax law. Finally, as the tax system has become more and more pervasive throughout society so there has been an increasing tendency by the government to use it for many purposes other than simply raising revenue, both to fulfil its own policy aims and to accommodate the demands of ever more vocal lobby groups.

It is impossible to measure the complexity of a tax system with any precision but there are figures available which may be used as an approximation. For instance, the increase in the length of the Income Tax Acts, from 135 pages in 1842 to the 1,600 pages or so that a 1976 Consolidation would require (see Table II–1), seems to indicate a considerable increase in complexity. The proportion of the population subject to these complicated provisions has also increased considerably in recent years. There were 3.8 million income taxpayers in 1938/39, 14.5 million in 1948/49 and 18.9 million in 1972/73.[2] In addition there is some reason to suppose that the personal circumstances of taxpayers are becoming more complicated. While it is relatively easy to ascertain gross incomes in the form of wages and salaries, other forms of income tend to be more difficult to establish precisely, and the number of assessments raised against these other forms of income has been increasing. Between 1964 and 1972 (the latest figures available) the number of assessments

Table II–1 Increases in the Length of the Income Tax Acts[1]

Date	Length
1842	135 pages[2]
1918	180 pages
1952	510 pages
1970	1,200 pages[3]
1976	1,600 pages[3]

SOURCE:
V. Grout; Paper delivered at the IFS conference on 'Tax Simplification and Anti-Avoidance Legislation', London 28 June 1974. And V. Grout and B. Sabine 'The First Hundred Years of Tax Cases' *British Tax Review*, 1976, No. 2.
NOTES:
1 There have been substantial increases in the numbers of Sections and Schedules.
2 This is as if the 1842 Act were printed in the same form as in 1918.
3 Approximately. This assumes that the Acts were consolidated.

[2] *Inland Revenue Statistics* 1970 and 1975.

on trading profits and professional earnings of sole traders and partnerships (Table II–6) rose from 1.7 million to 2.4 million. It is possible that, given the complexity of individuals' financial circumstances and the need for government revenue, the degree of complexity of the tax system in the United Kingdom is not unnecessarily high. We shall return to this proposition later.

Withholding at Source

The principle of withholding tax from incomes at source appeared in Britain in an Act of 1657, which permitted certain tenants to deduct tax from their rents.[3] It became thoroughly integrated into the process of collecting income tax in 1803, and is, for instance, reflected in the withholding of tax from dividends and some interest payments on a more extensive scale in the UK than in most other countries. Tax is effectively withheld from such income in the UK at the basic rate, 35 per cent in the tax year 1976/77, which is the relevant rate for most taxpayers since it covers the first £5,000 of taxable income. Tax on income from employment is withheld very accurately through the Pay-As-You-Earn system, a system that also enables tax to be collected on a current basis from some small investment incomes not taxed at source. This is achieved by reducing the taxpayer's allowances by the appropriate amount, in a manner described below.

Extensive withholding forms part of a wider traditional policy in the UK of organising the system so that the taxpayer has few opportunities to avoid or evade tax, rather than the more usual practice abroad of leaving such opportunities open, for example with more restricted withholding, but encouraging compliance by the active implementation of painful penalties. The unique version of Pay-As-You-Earn operating in the UK,[4] and discussed further below, takes tax administration almost entirely out of the hands of the taxpayer and ensures that tax is paid almost without regard to the degree of taxpayer co-operation. Earlier examples of this policy stretch back at least as far as 1806. So many people had been making returns stating that their income was just under the £60 exemption limit that rather than confronting them, the 1806 Act reduced the limit to £50, 'so that their former returns may be made use of'.[5]

2 The 1976/77 Income Tax Structure

We now turn to the 1976/77 structure of the British income tax, discussing in turn allowances and deductions, the rates of tax and the treatment of wives' earnings. A detailed account of the administration of income tax is left to later sections.

Allowances and Deductions

To clarify our terminology, in this and later chapters we shall use the terms

---

3 Sabine *op. cit.* p. 37.

4 Ireland has a somewhat similar system of Pay-As-You-Earn, but it differs from the British version in a number of respects (See p. 126 below).

5 *1st Report of the Commissioners of Inland Revenue*, London, 1857, p. 31.

'allowances' and 'exemptions' synonymously to refer to income that is tax-free as of right, while 'deductions' refer to income that is tax-free only in respect of certain types of expenditure. Thus a single person's allowance may be claimed by an individual regardless of his pattern of expenditure, while a deduction for life assurance is permitted only to the extent that a person has paid qualifying premia. Other examples of allowances include children's allowances, age allowance and blind person's allowance; and examples of deductions include those for mortgage interest, tools and industrial clothing.

Perhaps the two most significant characteristics of allowances against gross income in the United Kingdom are their complexity, and the rather paradoxical combination of equity in principle and inequity in practice.

To discover why the authorities have such a strong tendency to complicate the tax system would require a far longer study than ours. However, it does appear that there is a general theme of attempting to achieve a high degree of equity between taxpayers. For instance, we can see from Table II–2 that the married man's allowance (£1,085) was less than twice the single person's allowance (£735). There were different personal allowances in 1976/77 for children under the age of 11 years (£300), between 11 and 16 (£335) and over 16 years (£365), presumably on the basis that the costs of keeping a child are related to its age. There was also an additional personal allowance for children (£350) which could be claimed by a man or woman entitled to the single person's allowance or a married man whose wife was totally incapacitated. The dependant relative's allowance (£100; or £145 if the claimant was a single woman) was different again, and different from the blind person's allowance

Table II–2 Allowances Against Gross Income in the UK 1976/77

	£
Single person's allowance	735
Married man's allowance	1,085
Children:	
Aged not more than 11 years	300
Aged over 11 but not over 16 years	335
Aged over 16 (if receiving full-time education or training)	365
Additional personal allowance	350
Dependant relative allowance	100
Except if the claimant is a woman other than a married woman living with her husband	145
Housekeeper allowance	100
Daughter's services allowance	55
Blind person's allowance (each)	180
Age allowance:	
Single person's age allowance	1,010
Married man's age allowance	1,555

NOTE:
The age allowance is granted in place of the ordinary single person's and married man's allowance to people of 65 years or more who have a total income below certain limits (see text).

(£130) which in turn was different from age allowance. Age allowance varied between single people (£1,010) and married couples (£1,555) and was available to single people aged 65 years or over and to married couples if either partner was 65 or over, instead of the ordinary single and married persons' allowances. In the USA all these allowances had the same value ($750) in 1975 so that each person was entitled to one exemption for himself, two if he was either blind or 65 or over, and three if he was both. If his spouse had no income or did not file a separate return, he was entitled to the pattern of exemptions again, and he also received one for every dependant.

But the complexities in the United Kingdom do not end there. Several of the allowances are reduced if the taxpayer's income or that of his dependants exceeds a certain amount. Thus the children's allowance was reduced by £1 for every £1 by which the child's income exceeded £350.[6] The age allowance was reduced by £2 for every £3 of total income in excess of £3,250 until it reached the value of the personal allowance available to those under 65. Mention should also be made of the system widely known as 'clawback'. This arises because in addition to the allowances against taxable income for children, there were also direct cash payments to parents (Family Allowances) for the second[7] and subsequent children. To restrict the benefit of Family Allowances total personal allowances were reduced by £52 for each child for whom the allowance was granted.

Since deductions against gross income are worth more to people who pay higher rates of tax, attempts to ensure that everyone benefits equally have further increased complexity. In 1975/76 this principle was largely confined to the deduction for life assurance, and the following small extract from an Inland Revenue Guide[8] gives some idea of the complexity of the relief:

> The allowable premium, that is the amount of the premium which qualifies for relief must not exceed 7% of the capital sum insured at death (excluding any bonus or other additional benefit); nor must the total allowable premiums exceed 1/6th of your total income . . . Relief is given in terms of tax equal to one-half the basic rate tax on the whole of the 'allowable' premiums (or where the total premiums paid in the year do not exceed £20, at the basic rate on the amount of the premiums or on £10, whichever is the less).

or in other words, within limits, everyone gets relief of 17.5 per cent of the costs of life assurance premia. The restrictions arise from a decision not to extend the relief to the higher rates of tax, but despite the complexity of the deduction it still does not achieve the apparently desired result that wealthy taxpayers should not benefit from the relief more than poorer taxpayers. For instance, investing in a life assurance policy is one way of avoiding the investment income surcharge (see page 18). There has been some discussion about

6 But for children under 18 who were unmarried throughout the year and whose earnings were £235 or less, the allowance was reduced by £1 for each £1 by which investment income exceeded £115.

7 And to first children from 1977.

8 *Tax Return Guide 1975/76* p. 8 (issued by the Inland Revenue with Form 11).

extending the principle of flat-rate benefits to other deductions such as that for mortgage interest and indeed the option mortgage scheme[9] has already done so for non-taxpayers. Clearly any further moves in this direction would do little to simplify the system. Furthermore, the costs of administering complex allowances and deductions are considerable: it has been estimated that the total work involved in administering life assurance relief occupies the equivalent of between 1,000 and 1,500 Inland Revenue staff.[10]

There is some hope for the future. With regard to life assurance relief the 7 per cent rule has been dropped as from 1976/77, and there are proposals for a major reform of the system (see page 47) by allowing policy holders to deduct an appropriate amount from each eligible premium, rather than claiming a deduction from the Inland Revenue, with the Revenue reimbursing the life offices for the reduction in their premium receipts by direct payments. There are also proposals to reform the system of child relief (see page 47) by abolishing the tax allowances and 'clawback' and making weekly non-taxable payments to mothers. However, this simplification is to be introduced more slowly than originally planned: one result of the reform would be to transfer disposable income from husbands to wives, and it was thought that this might possibly have an adverse effect on the government's attempts to maintain a 'voluntary' incomes policy. There are no firm plans to simplify the many other complicated allowances.

Lack of simplicity may in itself promote inequity. Taxpayers may not claim some of their deductions because they find it too difficult to discover their full entitlement. An illustration is provided by the deduction allowed against income tax assessed under Schedule E for book purchases to teachers and lecturers taking courses of a standard above GCE 'O' level. A survey by Peter Dean[11] of 150 Polytechnic teachers found that of the 120 who responded to the survey, only 31 actually claimed the deduction. Of those who had previously not claimed, five said that they did not know how to and 43 had never heard of the deduction—an interesting result for one of the more highly educated sections of the community.

There is nothing inherently objectionable to complicating the tax system sufficiently to take an exact account of each person's circumstances. But there are considerable administrative costs of doing so and the increased complications can give an advantage to the astute, and to those who can afford the professional advice needed to take advantage of the intricacies of tax law. Presumably neither category is the intended benefactor of the complicated system of taxation resulting from the British emphasis on equity between taxpayers.

A more tangible inequity is that referred to by Lord Justice Harman in the following terms: 'Now it is notorious—and is, indeed a long-standing injustice

[9] A scheme whereby a mortgage is granted at a preferential rate but without any relief against tax.
[10] The Chancellor's Budget Speech, 6 April 1976 (*Hansard*, 6 April 1976, Col. 264).
[11] Peter N. Dean 'Do You Pay Too Much Tax?' *The Technical Journal* March 1971.

—that the scale of the taxpayer's allowances under Schedule E are on an altogether more niggardly scale than under Schedule D. Indeed it has been said that the pleasure of life depends upon the Schedule under which a man lives . . .'[12]

The reasons for the differential treatment are partly historical, partly on grounds of expendiency and partly on principle. Historically, Schedule E applied only to holders of public offices, e.g. Members of Parliament, and to certain others paid from public revenues. The only deduction permitted was for expenses 'wholly, exclusively and necessarily' incurred *'in the performance'* (authors' italics) of the duties of the employment—a provision that was, and still is, applied very strictly. Other employment income was originally assessed under Schedule D where the criterion is the less rigid 'wholly and exclusively'. The Royal Commission of 1920 recommended that employment income should be transferred to Schedule E because it was thought that public and private employees should have the same basis of assessment,[13] and the change came about in 1922 because a House of Lords decision in the case of the Great Western Railway v. Bater made it extremely difficult to decide who had a public office and who an employment of profit.[14]

Expediency is involved in the argument that if these deductions were left to the employee there would be no common standard and there would be great administrative difficulties in coping with the resulting claims. However, there is a system of flat rate deductions for tools negotiated in many different industries which seems to work reasonably. An element of principle arose because of the belief that it is the employer's duty to pay for all necessary expenses (and that any others therefore are *prima facie* suspect). A relevant example of the disparity is that the costs of employing assistance for one's tax affairs tends to be deductible in practice under Schedule D as part of the costs of preparing accounts, but not under Schedule E.

In practice, political expediency bears the major part of the responsibility for the complexities of tax law. A successful lobby group may win concessions for its special interest at the expense of principles, simplicity and general equity. For the best of reasons Members of Parliament rallied around the lobby for the blind some time ago and successfully secured a deduction for blind people from the government. But although this is superficially equitable, in that it attempted to compensate partially for the handicap suffered by blind people, like so many other similar actions it both increased the complexity of the system and introduced a whole new set of anomalies. The blind who pay income tax benefit from the deduction, but not those below the tax threshold. Secondly, it does not seem equitable to favour the blind and not the deaf, paralysed, or other handicapped people. Moreover, a concession for one group

---

[12] Mitchell and Edon v. Ross, 1959 TR 225, 1960 TR 79. Quoted in Gwyneth McGreggor, *Employees' Deductions under the Income Tax,* October 1960 p. 11.
[13] *The Royal Commission on Income Tax,* Cmd. 615, HMSO 1920 p. 109.
[14] *66th Report of the Commissioners of Inland Revenue,* Cmd. 1934, HMSO 1924 p. 63.

leading to an erosion of the tax base means that others have to pay more tax, or public expenditure has to be lower, than would otherwise be the case.

The general case for providing cash payments rather than tax concessions has been made extensively elsewhere,[15] and the debate sheds some light on possible reasons for the profusion of complicated deductions in the British system. Direct subsidies form part of government expenditure and are thus open to review, scrutiny and possible economy at regular intervals. Not so with tax concessions. Although deductions are a cost to government in a similar way to actual cash payments or provision in kind. they remain comparatively hidden and not so subject to review by e.g. the Public Expenditure Survey Committee. Therefore it is even more possible than with outright subsidies that deductions may remain when the case for them has diminished or even disappeared. Furthermore, there is a concentration effect. A concession to one section of the community can only be made at a cost to others, either in the form of a higher tax bill or a lower level of public expenditure. But even if the benefits gained by the recipients of a particular deduction are less than the cost to everyone else, nevertheless, because the benefit is concentrated on a specific group they may find it worthwhile to spend a lot of time, money and effort in defending their special privileges, whereas the share of total cost is so small for each individual concerned that no one finds it worthwhile to organise a counter-lobby. An additional effect is that as marginal tax rates rise and deductions become correspondingly more valuable, those who benefit may be expected to fight more tenaciously to keep their concessions. The effects that any programme of self-assessment may be expected to have on the government's propensity to complicate are discussed on page 193.

The Rates of Tax

Before April 1973 income tax was levied at a single 'standard rate' and surtax was levied at a series of more progressive rates on higher incomes. In 1973 the two were formally unified, with the standard rate becoming known as the basic rate and surtax as higher rates of tax.

One of the most striking characteristics of the income tax, both before and after 1973, is the very long basic rate band which applies to the first £5,000 of taxable income. This has some advantages in that the widespread withholding of tax from dividends and interest payments at the basic rate results in withholding at the correct rate for the majority of taxpayers. There may also be some advantage in that taxpayers are more likely to be aware of the marginal rate of tax they face, a figure that would be less easy to ascertain if the tax structure had a large number of rates close together. However, in a survey

---

16 e.g. Stanley S. Surrey, 'Tax Subsidies as a Device for Implementing Government Policy', in *The Economics of Federal Subsidy Programs,* a compendium of Papers, Joint Economic Committee, U.S. Congress, 1972; by the same author, *Pathways to Tax Reform—The Concept of Tax Expenditure,* (Harvard University Press, Cambridge, Massachusetts, 1974); Tax Institute of America, *Tax Incentives,* (Heath Lexington Books, Lexington, Massachusetts, 1969).

concerned with misconceptions about income tax[16] a group of weekly paid workers and a group of managers were asked if they knew the current standard rate of tax. Only 3 per cent of the workers replied correctly though 45 per cent of the managers did so. These low figures may be partially explained by the existence of an earned income relief (of 2/9ths of earned income, now abolished) which may have confused some respondents, but cannot possibly account for the extent of the ignorance on the subject. The main disadvantage of a long basic rate band is that the tax structure is lop-sided, as may be seen from Table II–3, or more clearly from Figure II–1, one result being that the lowest rate of income tax is very high (35 per cent in 1976/77). A single individual with an income of £736 a year pays tax on his marginal pound at the same rate as an individual in receipt of £5,735. This may well be incompatible with the apparent desire in Britain for a highly progressive tax structure.[17]

Table II–3 Rates of Tax on Taxable Income. UK, 1976/77

Slice of Income £	Rate of Tax
0– 5,000	35
5,001– 5,500	40
5,501– 6,500	45
6,501– 7,500	50
7,501– 8,500	55
8,501–10,000	60
10,001–12,000	65
12,001–15,000	70
15,001–20,000	75
Over 20,000	83

NOTE: There is also an investment income surcharge (see text).

In addition to income tax rates ranging from 35 to 83 per cent on earned income in 1976/77, there was an investment income surcharge. The surcharge is levied at an additional 10 per cent on investment income between £1,000 and £2,000 and at 15 per cent thereafter. The surcharge is imposed even if there is no other form of income. For people over the age of 65 the 10 per cent rate started at £1,500. The addition of the investment income surcharge means that the highest rate of tax was 98 per cent which applies to individuals with taxable income in excess of £20,000 provided that their income includes more than £2,000 from investment.

Separate Assessment and Separate Taxation of the Wife's Earnings

Normally a husband and wife are treated as one unit for tax purposes. The

16 C. V. Brown, 'Misconception About Income Tax and Incentives', *Scottish Journal of Political Economy* February 1968.

17 e.g. see the evidence of the Trades Union Congress to the Select Committee on Tax-Credit, Volume II, *Evidence*, HC 341–II, HMSO, June 1973.

Figure II–1 Marginal Rates of Income Tax in the United Kingdom 1976/77 (excluding investment income surcharge)

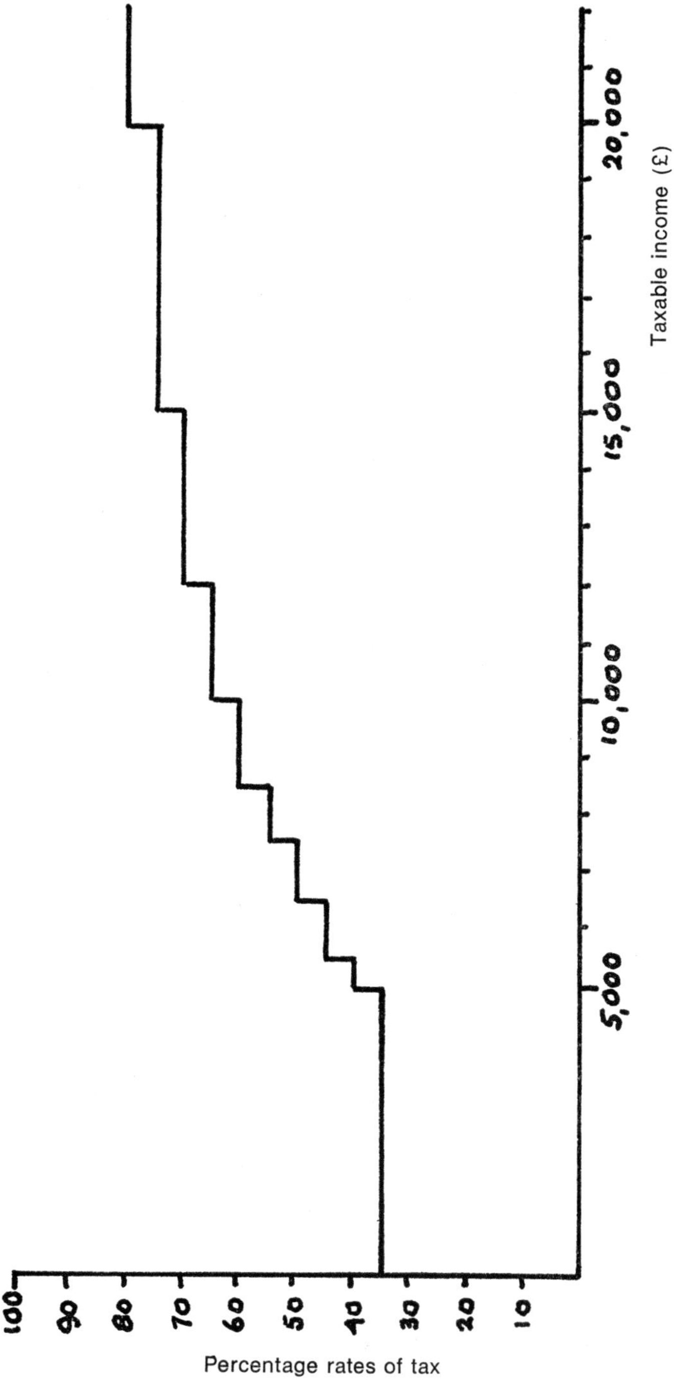

husband must enter his wife's income on his return as though it were his own, except that there are separate columns for his income and deductions and for those of his wife. This arrangement does not suit all married couples and there are two sets of provisions for the wife's income to be (i) taxed separately or (ii) separately assessed: the two procedures are quite distinct and should not be confused. Neither for separate assessment nor the separate taxation of the wife's earnings is it necessary for the wife to complete a separate return.

A separate assessment results in the same total tax liability for the husband and wife as a joint assessment. The couple's incomes are treated as one in order to calculate the amount of tax to be divided between them. Similarly, the allowances are the same as if a separate assessment had not been claimed and are apportioned between them. There are two main reasons why a husband and wife may elect to be separately assessed. The first is that the husband may not wish to be liable for the tax on his wife's income, especially if her income is very much larger than his own. The second is that a wife may be entitled to a tax refund in her own right which would be paid to her rather than her husband only if a separate assessment were chosen. Separate assessment may also be claimed for capital gains tax.

The separate taxation of the wife's earnings is quite different and may result in a saving of tax for the family as a whole. The reason is that, provided both the husband and the wife have earned income, their threshold for higher rates of tax is lower if the wife's income is counted as her husband's than if they are taxed separately. However, even if the wife's earnings are taxed separately, any investment income received by the wife will continue to be added to her husband's. There is also an offset to any gain from separate taxation in that a jointly taxed married couple received (in 1976/77) both the married man's allowance of £1,085 and a wife's earned income allowance of up to £735, but if the wife's earnings were taxed separately the couple each received only the single person's allowance of £735—resulting in most cases in a loss of £350 worth of allowances, and confining any advantage from separate taxation to those earning sums well into the higher rate tax brackets.

3 Income Tax Administration

The Inland Revenue Structure

At the time of writing (October 1976) the structure of the Inland Revenue had just been re-organised. The previous structure had been in existence for over 50 years and its emphasis on the decentralisation of authority was unique among Civil Service departments in the United Kingdom. The basic concept was that a small central unit should be responsible for policy work but that the actual implementation of tax should be left to the 750 or so local districts, each having a great deal of autonomy. Although the centre had overall responsibility the idea was that the District Inspectors should be encouraged to make their own decisions whenever possible and refer to Head Office only in exceptional circumstances. Within the local districts the normal organisation consisted of a District Inspector supported by perhaps two or three less senior Inspectors and 30 to 50 other staff. The inspectorate had both the technical job of assessing taxes and the responsibility for the general management of the local tax offices. A second important feature of this structure was the separation of the functions of assessment and collection; the Inspectors were responsible for the assessment of taxes while the actual process of collection was carried out by the quite separate Collectors of Taxes.

There were several reasons why it was considered that this structure could be improved.[18] The separation of assessment and collection has been a feature of the Inland Revenue since Inspectors first took a part in the administration of income tax and is logical in that those responsible for assessment have no interest in the process of collection. Indeed at one time it was 'thought so essential to the maintenance of security that Inspectors were even forbidden to lodge in the same house as a collector'.[19] However, the separation has been responsible for confusion amongst the public and has led to complaints when the actions of the local Tax Office and the local Collection Office have not been harmonised. The desirability of the Inspectors' dual responsibility as both technical experts and managers of establishments has also been called into question. The division of these functions would allow fully trained Inspectors to devote more attention to technical work such as countering evasion and avoidance, and would also mitigate the shortage of such Inspectors if much of their management work were to be taken over by specialist managers. This would have the further advantage of improving the career prospects of those individuals in tax offices who do not have a full technical Inspector training. Other reservations about the present structure have included the possibility that different branch hierarchies might have been breeding rivalries at the expense of co-operation within the Department; that many staff have tended to feel remote from the central Board; and that perhaps regional structures should be set up between the central unit and the local districts. If establishments work were to be devolved to regions there might be more staff transfers within regions and fewer between regions; and this might well improve staff morale.

The new system comprises a unified Head Office divided into Policy, Management and Technical Divisions, together with a Statistics and a Finance Division. Wherever appropriate, these Divisions will cover both income and capital taxes. Local Offices are being grouped into regions headed by regional managers, though this new hierarchy should be operated so that the present ability of the public to obtain decisions on individual cases at a local level will not be seriously affected. A small number of special offices are being set up in major cities, mainly to lead the drive against avoidance and evasion, with an

---

18 For a more thorough discussion see: 'Proposals of the Review Committee for the Structure of the Department', *Inland Revenue Management Review*, January 1975.

19 Sir Alexander Johnston, *The Inland Revenue* (George Allen & Unwin, London, 1965) p. 13.

under-secretary to co-ordinate such efforts. Staff is being re-graded and two new groups are being created. One will consist of the fully trained Inspectorate and the other is to be based on the Tax Officer class, though grades up to assistant secretary level are to be included in the latter.

The Valuation Office and the Solicitor's Office are largely unaffected by these changes. The main responsibilities of the Valuation Office include the valuation of real and leasehold property for estate duty and its successor capital transfer tax, stamp duty and local rates. The Solicitor's Office conducts the legal business of the Department.

Inland Revenue Districts

The well-established movement of Pay-As-You-Earn (PAYE) work out of London is continuing. Since 1945 some 7,500 posts have been moved from London to areas favoured by government regional policies, and two new London Provincial Districts[20] came into operation during 1976. The tendency for employees' files to be moved away from their local districts has been reinforced by two other factors. First, employees' records are normally kept at their employers' tax districts and as employers have become larger and made increasing use of computers, so payrolls have become more centralised—often well away from employees' homes. Second, the establishment of the computerised Centre 1 at East Kilbride in 1970 (see below) took over the work of the PAYE sections of 67 local offices in Scotland, dealing with around two million taxpayers. The result of these changes is that only about half of the taxpayers assessed under Schedule E are dealt with by their local district. Many individuals like to enquire personally about their tax affairs (apparently local buses make unscheduled stops outside Centre 1) and local enquiry offices have been set up in a number of areas. Although 70 per cent of taxpayers calling at local offices can be satisfied without recourse to their file, it can be sent temporarily to a local tax district where necessary.

Computerisation

Centre 1 at East Kilbride was designed to be the first, and smallest, of nine computer centres dealing with all Schedule E taxpayers. The computer itself has proved well able to cope with such mechanical operations as distributing tax returns and calculating and sending out coding notices and assessments, but for a number of reasons the plans for the other eight have been shelved. Apart from the implications of possible tax reforms such as a tax-credit system[21] at various times, there has been a substantial policy change away from centralising staff as well as computers. The disadvantages of large centres include difficulties in recruiting and keeping large concentrations of staff; lack of communication between staff; and an increased vulnerability to industrial disputes—there appears to be both a relatively high incidence of such disputes

[20] i.e. Districts situated outside London but dealing with taxpayers in London.
[21] *Proposals for a Tax-Credit System,* Cmnd 5116, *op. cit.,* HMSO 1972.

at a large centre and a possibility that any of them, however small, could paralyse the whole PAYE operation.[22] The Inland Revenue Staff Federation has also been forceful about the 'upheaval and human problems' associated with a 'nine centre' concept.[23] Small local districts on the other hand are thought to be more convenient for taxpayers, involve fewer unpopular staff transfers, and are more compatible with the Inland Revenue's concept of the independence of Inspectors. A solution appears to be centralised computers and de-centralised offices, and a pilot scheme has been devised to establish whether or not such a system is compatible with the existing pattern of local districts. It is also proposed to computerise the assessment and collection of capital gains tax, corporation tax, and income tax assessed under Schedule D. The computers to be used for this work will be based at three centres, Cumbernauld, Shipley and Bootle, and a full automatic data processing system is expected to be in operation by the mid-1980s.

Wages, Salaries and Pay-As-You-Earn

The British system of PAYE withholding of income tax at source is quite distinct from alternative methods employed abroad. It is not surprising that as early as 1951 Lady Rhys Williams remarked that 'Anybody who could invent the PAYE scheme and carry it through could do anything'.[24]

PAYE was developed in the United Kingdom largely as a result of the Second World War when wage earners first became subject to income tax in large numbers. A widespread scheme for wages and salaries was introduced in 1940 in place of the previous one of two half-yearly assessments. In effect, however, employees were paying tax on income they had earned some 10 months previously. What happened was that the tax charged on wages earned between 6 April and 5 October was withheld from the wages of the six months commencing the following February. The system attracted a considerable amount of criticism. As tax was collected in arrears there were many cases of hardship, especially in occupations with seasonally fluctuating earnings so that some of the tax due in respect of the high earnings of summer was deducted from much lower wages earned during the winter. There were similar difficulties when individuals moved to lower paid jobs. In addition much delay and inconvenience arose in effecting appropriate deductions of tax when a worker changed employment and it was thought that the system gave employees an incentive to do so, sometimes with a view to evasion.

Pressure to reform the system on to a more current basis grew steadily, despite unwavering opposition from the administration. The main problem was, as the Chancellor put it, that 'the income tax ... cannot be a simple tax

---

[22] This experience seems to extend outside the Inland Revenue; see for example the *Department of Employment Gazette,* 25 February 1976.
[23] *Taxes,* July 1975 p. 318 and other issues.
[24] Royal Commission on the Taxation of Profits and Income, *Minutes of Evidence* 21 June 1951, Question 103.

and a current tax, both at the same time.'[25] The Inland Revenue was able to produce a White Paper in 1942[26] 'proving with the most impeccable logic'[27] that income tax could not be administered on a 'Pay-As-You-Go' basis. However, the problems remained. As the rates of income tax rose to pay for the war so too did the difficulties associated with deducting tax in arrears. There was also widespread confusion and ignorance of income tax administration. The number of income taxpayers increased sixfold between 1940 and 1942 so that the Inland Revenue was faced with very large numbers of people who were totally inexperienced in complying with the requirements of income tax. Reform in Britain was further encouraged as both Canada and the United States introduced 'pay-as-you-go' methods of withholding, though on a non-cumulative basis. Finally, the Revenue relented and proposals for a cumulative PAYE system were put forward. The reasons given for a cumulative system were that it was necessary to make the weekly deduction of tax vary with weekly fluctuations in income; and also to avoid over-withholding tax and having to repay it after the end of the tax year (see page 67). The introduction of a cumulative rather than a non-cumulative system also neatly excused the Revenue's turn-around and hostility to previous plans for withholding on a current basis in that:

> 'The various proposals for collection on a current earnings basis which were considered in the White Paper of April 1942 . . . did not meet this serious difficulty [of over-withholding].'[28]

The form taken by the British version of PAYE also required very little co-operation or understanding by the taxpayer himself, a considerable advantage given the very large number of taxpayers inexperienced in the art of assessment at the time. The Pay-As-You-Earn mechanism (widely known at the time as Pay-ALL-You-Earn!) was finally introduced in the United Kingdom in 1944.

It is necessary to describe how the system works in some detail. The employee provides details of his personal circumstances to the Inland Revenue by completing a tax return, about once every five years in the majority of cases. The relevant allowances against gross income are then translated by the Revenue into a code number so that, for instance, a taxpayer with no allowances other than the single person's allowance (£735 in 1976/77) would find his entitlement represented by the code number 73L. A married man with two children aged 11 years or less would be entitled to the higher married man's allowance and two child allowances of £300, giving a total of £1,685 and a code number of 168H. The purpose of the suffixes L and H is described below; the numbers, like 73 and 168, each cover a band of allowances £10 wide, and as a result in the majority of cases, PAYE does not withhold tax with absolute accuracy. As any advantage is conceded to the taxpayer PAYE tends

[25] Quoted in *The Economist* Nov. 6 1943, p. 607.
[26] *The Taxation of Weekly Wage Earners,* Cmnd 6348, HMSO April 1942.
[27] *The Economist* Sept. 11 1943, p. 357.
[28] *A New System for the Taxation of Weekly Wage Earners,* Cmd. 6469, HMSO Sept. 1943 para. 3.

to underwithhold marginally, but discrepancies arising from this factor alone are not considered large enough to be worth assessing and collecting separately.

Having calculated the code, the Inland Revenue then forwards it to the taxpayer so that he may check it. He is warned to notify the tax office immediately of any change in his personal circumstances which may subsequently affect his code. It is then sent to the individual's employer.

If the Inland Revenue is informed of any changes in the circumstances affecting an individual's code a new one is issued, except that code numbers are not altered downwards in cases where the result would be a very large tax deduction in a single pay period to pick up past underpayments of tax. Note that a reduction in the code number results in an increase in the tax withheld. The cumulative feature of PAYE means that the amount of tax withheld by the employer is automatically adjusted in line with any change in the code or in gross earnings.

The working of the principle of cumulation may be illustrated by a simple example.[29] Let us suppose that the basic rate of tax on taxable income is 30 per cent and the taxpayer has a total of £520 a year allowable deductions, which accumulate at the rate of £10 per week (illustrated by column 4 in Table II–4). This sum is deducted from his cumulative pay to date (column 3) to give cumulative taxable pay (column 5), cumulative tax due (column 6) and thus the actual tax due (column 7) at any stage during the year. Thus in week 1 of the tax year, the individual's pay is £40 and free pay £10, so that £9 of tax is due on the taxable pay of £30.

Table II–4 Example of the Principle of Cumulation

1. Week	2. Gross Pay	3. Cumulative Pay	4. Cumulative Free Pay	5. Cumulative Taxable Pay (Col 3– Col 4)	6. Cumulative Tax Due (30% of Col 5)	7. Actual Tax Due
	£	£	£	£	£	£
1	40	40	10	30	9	9
2	50	90	20	70	21	12
3	0	90	30	60	18	−3

Similarly in week 2, when the employee's pay increases to £50 his tax liability rises automatically to £12 in the same week. When for some reason, such as sickness, unemployment or an industrial dispute, income falls to zero in week 3, free pay continues to accumulate and increases to £30. As a result taxable pay falls to £60 and cumulative tax due to £18. As £21 has already been paid in tax the individual automatically receives a rebate of £3, which is paid either by his employer or, if this is not possible for reasons such as unemployment, directly by the Inland Revenue (see page 30 below).

[29] See also Chapter III, Table III–7.

The code and the tax tables supplied by the Revenue provide the employer with sufficient information to assess and withhold the correct amount of tax from his employee's pay. Tax Table A is used to convert the code into 'free pay', which is the value of the allowances divided into weeks or months and then cumulated to give the total amount allowed up to and including the current pay period throughout the tax year. Hence, for example, in week 1 of the tax year an employee with a code of 168H would be entitled to free pay of £32.50 i.e. £1,680 ÷ 52. Table B is then used to establish the amount of tax due on the difference between cumulative gross pay over the year to date and cumulative free pay. Continuing our example, and supposing that the employee earned £42.50 in week 1, with a basic rate of 35 per cent then Table B would show tax due of £3.50 i.e. 35 per cent of (£42.50−£32.50). If the employer does not receive a code for a particular employee he must use the 'emergency code', which is equal to the single person's allowance only. In addition, he must operate the emergency code on a 'week 1' or 'month 1' basis so that each pay period is treated in isolation with no tax rebates being made by the employer i.e. the cumulative feature of PAYE is suppressed as previous earnings and tax paid are ignored. This procedure continues until a revised coding is received from the tax office.

As indicated earlier, the suffix L refers to the (lower) single person's allowance, and the suffix H represents the (higher) married man's allowance. T is used either in complicated cases, such as coding for a second job, where the amount of a person's allowances is immaterial, or if the employee does not wish his marital status to be revealed. From 1976/77 this system was extended to people over retirement age entitled to age allowance and who had tax withheld through PAYE e.g. in respect of occupational pensions. In such cases the suffix letters are P for the single allowance and V for the married allowance.

The tax withheld by employers during an income tax month, less any tax refunded, must be paid over to the Collector within 14 days of the end of that month. Should refunds to an employer exceed the amounts withheld, he may apply to the Collector for reimbursement. After the end of the tax year (5 April), the employer is required to issue a certificate (P60) to each person employed by him on 5 April and from whose pay tax had been deducted during the year. The certificate should give the total pay and net tax deducted or refunded by the employer together with pay and tax withheld from any previous employment during the tax year. At the same time the employer must send the Collector a list of people employed by him at any time during the tax year with yearly totals of pay and tax deducted. The Inland Revenue then checks the position of each taxpayer but if his code has been correct there will be no need for any further adjustment.

As well as dealing with employees' income tax, the PAYE system plays an important role in collecting National Insurance contributions. It has been estimated that while some £12,000 million in income tax was due to be collected in 1975/76, in the same year the PAYE machinery was also responsible for collecting some £6,000 million employees' and employers' National Insurance contributions.[30] Although they are related to income,[31] the contributions are calculated quite separately from PAYE; but they are withheld at the same time as income tax and remitted with the tax and the employers' contributions to the Collector each month.

The PAYE system applies only to emoluments assessable to income tax under Schedule E, but the liability on small amounts of other income e.g. interest on bank deposits or on government stock held through the National Savings Stock Register, can be dealt with by an arrangement known as 'coding-out'. Under this arrangement the amount of the other income is deducted from the taxpayer's coding allowances, resulting in a lower code and consequently higher tax deductions.

If for some reason the taxpayer has under-paid tax on his earnings at the end of the tax year, then instead of demanding immediate payment, the Inland Revenue may recover the amount due slowly (and less painfully) over the following year, again by reducing the taxpayer's code—a practice known as 'coding-in'. If, on the other hand, anything is due to the taxpayer it is repaid in a lump sum.

The main advantage of PAYE is that current tax payments are matched with current tax liability; in other words, taxes are paid as liability accrues. The taxpayer does not have to worry about the possibility of having to meet a large tax bill sometime after the end of the tax year. The Inland Revenue also has fewer problems (at least with incomes assessed under Schedule E) about collecting arrears of tax after the income has been spent. In addition, there is no need for a large number of end-year adjustments with taxpayers having to file returns every year to re-claim overpayments of tax. Only about 4 million out of 20 million PAYE cases require adjustment each year.[32] In the UK repayment can be and is made without completion of a return; the Revenue used to insist on a return in every such case but no longer does so provided it is satisfied that there is no other income. It has been estimated that in the future about 60 per cent of PAYE taxpayers will normally be asked to make a return only once every five years.[33] Furthermore, the system does not break down if returns are not filed. Indeed, of the 10 million or so returns sent to PAYE taxpayers in any one year, only about 7.8 million are completed or sent back.[34] A further advantage sometimes claimed for PAYE is that even the average taxpayer is not the most suitable person to undertake the complicated job of income tax assessment and PAYE relieves him of much of this work and places it in the more professional hands of the Inland Revenue and employers. These arguments will be discussed at length in Chapter IV.

[30] *118th Report of the Commissioners of Inland Revenue,* Cmnd. 6302, HMSO, 1974.
[31] For 1976/77 the National Insurance contribution for employees earning over £13 per week was 5.75% of gross earnings up to a ceiling of £95. The employers' contribution was 8.75% of all earnings.
[32] Inland Revenue estimate.
[33] *118th Report of the Commissioners of Inland Revenue,* 1974–75 Cmnd. 6302.
[34] Inland Revenue estimate.

Some of the biggest complications of PAYE have been simplified since 1943 (e.g. the original PAYE tax tables in 1944/45 contained some 30 million computations). However, several complications remain. Because PAYE is a cumulative system employers need to take into account an employee's previous earnings during the tax year in order to be able to withhold the correct amount of tax. This leads to a considerable amount of work when a person changes his employment. When an individual leaves a job his employer issues a form P45, which shows the employee's code number, gross pay and tax paid to date. Part 1 of the P45 is sent to the employee's present tax district, parts 2 and 3 are given to the employee to give to his new employer, who in turn, retains Part 2 for authorisation to make deductions of tax, and sends Part 3 to the new tax office. The first tax office then sends the person's file to the second tax office. In a tax district dealing with PAYE this P45 work alone is likely to occupy at least 10 per cent of total staff resources.

The P45 system may also impinge on an individual's privacy. If a person changes his occupation his new employer can readily establish how much he earned in his previous job during the tax year and it may therefore affect a man's bargaining strength when negotiating pay for a new job, i.e. he knows he may be found out if he exaggerates his previous earnings. It is possible for an individual to avoid this disclosure by asking the tax office to arrange for his tax to be paid on a 'week 1' (non-cumulative) basis, but it is not known how many people are aware of this facility or would wish to draw attention to their financial affairs by using it.

Another difficulty arises in the process of coding. The tax year in the United Kingdom commences on 6 April, and by this date the process of calculating taxpayers' code numbers should have been completed. However, a budget at the start of the fiscal year may change the value of at least some of the allowances and so necessitate changes in code shortly after the codes determined for the year have been brought into use. To meet this contingency a rather ingenious device was developed. The Inland Revenue examined the largest change e.g. a change that affected the personal allowance, and if the taxpayers affected by this change were in the majority, Table A (converting codes into total free pay to date) was adjusted to suit the majority, and only the remaining taxpayers had to be recoded. This may be illustrated by a numerical example. Suppose that in some year the single person's allowance was originally £225, represented by code 200. The allowance was increased in the Budget by £135 to £360 but the code was left at 200 and the table was revised so that code 200 then represented allowances of £360. Since 1973, however, this device has been replaced by the system of suffixes described above. If the values of personal allowances change the Revenue can instruct employers to alter those codes with suffix L or H by the appropriate amount but not those with suffix T unless the employer receives individual notification from the Tax Office.

It is difficult to ensure cumulation in all cases. PAYE is able to withhold tax on a cumulative basis from a higher rate taxpayer who derives his income from one job only by the use of a supplement to Table B (Table C). For example, one line from the Table C for monthly pay, issued in 1974, reads: 'if total taxable pay to date (month 12) exceeds £4,500 but not £5,000, then total tax due is £1,485 plus 38 per cent of the excess over £4,500'. However, accurate withholding is not so easy where a higher rate taxpayer has income from more than one employment source. Potentially tax would be under-withheld if the PAYE system treated each employment separately and so deducted more tax at the basic rate than it should, and less at higher rates. To overcome this problem there is a system of D code prefixes. What happens is that all the individual's allowances against taxable income, and all pay subject to tax at the basic rate, are absorbed by one (or possibly more) employment(s); then he receives a D code for any further jobs. There is a separate D code for each rate bracket starting with D0 for deductions at 40 per cent, D1 for 45 per cent and so on up to D8 for the top rate of 83 per cent. Codes with a prefix D are operated on a non-cumulative basis and the relevant rate of tax is deducted from the whole of the payment, irrespective of the size of that payment. The appropriate amount of tax is calculated by reference to Tax Table D which consists of a set of ready reckoners, one for each of the D codes. Thus for code D0, one line in the Table might read: 'income £100—tax £40.' While in many cases the use of D prefixes may increase the accuracy of withholding through PAYE, inaccuracies remain because of the non-cumulative element. For example, should the income from the taxpayer's main employment fall and his allowances and basic rate entitlement not be fully used up, then too much tax would be deducted. At the moment people in this category form only a small minority of taxpayers, though clearly the number subject to this form of non-cumulative withholding will rise if the threshold for higher rate tax is not increased in line with increases in incomes and if secondary sources of income become more common.

Cumulation itself has attracted criticism because a rebate may be payable during the tax year should an employee's earnings drop or cease altogether. It has been said that this may encourage workers to strike more often and for longer periods than they otherwise might, and that there may be an incentive for some workers to become unemployed for part of the tax year. The issue has received some attention both from the financial press and the Conservative Political Centre.[35]

It can be seen from Table II–4 and the accompanying discussion, that a rebate will become payable when an employee's earnings during a pay period are less than the value of the free pay (i.e. the value of his allowances and deductions) allocated to him for that pay period. If his earnings fall to nothing, the value of the rebate will be equal to the rate of tax multiplied by his free

[35] *See Financing Strikes*, July 1974 and Ralph Howell *Why Work?*, March 1976, both published by the Conservative Political Centre, London.

pay. Thus in our example on page 25, the employee's allowances are accumulating as free pay at the rate of £10 a week, and assuming a tax rate of 30 per cent, the rebate to which he is entitled when his earnings fall to zero in week 3, is £3. Should the individual continue to earn nothing the same amount of rebate will continue to be payable until he has received back all the tax paid during the current tax year. The amount of rebate due in any one pay period does not depend on the time of the year (apart from right at the beginning of the tax year when little or no tax has been paid) but the possible duration of the re-payments will be longer towards the end of the year as there would normally be more tax to be refunded.

Clearly refunds may fall due in a number of situations, including strikes. The publication *Financing Strikes* states that this is 'a fact not lost upon Trade Union secretaries, and which partially explains the high incidence of strikes in the later part of the PAYE tax year'.[38] However, in practice the situation is not as automatic as may appear at first sight. Confronted by a strike, an employer may either pay the rebates to the strikers himself or provide sufficient information to the Inspector of Taxes to enable him to do so.[37] Failure to do either will render the employer liable to prosecution. But there are a number of reasons why rebates may not be paid during strikes. A great many disputes are settled within a few days so that a rebate does not fall due, and even for more lengthy strikes there are difficulties. For instance, whether an employer decides to pay rebates himself or let the Inland Revenue undertake the operation is irrelevant in an industry-wide strike such as that of the Union of Post Office Workers (UPW) from January to March 1971, when the staff manning the payroll sections also withdrew their labour. It may be possible for the Revenue to extract accurate information concerning the tax paid, earnings to date and code of a person on strike even when the employer is not in a position to provide it. But there would be problems; and a study of the Post Office strike by Gennard and Lasko[38] found that none of the UPW members interviewed even applied to their tax office for a rebate. Additionally, while an employer may pay refunds at the appropriate time, i.e. weekly or monthly, the Inland Revenue's procedure is much more complex and lengthy. First of all, the employer is not obliged to inform the Revenue of his decision not to pay rebates until the first pay day on which the employees do not receive wages. Where employees are paid in arrears therefore, there may be a delay of up to two weeks in the case of weekly-paid workers and up to two months for those paid monthly. Secondly, the length of time before the Revenue will pay out rebates is about four weeks, and it is usual for the rebates to be made only fortnightly for weekly paid employees and once a month for the monthly paid.

---

[36] Howell, *op. cit.* p. 9.

[37] The procedure in both cases is presented in Regulation 24 of *Statutory Instrument 1973 No. 334* 'The Income Tax (Employments) Regulations 1973', made under Section 204 of the *Income and Corporation Taxes Act* (1970).

[38] John Gennard and Roger Lasko, 'The Individual and the Strike' *British Journal of Industrial Relations,* November 1975.

Nevertheless, refunds are made during strikes: often by the employer directly, perhaps because it is less costly in terms of administration or because it may be detrimental to future industrial relations to do otherwise. There is also some evidence to suggest that the sums may be significant. For instance, Cole undertook a study into the finances of 30 workers in the Midland area involved in the national building industry stoppage of 1972.[39] He found that although there were wide variations in the total income received by strikers, on average 10 per cent of that income came from tax rebates.

A slightly different issue is that tax rebates combined with social security payments may result in some employees finding it profitable to become unemployed for part of the tax year. This area has been explored by Mr. Ralph Howell who has asked some two hundred Parliamentary questions in the House of Commons on the subject since 1970. The main reason for this situation is that short-term national insurance benefits (unemployment and sickness benefits) are not taxable because of the difficulties of taxing such payments through a cumulative PAYE system.[40] An individual in receipt of unemployment benefit would therefore be treated for tax purposes as though he had no earnings, and so may receive a full tax rebate as well. Howell discovered that 'nearly all persons at the present time, married or single, with or without children, and earning up to as much as £70 per week (well above average manual earnings) can find themselves better off by being unemployed for an average of 15 weeks per year'.[41] It was also revealed that £400 million more was paid in rebates in 1974 than would have been the case had short-term benefits been taxable, and that the figure had risen from £150 million in 1970.[42]

Direct Collection

A further limitation on the usefulness of the PAYE machinery is that it does not cover all incomes under Schedule E, despite the 'coding-out' process. This arises because many retired people are in receipt of taxable incomes that are not subject to withholding, for example, the National Insurance pension, some interest receipts, and many casual jobs. As a result it may not be possible to 'code-out' the tax liability incurred on these incomes by reducing the code applied to another source of income, such as an occupational pension. Instead, a direct collection assessment is raised on the pensioner's income. The tax due during the tax year is calculated and a quarter of that tax is payable 30 days after each quarter of the time remaining between the date of the assessment and the end of the tax year. Ideally, the payments should be made quarterly but it is not always possible to raise the assessment at the beginning of the tax

---

[39] W. J. Cole 'The Financing of the Individual Striker: A Case Study in the Building Industry' *British Journal of Industrial Relations,* March 1975.

[40] See Sir Stafford Cripps' Budget speech, 6th April 1949, *Hansard,* cols. 2090–1. Also Ch. IV, p. 146.

[41] Howell, *op. cit.* p. 7.

[42] *Ibid.* p. 6.

year. The Inland Revenue makes considerable efforts to issue assessments to pensioners who are subject to direct collection assessments early in the tax year, but some slip through the net, particularly the newly retired, and as their tax liability accumulates they may find themselves faced with a bill for past tax as well as a reduced income following retirement. If there are changes in pensioners' financial circumstances, for instance if the National Insurance pension rises, the whole estimation process may have to be reworked.

Some aspects of the system were reformed in 1976. New prefix F codes were introduced enabling tax to be withheld at rates higher than the basic rate. Prefix F codes are designed for those cases where the full amount of a pensioner's tax liability cannot be collected through PAYE by the use of other codes i.e. with those suffix H, L, T, P or V. Although the introduction of F prefixes may reduce the difficulties and worries of some pensioners they cannot be regarded as a complete solution to the problems associated with direct collection assessment.

Roman Catholic Priests

Although Roman Catholic priests are assessed under Schedule E they are not covered by the normal PAYE process. The reason is that unlike, say, Ministers of the Church of England, they are not paid from a central source but their main income arises directly from the parish. As a result these priests are issued with their own Tables A and B and instructed to make their own peace with the Collector of Taxes. This case provides one instance of self-assessment operating in the United Kingdom today under the unfavourable circumstances of a system designed for non-assessment on the part of the taxpayer.

To summarise, the main issue with regard to self-assessment and PAYE is whether any net benefits gained by keeping assessment out of the hands of most people earning wages and salaries are worth the considerable costs imposed by the sophisticated PAYE machinery on employers and the Inland Revenue. We now turn to examine incomes assessed under Schedule D which raise quite different issues concerning self-assessment.

Schedule D and Other Incomes

Incomes assessed under Schedule D consist in the main of profits and interest payments and the Schedule is sub-divided into the following cases: Cases I and II cover profits of trade, business and the professions; Case III covers interest and annuities other than those payable from public revenues; Case IV is concerned with foreign securities; Case V with income from possessions or business conducted abroad; and Case VI with casual and miscellaneous profits such as the income from furnished lettings. Schedules A, B, C and F are less important and so will only be touched on briefly.

CASES I AND II (PROFITS)

We have seen that tax is collected from wages and salaries more or less at the time that liability is incurred, i.e. on a 'current year' or even a 'current week' basis. With the exception of Case VI and of what amounts to withholding at the basic rate from dividends and some interest payments, assessment for Schedule D incomes is normally on a 'preceding year' basis. In the case of profits (Cases I and II) the assessment (except when firms are just opening or closing) will be based on the profits shown in a person's accounts for his financial year ending in the tax year (i.e. the year ending 5 April) preceding the year of assessment. Payment of half the liability is then due by the following 1 January, and the rest by the following 1 July. To give an example: suppose a trader makes up his accounts to 31 December each year, then in the tax year 1976/77 he would be assessed for income tax on the profits he made in the year ending 31 December 1975. Half the tax liability on those profits then falls due on 1 January 1977 and the rest on 1 July 1977. A major problem with the preceding year basis is that it necessitates some very complicated arrangements for firms just starting business as there is no preceding year on which to base an assessment. Other provisions apply to the closure of businesses. Because of their complexity it is easier to illustrate the provision for new businesses with the example of our trader who makes up his accounts to 31 December each year. Suppose that he commences trading in August 1974. Effectively what happens is that in one way or another the first three payments of tax are based on the first year's profit. The first payment for the tax year 1974/75 would be based on the profits made from August 1974 to 5 April 1975. The bill for the second tax year 1975/76 would be based on the profits of the first 12 months' trading, i.e. August 1974 to August 1975. For the third tax year, 1976/77, the usual basis of assessment is the profit of the 12 months up to the end of the trader's accounting period preceding the start of the tax year, i.e. the year to 31 December 1975. Thereafter the preceding year is used. As this procedure for the first three years of a business may bear unfairly on the taxpayer, he has the right to have the assessments for the second and third years (but not one year only) based on the actual profits of those years. Clearly, for the purposes of making up one's accounts not all dates are equally advantageous. As one tax guide points out,[43] the best year-end dates for making up one's accounts are 31 March or 5 April if one is considering convenience, and 30 April or 31 May if one is considering deferral of tax liability.

The last years of a business are also subject to different rules. The assessment for the final year is based on the actual profit made from the previous 6 April to the date the business closed. However, if the actual profits of the two tax years preceding the final year were more in total than the two years' assessments made on the preceding year basis, the Inland Revenue has the power to decide that the assessments be based on the actual profits for each of those two years (but not one year only). The total profits over a lifetime of a business therefore, would not usually be the same as the total amount of

---

[43] J. D. Finnigan and G. M. Kitchen, *Check Your Tax*, 1975/76 ed. (Foulsham, London), p. 45.

Schedule D assessments on the business, and in fact cannot be so if the trade continues for longer than six years.[44]

The upshot is that Schedule D assessments may have an advantage over Schedule E in addition to the more generous deductions discussed above.[45] While tax is payable in each year of trading, liability is measured with reference to the income of the previous year. If incomes are rising, either as a result of inflation or increases in real income or both, then tax on the additional income is delayed until the following year. Such a delay in payment confers a benefit which may be interpreted as an interest-free loan from the government. During a period of inflation it may be interpreted as the ability to pay the delayed part of the tax bill in depreciated currency. In the above example, if our trader receives an even flow of income throughout the year, he is able to delay his tax payments on average by approximately 21 months, without even the need for an appeal against an assessment.

There are several difficulties with this arrangement. If it is generally thought that individuals assessed under Schedule E have to pay tax on income as soon as it is received whilst others do not, and that this situation is inequitable, we may have a loss of 'tax morale' and taxpayer co-operation. Wage and salary earners have also to pay more tax than otherwise to make up for the loss of revenue. Together with other benefits associated with a Schedule D assessment[46] the ability to delay tax payments will lead to advantages, other things equal, in being self-employed even though from an economic viewpoint it may be more efficient to work as an employee. There may also be costs incurred by the

Table II–5 Assessments Under Schedule D, Cases I & II (Trading Profits)

	Number (in '000s)
1964	1,741.4
1965	1,814.5
1966	1,859.7
1967	1,915.5
1968	1,971.5
1969	2,046.2
1970	2,107.9
1971	2,222.2
1972	2,410.0

SOURCE: *Inland Revenue Statistics*.

NOTE: The figures generally relate to the earnings in accounting periods ending in the fiscal year to the following 5 April.

---

[44] See P. C. Whiteman and D. C. Milne, *Whiteman and Wheatcroft on Income Tax*, Sweet & Maxwell, 1976, pp. 312–317 for further discussion.

[45] Cf. p. 16.

[46] *Ibid.*

Inland Revenue. If it should happen that a taxpayer has either spent the money or disappeared before he actually pays his tax there is an additional loss of revenue and perhaps further costs faced by the Revenue in attempting to recover it.

Self-assessment in the form of estimated payments of current tax liability would minimise the difficulties and complexities of the preceding year basis of assessment. The complicated provisions for businesses that are either starting or finishing would no longer be necessary; there would be less inequity between the employed and the self-employed; a shorter interval between actual tax payments and accruing liability; and perhaps less difficulty in ensuring the payment of tax that had long been spent or had otherwise disappeared. Reform in this area would appear particularly relevant given the increase in the number of assessments under Schedule D cases I and II, e.g. from 1.7 million in 1964 to 2.4 million in 1972 (Table II–5). We shall revert to these matters in more detail in both Chapter III and Chapter IV.

CASE III (INTEREST PAYMENTS FROM NON-PUBLIC SOURCES)

Like Cases I and II, the basis of assessment for Case III is the preceding year and there are provisions for years when a source of income first arises or terminates.

In certain circumstances tax must be withheld from interest payments, but in most cases it is not, the most common example being bank deposit interest. The arguments against withholding tax from bank deposit interest are based not only on the convenience of the banks, but also on the fear that the Inland Revenue might be involved in large numbers of repayment claims from individuals who are in receipt of interest but not liable to tax. However, non-withholding in this case has its problems; a large number of taxpayers fail to disclose small interest receipts on their returns (some 140,000 were discovered in the year from mid-1975 to mid-1976). This in turn involves the Revenue in a considerable amount of correspondence. Banks (and individuals) are obliged to report to the Revenue interest payments exceeding a certain amount together with the name and address of the recipient. In 1976/77 the amounts were £40 in the case of the National Savings Bank and Trustee Savings Bank ordinary accounts; and £25 for other bank accounts.

There are special arrangements for most building societies. Their rates of interest paid to investors are quoted net of tax, which is paid by the societies at an average or composite rate that is less than the basic rate. Investors not liable to tax cannot, however, claim a refund, which avoids the considerable number of claims for repayment of tax that would otherwise have to be dealt with by the Revenue. Recipients of building society interest who pay tax at the basic rate have no further liability. Higher rate taxpayers are regarded as having received the net interest after deduction of tax at the basic rate, and are liable to higher rates of tax on the gross amount.

CASES IV AND V (INCOME FROM FOREIGN SECURITIES AND POSSESSIONS)
The whole area of income from abroad is very complicated and we shall not attempt a thorough explanation here.[47]

Most of the income assessed under Cases IV and V is taxed on the full amount of the income arising in the foreign country, whether or not it is received in the United Kingdom, i.e. the 'arising basis of assessment'. But in two cases income is taxed only on a remittance basis, that is only to the extent that the income is received in the United Kingdom. The two exceptions are income received (i) by individuals not domiciled[48] in the United Kingdom and (ii) by citizens of the United Kingdom or the Irish Republic who are not ordinarily resident in the United Kingdom.

The bulk of the income in this category received by residents in the United Kingdom consists of interest and dividends from overseas companies. Where the income is paid by a paying agent in the United Kingdom or received by an agent in the United Kingdom there are provisions in tax law for the agent to be assessed to tax on the sums paid or collected and to deduct British income tax at the basic rate (after crediting any appropriate amounts in respect of foreign taxes already paid) before passing them on.

CASE VI (CASUAL AND MISCELLANEOUS PROFITS)
Unlike the normal rule for Cases I to V of assessments based on the preceding year, income charged under Case VI is assessed on a current year basis. One interesting aspect of assessments under this Case is a form of standard deduction. In practice many Inspectors allow the landlords of furnished lettings a deduction for the depreciation of furnishings in the form of an annual percentage, usually 10 per cent, of the gross rents receivable. It is possible to itemise the deductions but this entails considerably more work. Landlords also have the right to have the rent other than that attributable to the furnishings charged under Schedule A if they so wish.

Schedule A
The scope of Schedule A has been altered in recent years and at present basically covers rents and other receipts from the ownership of land and other property. Income is taxable under this Schedule if it is receivable—regardless of whether it has actually been received or not. However, there are exceptions where non-receipt is attributable to default by the tenant and where it can be proved either that reasonable steps to enforce payment have been taken, or that payment was waived in order to avoid hardship.

[47] For further information and discussion see Board of Inland Revenue, *The Taxation of Foreign Earnings and Foreign Pensions: Finance Act 1974,* Oct. 1974; and M. A. Pickering and A. R. Prest 'Some Aspects of the Remittance Basis for the Taxation of Overseas Income', *British Tax Review,* 1974 No. 6.

[48] Basically domicile is determined either by origin which is taken at birth from the domicile of an individual's father, or by choice which largely centres on the revealed intention to remain permanently in a country which is not the country of origin. Domicile is distinct from nationality, citizenship, residence or ordinary residence.

The collection of tax under Schedule A is on a current basis and represents a crude version of the estimated tax payments found in many systems of self-assessment abroad. The tax is payable on 1 January during the tax year in which the income is received. As is inevitable in the case of estimated tax payments, liability cannot be determined accurately at that stage in the tax year and so tax is payable on the assumption that taxable income is the same as in the preceding year. Any necessary adjustments are made soon after the end of the tax year. If a taxpayer ceases during the current year to possess a source of income assessed under Schedule A since the beginning of the preceding year he may present a written statement to that effect to the Inspector. If the Inspector is satisfied that the statement is accurate the assessment will be reduced accordingly.

Schedules B and C

Tax is chargeable under Schedule B on the occupier of commercial woodlands on the 'assessable value of his occupation'. The basis of assessment is one-third of the estimated annual value of the land on the assumption that, instead of being woodlands, the lands are let and occupied in their natural and unimproved state. The occupier may not deduct any expenditures, but on the other hand the assessment to tax will be based on the same notional amount regardless of the level of his profits. An occupier of commercial woodlands has the right to be assessed under Schedule D rather than Schedule B; a right that may lead to a certain amount of manipulation. While the trees are growing losses are incurred and it is normally beneficial to the occupier to be assessed under Schedule D so that he may claim loss relief and capital allowances, and when the trees mature and are sold, to form a company to take over the woodlands and be assessed under Schedule B.

Schedule C covers the taxation of interest and annuities payable out of public revenues. Income is assessed on a current basis and there are provisions for the tax to be withheld at source by deduction at the basic rate.

Schedule F

Schedule F applies to certain dividend income. Dividends receivable from companies resident in the UK are distributed with a tax-credit which is sufficient to satisfy tax liability at the basic rate on the combined dividend and credit. So assessment under Schedule F will only be made in cases where liability to higher rates of tax is incurred.

Capital Gains Tax

Capital gains are not taxed under the personal income tax as is common in other countries. Instead, capital gains tax is chargeable on gains on the disposal of assets at a rate of 30 per cent. However, if it is to the taxpayer's advantage an alternative method of calculation may be used by which the tax payable is restricted to the additional income tax (including investment income surcharge) chargeable if half of the gains up to a maximum of £5,000 and the whole of any gains in excess of £5,000 were added to the individual's income for the tax year. Capital gains tax is not chargeable where gross disposable proceeds in any one year do not exceed £1,000, nor is it chargeable on death. Some of the main forms of property that are exempt from the tax include gilt-edged stocks held for 12 months or more, any gains an individual may make by selling his principal private residence, chattels worth £1,000 or less, and winnings from betting. Although individuals are asked to compute the value of their capital gains, self-assessment does not play a significant part in the administration of the tax as the Inland Revenue calculates net gain and liability and no payment is due until an assessment has been received from the tax office.

Enforcement

APPEALS

Appeals against a notice of assessment for income tax must be made in writing within 30 days of the date on which the assessment was issued, though late appeals may be considered if the taxpayer can provide a satisfactory explanation, such as being in hospital or abroad, and his application to appeal is made without unreasonable delay. In practice, a late appeal may also be considered if the Inspector considers the responsibility for any mistake to be his, though in such a case an appeal may not be necessary. An appeal may be made even if the assessment is based on an inaccurate return made by the appellant. Most appeals can be settled between the Inspector and the taxpayer, but cases where no agreement can be reached are heard by the Commissioners of Income Tax.

There are two separate types of Commissioners who enjoy equal status: the General and the Special Commissioners. Neither should be confused with the Commissioners of Inland Revenue who form the Board of Inland Revenue. The General Commissioners of Income Tax are unpaid members of the public normally sitting in a quorum of two in their own particular locality. They are appointed in England and Wales by the Lord Chancellor, in Scotland by the appropriate local authority, and they are subject to a retiring age of 75. There are no bodies of General Commissioners in Northern Ireland, their duties being undertaken either by the county court, with the judge sitting alone and in private, or by the Special Commissioners. The Special Commissioners are full-time salaried civil servants appointed by the Treasury and include barristers and solicitors with extensive experience of tax law gained either in practice or in the Inland Revenue, though as Commissioners they operate independently of the Revenue. They are based in London but go on circuit to hear appeals, and under certain circumstances (which obtain at most hearings) sit alone. With the exception of Northern Ireland where there are no General Commissioners, and within certain statutory limits,[49] the choice between the General and Special Commissioners lies with the taxpayer. It has been said that an appeal to the heart would do better before the General Commissioners with their local knowledge, and an appeal to the head before the Special Commissioners with their technical expertise.[50]

The hearing itself is informal. The Inspector will normally represent the Inland Revenue though the taxpayer may conduct his own case or be represented by an accountant, solicitor or barrister. During the hearing the onus is on the appellant to show that the assessment is erroneous, rather than on the Revenue to prove that it is correct even though the assessment is based on an estimate made by the tax office—a procedure that has been interpreted as the taxpayer being considered guilty until proved innocent. The Commissioners have the power to require the appellant to provide such information and to make available for inspection such documents or accounts in his possession as are relevant to the appeal, and the Revenue may take copies of such documents. The Commissioners may also summon witnesses to be examined under oath. Although notice of appeal against an assessment must specify the grounds of appeal, the taxpayer may be permitted by the Commissioners at the hearing to go into grounds of appeal not specified in the notice if they are satisfied that the omissions were not wilful or unreasonable. The Commissioners have no power to enquire into matters not under appeal. After the hearing they may confirm, discharge, reduce or increase any assessment under appeal and their decision is a majority one except that if only two Commissioners sit and they disagree, the practice is that the taxpayer may be given the benefit of the doubt or the case may be re-heard by three Commissioners. Since August 1975 an appeal no longer affects the liability to pay the tax assessed. However, if the Commissioners are shown reasonable grounds to believe that the appellant has been overassessed, they have the power to determine that all or part of the payment of tax should be postponed pending the determination of the appeal.

Decisions by the Commissioners on questions of fact are final. On questions of law however, the loser at the hearing before the Commissioners may take the case to a court of law. Such an appeal would come before a judge of the Chancery Division of the High Court in England and Wales, the Court of Appeal in Northern Ireland, or the Inner House of the Court of Session in Scotland. In England and Wales an appeal from a decision of the High Court would be made either before the Courts of Appeal or, in certain circumstances, directly to the House of Lords. In Scotland and Northern Ireland further appeals would be made directly to the House of Lords. While each party is responsible for his own costs before the Commissioners, the loser usually pays if the case is taken further. The costs of appeal are not deductible against

---

49 A thorough discussion of this and other related areas of tax law appears in P. G. Whiteman and D. C. Milne, *Whiteman and Wheatcroft on Income Tax,* 'British Tax Encyclopedia' 2nd ed. (Sweet and Maxwell, 1976).

50 M. Z. Hepker, *A Modern Approach to Tax Law* (Heinemann, London, 1973) p. 29.

taxable income but the Revenue will sometimes undertake to pay all the costs in test cases.

PENALTIES

One of the traditional policies of British tax administration has been to reduce the number of opportunities for tax evasion as much as possible. As is shown in more detail in Chapter III this contrasts with the practice in many other countries where the emphasis has been to leave such opportunities open (for example, by not withholding tax at source from dividend and interest payments) and to discourage fraud by various methods of checking and penalising those caught. As well as formal penalties, taxpayers abroad may suffer in other ways; for instance, in Australia the names of those convicted are listed and published including—in 1974 at least—ministers of religion!

In the United Kingdom tax enforcement is a little less aggressive, both as regards criminal prosecutions and penalties imposed without reference to a court of law—Inland Revenue prosecutions were unknown before 1916. During the fiscal year 1974/75 criminal proceedings were taken in only 140 cases, or one for approximately every 143,000 taxpayers.[51] Of these 140 Revenue prosecutions only ten were for false accounts and returns of income etc., one for every two million taxpayers. Most of the rest were in areas more commonly dealt with by the police, such as 76 for sub-contractor exemption certificate frauds and 28 for such crimes as the theft of payable orders and Giro cheques; or in areas that may be considered potentially less rewarding in terms of tax evaded, such as 18 for false claims to personal allowances, deductions etc., and three for assaults on Inland Revenue officers. Only 14 out of the 140 were acquitted, which may indicate some reluctance on the part of the Revenue to undertake criminal proceedings unless they are confident of winning.[52]

It may be that the relatively small number of criminal prosecutions in the United Kingdom is a result of honesty on the part of British taxpayers. However, similar restraint is shown by the Inland Revenue in the imposition of other penalties. On paper these penalties are severe, for example up to £50, plus £10 a day, for overdue returns and up to three times the amount of unpaid tax liability. But such penalties are rarely used. A British taxpayer failing to file a return when required will normally find his allowances disappearing until he does so. As his allowances would be returned at that stage his only loss is the net-of-tax interest foregone by paying tax earlier in the year than would otherwise have been necessary. The practice in the United States and many other countries provides something of a contrast as taxpayers filing late returns face formal penalties based on a percentage of the tax due and imposed automatically (see Chapter III). Similar penalties might improve the

[51] Based on an updated estimate of the latest figures available in *Inland Revenue Statistics 1975*. Married couples are counted as one.

[52] There is a great contrast between the unwillingness of the Revenue and the willingness of the social security authorities to prosecute in this country. See also Chapter III for further discussion on prosecutions in other countries.

extent to which taxpayers comply with the tax system in the United Kingdom. The large number of small cases of under-payments of tax might be reduced if individuals faced automatic penalties; there were 140,000 such cases in 1975/76 (mid-year to mid-year), mainly as a result of interest which had been received or credited without deduction of tax and had not been shown on taxpayers' returns. It is also of interest to note that while the amount of tax collected by the Revenue has risen threefold between 1964/65 and 1974/75, the total penalties including interest raised during that period in cases of under-assessment rose from £4.9 million to only £5.9 million. The informal penalties employed in Britain may provide a more gentlemanly method of encouraging compliance than methods used abroad, but the greater use of more formal penalties might be more effective as taxpayers would know exactly where they stood. Formal penalties may also appear less arbitrary.

Evening Standard

You've been most helpful, co-operative and honest—what's your little game?

POWERS OF INVESTIGATION

Historically Inspectors have had few formal powers to enable them to require information and documents for inspection from taxpayers or third parties dealing with taxpayers. Methods have evolved to fill the gap at least in part. Should a person be suspected of paying less than his true liability to tax and should he refuse to provide the information required to disprove those suspicions, the Inspector may raise an estimated assessment. If the person so assessed considers the estimate excessive he may appeal to the Commissioners but the onus is on him to provide any information necessary to disprove the assessment. An Inspector may not have the formal power to demand an individual's bank statements, for instance, but it may be necessary for the individual to produce them in support of an appeal before the Commissioners.

The current tendency however, is to extend the powers of the Inland Revenue to demand information. Banks are required to disclose certain details of their customers' accounts and people such as stockbrokers may also be required to provide information on the transactions they undertake for their clients. Although the scope of the relevant provision is very limited, the Inland Revenue were empowered in 1972, for the first time, to exchange information relating to taxpayers' affairs with Custom and Excise. The 1976 Finance Bill proposed further extensions to the Revenue's powers. These were in fact modified in Parliamentary discussion, but even if implemented in full they would still have been less than those available to many tax authorities overseas.[53]

4 Taxpayer Assistance

Inland Revenue

Revenue assistance to taxpayers is more widespread than is usually supposed. It consists of direct communication—by telephone, personal visits to tax offices and written queries—the issue of general guides with tax returns and the provision of more detailed guides on specific areas which are obtainable on request. As Appendix III–2 deals with various aspects of tax returns and return guides we shall confine ourselves here to the other methods of assisting taxpayers.

It is difficult to estimate the number of enquiries received by the Inland Revenue each year as full records are not maintained and enquiries may vary considerably from year to year. One informed estimate however, was that on average over 10 million enquiries are made in person to tax offices and about the same number are made by telephone. Perhaps over 20 million enquiries are made by post. As these figures are only estimates we should not push comparisons too far, but with all reserve the figures do permit a rough contrast with the enquiries made to the Internal Revenue Service in the USA. As we can see from Table II–6 the 40 million or more enquiries in the UK are roughly comparable with the number in the USA, but one must remember the difference between the two countries in the size of population (USA 210 million, UK 56 million).

[53] See e.g. Chapter III, p. 109.

Table II–6 Number of Taxpayer Enquiries USA and UK (millions)

	USA	UK
Personal visits	11	(10+)
By telephone	29.4	(10)
By post	0.2	(20+)
Total	40.6	(40+)

SOURCE: US figures: Commissioner of Internal Revenue *Annual Report 1975*, US Government Printing Office, Washington, p.2.

It is interesting to speculate why proportionately more people would appear to require Revenue assistance under the British system of official assessment or non-assessment than under a system of self-assessment. We shall return to the point later.[54]

A further technique for enlightening taxpayers is the issue of detailed guides on particular aspects of tax law and administration. As can be seen from Appendix II–1 the Inland Revenue produces a wide range of these publications. One advantage of producing a range of pamphlets rather than one large master tax guide is flexibility: a new pamphlet can be produced, or an old one revised as soon as necessary, without having to wait until a complete version is worthwhile. Secondly, taxpayers with a specific query have to read only the relevant literature, rather than a whole mass of detail. But the production of a range of pamphlets can have a major drawback, as the present authors discovered when they tried to collect a copy of each of the Revenue publications. As often as not the required pamphlet was not available at the local tax office. There might be room for the production, as in other countries, of both an annual master guide (possibly in looseleaf form), plus a number of specific leaflets issued during the year when necessary. We shall return to this subject in Chapter VI.

The Private Sector

Although British income tax administration is based on official assessment, or non-assessment in the case of most wage and salary earners, the private sector is quite intimately involved in satisfying the needs of taxpayers for assistance. Sandford has estimated[55] that some 2,121,000 people pay someone to help them with their tax affairs. This figure includes some 1,854,000 individuals employing qualified accountants, 138,000 cases dealt with by banks, together with a number of enquiries of solicitors and unqualified accountants. Perhaps a further 850,000 are assisted by unpaid advisers. There are also a number of

[54] See Chapter III, p. 92 and Chapter VI, p. 188.
[55] C. T. Sandford, *Hidden Costs of Taxation* (Institute for Fiscal Studies, London, 1973)

tax guides, including the *Money Which? Tax Guide* with a circulation of over 565,000 in 1975, the Daily Mail's *Income Tax Guide* and the Daily Telegraph's *Guide to Income Tax* with circulations of 170,000 and 20,000 copies respectively in 1975.[56] In addition, a large number of miscellaneous articles on the subject appear in a wide range of publications: the authors' attention has even been drawn to such an article nestling between the ladies featured in a magazine for gentlemen![57] Press enquiry bureaux appear to answer about 40,000 queries a year and Citizens' Advice Bureaux a further 25,000.[58] There is also an Income Tax Payers' Society which 'fights for taxpayers' and provides a comprehensive service for its 6,000 members. The amount of assistance provided by the private sector also appears to be growing rapidly. The circulation of the Daily Mail's *Guide,* for instance, has risen from 20,000 copies in 1964 to 170,000 in 1975. Thus there are many sources of assistance for taxpayers even without self-assessment, and given their diversity and scope they could be very helpful should any system of self-assessment be introduced.

The Tax Guides

The guides vary considerably in their style and presentation, from the formal layout of the Daily Telegraph's[59] publication to the eye-catching format of *Check Your Tax.*[60] The latter boldly asserts on its cover that '30 per cent of us pay too much [tax]' a claim that it does not substantiate. The complexity of language, and details covered also vary significantly between guides. The diversity presumably indicates that the publications are designed to satisfy different sections of the taxpaying population, a flexibility not found in the administration's literature. In addition the commercial guides are able to offer the sort of advice that the Inland Revenue does not normally provide, such as opening a bank account for one's business, and how to go about employing one's wife as a partner. The flavour of this direct advice on tax planning may be illustrated by the example from the *Money Which? Tax Guide:* 'When you decide to have children, plan for your baby to be born towards the end of the tax year—which makes May or June good months to conceive. You still get a full year's tax saving of £79.20 . . . even if the baby isn't born until the last hour of the last day of the tax year'. In other words April 1 is not such a foolish day on which to be born after all!

Taking the guides together, the intention and/or result of both the Daily Mail and The Daily Telegraph's publications is basically to provide the same sort of information as the Inland Revenue's Tax Guides, only better, and perhaps with slightly different aims in mind. However, one is reminded of a quotation from Keynes: 'The important thing for government is not to do things which individuals are doing already, and to do them a little better or a little

[56] Figures supplied by the publishers.
[57] Victor Selwyn, 'Do You Pay Too Much Tax?' *Knave* Volume 8 No. 3.
[58] Sandford, *op. cit.* p. 73.
[59] Bryan Budibent, *Daily Telegraph Guide to Income Tax,* (Collins, London 1975).
[60] J. D. Finnigan & G. M. Kitchen, *Check Your Tax,* (Foulsham, London 1975).

worse; but to do those things which at present are not done at all.'[61] In this case it is the other way around. The private sector has a quite different role to that of the Inland Revenue. It should be able to provide the sort of assistance and information that the Inland Revenue is not there to provide such as unembarrassed guidance for the taxpayer in dealing with the tax system (both tax law *and* Revenue practice) to minimise his liability. It should be able to present the relevant information in simple, straightforward prose that the Inland Revenue, constrained by the intricacies of statute, is either unable or unwilling to use. *Check Your Tax* and the *Money Which? Guide* have taken this approach with some success and have the potential to assist a large number of taxpayers in the event of any element of self-assessment being introduced.

Punch

'An individual is resident and ordinarily resident in the United Kingdom if he is living here in the ordinary course of his life, or for an extended period; also though normally he lives here, if he is abroad for occasional residence only; or if he visits the United Kingdom, year by year, even though his main home is abroad' . . . who on earth wrote this, Harold Pinter?'

PRESS ENQUIRY BUREAUX

In his study of compliance costs,[62] Sandford found that in 1970 around 40,000 queries regarding taxation were put to the enquiry bureaux of press combines based in England and Wales. As part of the study a survey was undertaken of the questions received by the Westminster Enquiry Bureau which revealed a number of interesting characteristics of the people seeking assistance. First

[61] J. M. Keynes, *The End of Laissez-Faire* (Hogarth Press, London, 1927) p. 46.
[62] C. T. Sandford *op. cit.*

there was a disproportionate number of men, resulting presumably from a man's responsibility for his wife's income tax return. Secondly, compared to the sample census of 1965 there was a lower proportion of single people and a relatively high proportion of widows and, thirdly, over two-thirds of the survey population whose age was identified were either retired or about to retire. Finally, the typical enquirer appears to have been in receipt of an income considerably below the national average.

Of the requests themselves, 39.9 per cent were requests to check Inland Revenue calculations, 31.9 per cent to predict future tax payments and 25.1 per cent were requests to explain some aspects of the tax code. Only 3.1 per cent asked for advice on the tax implications of a particular course of action. A survey of enquiries to a second bureau showed that 26 per cent of retired people making enquiries had part-time jobs.

The results of the surveys have several implications for self-assessment. Even under the British system of official assessment a large number of people take the trouble to check the official calculations. Almost as many people appear to be unable to calculate their own future liability with confidence—which is not surprising as the existing system is not designed to enable people to ascertain their liability easily. The same situation applies to the number of people who wanted further explanation of some aspect of the tax code. It is not necessary for the British taxpayer to understand the tax system in order to pay tax. One wonders, therefore, how many other taxpayers there are who do not trouble to establish their tax position and are content to make economic decisions in ignorance of their tax implications.

CITIZENS' ADVICE BUREAUX

As part of the study in *The Hidden Costs of Taxation* the organiser or tax adviser of ten Citizens' Advice Bureaux (CABs) was interviewed. The results of the interviews supported the conclusion from the press enquiries that a large proportion of the people seeking help were retired—possibly a majority in the case of the CABs. Both sources appear to indicate that a further group of people in need of tax advice are those experiencing changes in their marital status. Some 25,000 tax queries were put to CABs in England and Wales in 1970.

Under the existing British system of official assessment many taxpayers of average and below average means seek assistance from sources other than the Inland Revenue. Assistance such as tax-planning is quite understandable as this type of work does not, and perhaps should not, form part of the work of the Inland Revenue. But most of the queries received by the Press and Citizens' Advice Bureaux are not concerned with tax avoidance so much as information; or they seek to check Inland Revenue calculations or to predict future liability. Many of the enquiries appear to be from people who have not fully understood explanations given to them by the Revenue, or who were reluctant to ask the Revenue. Most of the contents of the published tax guides are devoted only to explanations of how to complete a return successfully. These are operations that might be performed successfully by the Inland Revenue if the tax system and administration were designed to be more easily understood and operated by taxpayers. Any increase in the compliance burden on the private sector as a result of self-assessment might be less than would at first be supposed.

5 Proposals for Reform

Proposals involving major reform or extension of the income tax system in the United Kingdom have been put forward from time to time. For instance, a number of alternatives to the cumulative PAYE mechanism were suggested to the 1955 Royal Commission on the Taxation of Profits and Income.[63] However, to keep our discussion within reasonable bounds, we shall confine ourselves here to the proposals for a tax-credit scheme and the possibility of a local income tax.

Tax-Credits

The 1972 Green Paper on tax-credits[64] raised a number of points of interest, not least of which was the following condensed critique of PAYE:

> 'It [PAYE] is complicated and difficult to understand. It requires the employment of some 35,000 staff in the Inland Revenue and perhaps as many again in industry. It has been found to lack flexibility and governments of both political parties have found it difficult to adapt it to accommodate changes that they have felt desirable. Nor would these handicaps have been removed even if the system had been operated fully by computers. The complexities of PAYE arise partly from the annual coding, and partly from its cumulative basis which requires the tax office to maintain contact with all employees through their employer no matter how frequently they change jobs—and there are about 10 million job changes a year.'[65]

Attention was drawn to the overlap between income tax and social security due to the fact that there is a system of allowances against income tax for individuals, spouses and children (see page 13) as well as cash payments to families with children (see page 14). This combination of tax exemptions and cash payments resulted in allowances being given at nine different rates and a 'system of family support (that) is more costly to administer and more difficult to understand than is necessary'.[66]

The Green Paper therefore proposed to replace the main personal allowances against income tax and family allowances with a system of tax-credits. Three rates of credit were suggested: one for a single person, one for a married

[63] Royal Commission on the Taxation of Profits and Income, 1955, *Minutes of Evidence*.
[64] *Proposals for a Tax-Credit System*, Cmnd. 5116, *op. cit.*, HMSO, October 1972.
[65] *Ibid.* para. 2.
[66] *Ibid.* para. 3.

couple, and one for each dependant child, the figures suggested being £4, £6 and £2 weekly. All income from the first £ to the top of the basic rate band was to be taxed at the basic rate—30 per cent at the time. It was proposed that the tax-credit be set against tax liability and if in any period it was not fully absorbed, the unused part of the credit would be paid out as an addition to the wage or salary. As no questions of carrying forward unused tax-credits could arise, the need for cumulation would have been greatly diminished and so it was proposed to abolish the cumulative element of PAYE. Any overwithholding that would have resulted from a combination of higher rate taxation and non-cumulative withholding was to be dealt with by an assessment at the end of the tax year.

The administration of the scheme would have been as follows. Every employed person within the scheme would receive a card showing his credit entitlement and this would be passed to the employer who would then be in a position to pay the appropriate credits.[67] When a person moved between jobs the card would be given back to him to give to his next employer. His former employer would also give him a certificate of pay, credits received and tax and national insurance contributions paid in that employment. If for some reason an employee was temporarily without a card, an emergency procedure would allow him a single person's credit until a card was issued. It was estimated that the Green Paper proposals, if implemented, would lead to an eventual saving of some 10,000 to 15,000 civil servants, and that it would take some five years to bring the scheme into operation.

A number of other proposals arose from the scheme. As the main personal allowances were to be replaced by tax-credits and PAYE coding would disappear, it would no longer have been possible to give tax relief such as that for life assurance by increasing the taxpayer's code number. Neither would it have been possible to collect the tax due on income not subject to withholding at source by altering the code. Two areas of change were envisaged. The first related to the deductions for life assurance, interest paid, and work expenses. It was proposed that for life assurance relief (claimed by over 14 million taxpayers a year), policyholders would deduct tax from qualifying premia at half the basic rate, and the life offices would then recover the money directly from the Inland Revenue. It was suggested that the relief for interest paid on loans for buying or improving property in the United Kingdom (over 5 million claimants) be given by permitting borrowers to deduct tax at the basic rate from the interest payments. This would take care of the basic rate[68] relief due to all borrowers and would do so normally at the time that the interest was paid. Work expenses (11 million claims) are allowed for expenses incurred 'wholly,

---

[67] This proposal was modified by the Select Committee so that employers would be notified directly by the Revenue of employee tax-credits. See Select Committee on Tax-Credit, Volume I, *Report and Proceedings of the Committee*, HC 341–1, HMSO, June 1973, p. 46.

[68] Special arrangements were envisaged for higher rate taxpayers.

exclusively and necessarily' in the performance of an employee's duties. It was proposed that a new standard deduction for such expenses would be introduced and would be given without reference to the actual amount of expenses incurred; except that if the expenses were larger than the standard deduction, the employee could claim the difference, subject possibly to a *de minimis* rule. These suggestions would have meant that reliefs could be given without changing a PAYE code, and under the tax-credit proposals in most cases there would have been no need for an end-year adjustment. Secondly, the collection of tax on incomes not subject to withholding posed potential difficulties. The Green Paper considered that these might be dealt with by more extensive withholding at source, e.g. from bank deposit interest; there was also an allusion to self-assessment in the case of other forms of income, such as from self-employment.

A number of relevant reactions to the possibility of non-cumulation and self-assessment appeared in the evidence submitted to the Select Committee[69] appointed to consider the Green Paper proposals. The Inland Revenue Staff Federation expressed 'grave doubts about the efficacy of self-assessment in any other than very straightforward cases'. In such cases, however, they conceded that 'a simple system of self-assessment might well be useful and economical'.[70] When representatives of the Federation were questioned by the Select Committee, the grave doubts appeared to be two-fold: first, there was the 'very natural one that we have about compliance on the part of the tax-paying public', and secondly, the 'readily forecastable failure on the part of the public in getting the answers right'.[71] The representatives of the Trades Union Congress were worried about non-cumulation on the grounds that the unemployed and sick would not receive tax rebates until after the end of the tax year.[72] The TUC was also in favour of a more progressive tax structure; and further reservations were raised about the assumption that it might be costly to operate a more progressive tax structure under a non-cumulative system in that such progression might imply a lower threshold for higher rate tax and a resulting increase in the number of adjustments.[73] The representatives of the Confederation of British Industry on being asked if the CBI had any views on the desirability or otherwise of self-assessment, replied 'No—it is a tricky question as you very well know'.[74] However, the point was made that individuals are unlikely to lose documents that might have a favourable effect on their financial circumstances. The actual comment was: 'this [tax-credit] card will be a passport to something positive, almost like a successful coupon on the football pools. He never loses those, even though he may lose his tax returns'.[75] Presumably therefore, if there were some financial incentive such as a rebate,

[69] Select Committee on Tax-Credit, *op. cit.*
[70] *Ibid. Evidence,* Vol. II, p. 136.
[71] *Ibid.* p. 148.
[72] *Ibid.* pp. 267 and 274. See also Chapter IV p. 00.
[73] *Ibid.* pp. 262 and 267.
[74] *Ibid.* p. 294.
[75] *Ibid.* p. 283.

the taxpayer might not lose his tax returns either. While these points are discussed in more detail in Chapter IV, it is worth noting that very few of the comments of substance relating to non-cumulation and/or self-assessment were actively hostile.

The Select Committee's report concluded that 'the scheme as a whole . . . offers a rationalisation and simplification of the present separate tax and benefit systems, so far as that is reasonably practicable and desirable'.[76] However, despite the considerable amount of work done in preparation for the implementation of such a tax-credit scheme, the proposals were shelved following the change of government in 1974, though it may be pointed out that at least two of the features of the scheme have been proposed in their own right, namely the arrangements for life assurance relief (see page 15) and the reform of children's allowances (see page 15), and one may speculate over the possibilities that other features may eventually be adopted.

Local Income Tax

The Layfield Committee on local government finance[77] considered that a local income tax was a 'serious candidate' as a new source of local revenue. It was the only source that appeared to offer both a substantial yield and at the same time contributed something towards the accountability of local government to the electorate.

A number of possible schemes were considered by the Committee.[78] Scheme A was based on local assessment and collection whereby the Inland Revenue would provide local authorities with the necessary information to assess the tax at locally determined rates. The Committee did not consider this scheme as a serious possibility given the estimated administrative costs of operating it of £120 million a year (1975 prices), representing an increase of 15,000 in Inland Revenue and local authority staff.

Scheme B was on the lines of that operating in a number of other countries whereby the local income tax is based on an end-year assessment for both national and local tax liabilities. This system has a number of advantages. There would be no problems in establishing total income for local tax purposes only. Provision could be made on the annual return for a declaration specifying the taxpayer's residence—a necessary requirement if local authorities were to have the power to alter the rates of tax. Finally, so far as accountability is concerned, it would be possible to make a sharp distinction between revenue raised by central government and that by the local authority. However, in the United Kingdom such a scheme would not be economical given that the Inland Revenue's present policy is to minimise the number of taxpayers requiring an end-year assessment. With a system of self-assessment for national income tax

---

[76] *Ibid.* Vol. I, para. 37.

[77] *Local Government Finance,* Report of the Committee of Enquiry, Cmnd. 6453, *op. cit.*

[78] *Ibid.* pp. 197–208 and Annexes 24 and 25.

such a constraint would no longer apply as returns of total income would have to be filed annually in any case.

Scheme C was based on self-assessment, as operated in some parts of the United States. All taxpayers would receive an annual return and would calculate and remit the local income tax due. The annual return could also be used as an annual declaration of residence. This scheme was rejected on the grounds of cost in that the Inland Revenue estimated the annual administrative costs at between £200 and £250 million (1975 prices) representing 50,000 or more additional Revenue Staff. No satisfactory explanation was provided of how this remarkable high figure was derived. Not only does the £200–£250 million estimate for self-assessed local income tax wildly exceed the estimated costs of an officially administered version, but it is in the same league as the £249.8 million that it cost to collect *all* Inland Revenue duties in 1974/75.[79] Perhaps the idea was to have officially administered self-assessment. The only clues were that 'a percentage sample of returns would need to be examined by the Inland Revenue and discrepancies pursued with taxpayers', and 'reminding action would be necessary, probably extensively since there would be little incentive to render prompt returns'. [80] However, neither of these operations incur such staggering costs abroad, and as we shall show later, there is no reason why taxpayers cannot be provided with an incentive to file returns that have been completed accurately by a specified date. The Committee did not recommend self-assessment for local income tax, and with the lack of evidence to the contrary, one can only conclude that the idea was not taken seriously.

The scheme considered to be the most feasible was the integration of a local tax within the present administrative framework for national income tax. Thus income assessed under Schedule E would be taxed through PAYE. A number of problems would arise from this arrangement; for instance, one of the benefits of PAYE that most taxpayers do not have to file a return annually would be partially offset as everyone would have to complete an annual declaration of residence. But given the procedures of tax administration established in this country the scheme was considered feasible despite, according to the Inland Revenue's estimates, an annual cost of £100 million and an increase in Revenue staff of around 12,000.

6 Self-Assessment and Other Taxes

Although few characteristics of self-assessment, as defined on page 4, are to be found in the operation of the income tax in the United Kingdom, they do play a much larger part in the administration of other taxes and also appear to be spreading. Estate duty and its successor capital transfer tax provide notable examples. Value added tax, introduced in 1973, contains many such

[79] *118th Report of the Commissioners of Inland Revenue,* Cmnd. 6302, January 1976, p. 36.
[80] Layfield Committee *op. cit.* p. 449.

features and a considerable degree of self-assessment was envisaged for the proposed wealth tax.

Estate Duty

Estate duty was applied to the capital value of property passing, or deemed to pass, at the time of the death of an individual, but liability to the duty has ceased entirely for deaths occurring on or after 13 March 1975. It is of interest to us here because an element of self-assessment was introduced into the administration of estate duty in 1970[81] and it continues to feature in the assessment of its successor, capital transfer tax. Prior to 5 October 1970 completed Inland Revenue affidavits (estate duty forms) were sent to the Estate Duty Office for assessment before any duty was paid. After that date the solicitor preparing the affidavit made the preliminary assessment of estate duty and interest payable which he sent, together with the affidavit, to the Accountant-General at Somerset House. This form of self-assessment did not apply in all cases e.g. where the deceased was domiciled outside the United Kingdom, or exemption from duty was claimed for articles of national, scientific, historic, or artistic importance, and solicitors having difficulty were still able to let the Estate Duty Office make the assessment. This switch to self-assessment was made following representations by the Law Society and was thought[82] to save about ten days in obtaining the grant at the Probate Registry.

Capital Transfer Tax

Capital transfer tax is chargeable on the gifts and other gratuitous transfers of value made during a person's lifetime and the property left at death. It is applied on a lifetime cumulative basis and there are a number of exemptions such as transfers between husband and wife either in life or at death, and transfers up to a value of £2,000 made by a person in any one tax year. In the case of transfers of value at death the self-assessment procedure described for estate duty continues as before. Generally the tax on transfers at death becomes due at the end of the sixth month following the death; and the tax on a transfer during life is due at the end of the sixth month after the transfer or if the transfer were made between 5 April and 1 October in any year, on 30 April the following year. Overdue tax is subject to an interest charge from its due date at a rate of 6 per cent for transfers at death and 9 per cent for other transfers.

The Proposed Wealth Tax

There was a large element of self-assessment in the proposed wealth tax. Although the Select Committee on Wealth Tax[83] produced five draft reports, the

---

[81] Inland Revenue Press Notice dated 11th September 1970. Reproduced in *Green's Death Duties,* 7th ed. p. 397.

[82] Reported in the *British Tax Review,* No. 5 1970, p. 282.

[83] Select Committee on a Wealth Tax Session 1974/75 Volume I, *Report and Proceedings of the Committee,* 1975 H.C. 696–I, HMSO, 1975.

role of self-assessment in any future British wealth tax was not seriously disputed. The Chairman's Report as amended by the Committee but not adopted [84] proposed a system of self-assessment with an audit of about 10 per cent of cases by the Inland Revenue each year. The main difficulty with this form of assessment is that even if a taxpayer conscientiously values his assets, he may find that when he is audited the Inland Revenue declares them to have been undervalued for a number of years and presents him with a large bill for past tax. At the same time a limit on reopening past years may be seen as unfair on taxpayers who had paid wealth tax on correct values. The Report therefore recommended that reopening should be allowed subject to a time-limit of three years where the taxpayer's valuation, though erroneous, had been made to the best of his ability and no question of fraud or negligence was involved. It was also felt that outstanding tax arising from under-valuations made in good faith should not be regarded as the fault of the taxpayer and should not be subject to interest; but if interest was charged then it should be at less than a commercial rate.

Value Added Tax

The assessment and collection of Value Added Tax in the United Kingdom exhibit many of the characteristics of self-assessment found abroad. A person registered for VAT must file a return not later than one month after the end of each tax period, which is normally three months. The return must be filed even if the person has no taxable outputs or inputs during the tax period, or if the amount payable or repayable is under £1. The registered person must calculate the total due and the net amount of VAT payable by him or repayable to him. Provided that the net tax payable is £1 or more the full amount must be paid at the time that the return is filed.

Customs and Excise possess more formal powers to ensure compliance with VAT than does the Inland Revenue for Income Tax. An Inspector of Taxes does not have the same easy authority, even after recent changes to enter premises, for example. Customs and Excise may require the production of documents, may take copies of them or remove them at a reasonable time or for a reasonable period and samples of goods may also be taken; they may also enter and search premises and search people. In addition, an appeal to a VAT tribunal will be entertained only if the taxpayer has made all the required returns and paid the tax shown to be due by those returns.

[84] *Ibid.* p. ccxxiv.

APPENDIX II–1

The Main Inland Revenue Forms and Explanatory Literature

This list is not comprehensive, but covers all forms etc. of importance.

Forms

1	For partnerships, trustees and estates.	Each form is issued with a tax return guide.
11	For taxpayers in general other than PAYE cases.	
11P	For taxpayers subject to PAYE withholding and with substantial other income.	
P1	For taxpayers subject to PAYE withholding and with little other income.	
P2	Notice of Coding.	
P3	PAYE Coding Guide.	
P6	Notice to employer of code or amended code.	
P8	Blue card. Instructions to employers.	
P9D	Return of expenses payments, fees, bonuses, etc., for employees to whom form P11D is not applicable.	
P10	(Tax Tables) Instructions to employers.	
P11	Deduction card.	
P11D	Return of payments, benefits, etc. to or for directors and certain employees.	
P11D(a)	Return of payments, benefits, etc. to or for directors and certain employees—nil certificate.	
P11(S)	Deduction card.	
P24	Covering form to be issued with Deduction Cards before the beginning of the year.	
P24N	Covering form to be issued with Deduction Cards to a new employer.	
P30	Remittance Card.	
P30 (Payslip)	Payslip—employer's remittances.	
P34	Employer's requisition form.	
P35	Employer's Annual Declaration and Certificate.	
P35X	Notes for guidance on completion of Form P35.	
P38	Employer's Supplementary Return.	
P38(S)	Students employed during vacation: declaration by employer and statement by student.	
P43	Particulars of employee leaving.	
P44	Commencement of employment.	
P45	Part 1: Particulars of employee leaving. Part 2: Employee leaving: copy of employer's certificate. Part 3: New employee: particulars of old employment.	

P46	Particulars of employee for whom no code has been notified to the employer.
P47	Employer's application for authority to refund tax exceeding £20 to new employee.
P48	Authority to refund tax exceeding £20 to new employee.
P50	Refund during unemployment: employee's application.
P60	Employer's certificate of pay and tax deductions to be given to employee at end of year.
P70A	Schedule E Assessment: File Copy.
P70B	Income Tax Assessment.
P70C	Notice of Assessment and Statement of tax unpaid or overpaid.
P85	Claim for repayment of any tax due on leaving the country.
P87	Schedule E expenses claim.
P160	Notification of retirement of an employee to whom a pension is paid by the employer.

Pamphlets

46Q	Returns of Payments made to Entertainers, etc., under section 20 of the Finance Act, 1956—Explanatory notes.
480	Income Tax—Notes on Expenses Payments and Benefits for Directors and Certain Employees.
530	Notes on the Taxation of Income from Real Property.
CA1	Income Tax and Corporation Tax—Capital Allowances on Machinery and Plant.
CA2	Income Tax and Corporation Tax—Capital Allowances on Industrial Buildings.
CA3	Income Tax and Corporation Tax—Capital Allowances on Agricultural Forestry Buildings and Works.
CA4	Income Tax and Corporation Tax—Allowances for Scientific Research.
IR1	Extra-statutory concessions in operation at 1 August 1970.
IR2	Paying tax for the First Time.
IR4	Income tax and the Elderly.
IR6	Double Taxation Relief.
IR6–1	Double taxation Relief—Withdrawal of Relief for overseas underlying tax.
IR7	Some hints on Income Tax for Commonwealth Immigrants.
IR8	Special Charge.
IR9	Income Tax and Corporation Tax—Notes on Treatment of Livestock kept by Farmers and other Traders.
IR11	Tax treatment of Interest paid.
IR12	Occupational Pension Schemes—Notes on approval under the Finance Act 1970.
IR13	Income Tax—Taxation of Wife's Earnings.

IR14	Income Tax—Subcontracting in the Construction industry—Explanatory Pamphlet for contractors.
IR15	Income Tax—Subcontracting in the Construction industry—Explanatory Pamphlet for Sub-contractors.
IR16	Share Option and Share Incentive Schemes.
1R18	Corporation Tax.
IR19	The New Unified Tax System.
IR20	Residents and Non-residents—Liability to Tax in the United Kingdom.
IR21	Income Tax Tables.
IR22	Income Tax—Personal Allowances.
IR23	Income tax and Widows.
IR24	Class 4 National Insurance Contributions.
IR25	Taxation of Overseas Income.
C.G.T.1	Capital Gains Tax—How to calculate your gains.
C.G.T.2	Capital Gains Tax—Quoted shares and securities.
C.G.T.3	Capital Gains Tax—Individuals—Rate of Tax Alternative basis of charge and exemption for small amounts.
C.G.T.4	Capital Gains Tax—Owner-occupied houses.
C.G.T.5	Capital Gains Tax—Unit and Investment Trusts.
C.G.T.5A	Capital Gains Tax—Unit and Investment Trusts (September 1972).
C.G.T.6	Capital Gains Tax—Retirement: disposal of a business.
C.G.T.7	Capital Gains Tax—Individuals; gains accruing at death.
C.G.T.7A	Capital Gains Tax—Individuals: treatment of assets on death.
C.G.T.8	Capital Gains Tax (a comprehensive pamphlet).
C.G.T.9	Capital Gains Tax—Land with development value.
C.G.T.9A	Capital Gains Tax—Land with development value: abolition of Betterment Levy.
P7	Employer's Guide to PAYE.

Chapter III

Income Tax Systems in other Countries

1 An Outline of the US Tax System

Allowances, Deductions and the Tax Structure

This chapter discusses in some detail the structure of income tax in the USA and Canada, with some mention also of Sweden. The experience of other countries is alluded to in passing. Initially we discuss the tax system in broad outline, leaving until later in the chapter a more detailed discussion of those aspects of the system that are particularly relevant to self-assessment. Unless otherwise stated all data refer to 1975.

As stated in the Glossary we use the terms 'allowances' and 'exemptions' synonymously to refer to income which is tax-free as of right, while 'deductions' refer to income that is tax-free only as an offset to certain types of expenditure. Federal individual income tax in the USA has only one major exemption—a flat rate amount of $750 per person.[1] A family consisting of husband, wife, and two children can thus claim four exemptions. Two exemptions per taxpayer (but not per dependant) may be claimed if the taxpayer is over 65 or blind (three exemptions if the taxpayer is both over 65 and blind). The number of exemptions claimed and the total income untaxed because of them is given in Table III–1 along with similar figures for deductions.

In contrast to the UK, income tax in the USA allows the individual to claim as deductions against income a large variety of personal expenditures, as laid out in Table III–2. In quantitative order of importance these deductions are for state and local taxes (including most indirect taxes), interest payments,

[1] In 1975 there was also a tax credit of $30 per exemption (other than age or blindness exemptions). It may or may not be retained in subsequent years. Also, beginning in 1975, there was an 'Earned Income Credit' for parents with income less than $8,000. There were also various other minor credits in 1975 only. Tax credits are paid to the taxpayer even if he has no tax liability.

charitable contributions, and medical expenses. Medical deductions are relatively low because such expenditures are allowable against income only where they exceed 3 per cent of the taxpayer's gross income, or are premium payments for medical insurance not exceeding $150.

Table III–1 Exemptions, Deductions and Tax Liability, USA, 1974

	Number millions	Amount $ thousand million
Total number of returns and adjusted gross income	83.3	906.1
Total number of exemptions claimed	215.2	161.3
Number of returns claiming the standard deduction	53.1	75.8
Number of returns claiming itemised deductions	29.7	119.7

SOURCE: *Preliminary Statistics of Income, 1974, Individual Income Tax Returns*, US Department of Treasury, Internal Revenue Service, Table 4.

Table III–2 Itemised Deductions, USA, 1974

Type of Deduction	Amount $ thousand million	As percentage of total itemised deductions
Total itemised deductions	119.7	100
State and local taxes	43.6	36.4
Interest paid	37.2	31.1
Charitable, etc. contributions	15.0	12.5
Medical and dental expenses	11.5	9.6
Casualty or theft loss (net)	1.3	1.1
Other miscellaneous	12.5	10.4

SOURCE: *Preliminary Statistics of Income, 1974, Individual Income Tax Returns*, US Department of Treasury, Internal Revenue Service, Table 5.

As a substitute for these so-called itemised deductions there exists also the so-called standard deduction. Instead of itemising his deductible expenditures, the taxpayer is allowed to treat as tax-free a certain percentage of his income (subject to a floor and ceiling) *irrespective of his expenditures*. To this extent the standard deduction is analytically a further exemption.

Table III–3 The Standard Deduction, USA, 1975

Type of taxpayer/return	Minimum Standard Deduction	Percentage of Adjusted Gross Income	Maximum Standard Deduction	No return to be filed if gross income less than [a]
Joint return	$1,900	16%	$2,600	$3,400
Surviving spouse	$1,900	16%	$2,600	$2,650
Single	$1,600	16%	$2,300	$2,350
Married, filing separately	$ 950	16%	$1,300	$ 750

a Plus $750 for each additional exemption.

NOTE: the standard deduction is 16% of Adjusted Gross Income, but no smaller than the minimum given in the first column and no larger than the maximum in the third column.

Details of the size of the standard deduction are given in Table III–3, while the number claiming it is given in Table III–1. The taxpayer is free either to itemise or to take the standard deduction, and will normally take whichever is the greater; thus house-buyers with large mortgage interest payments, or those with heavy medical expenses will normally itemise. The main reason for the existence of a standard deduction is its convenience to the taxpayer and to the tax administration. For both reasons, the real value of the standard deduction has steadily increased in recent years and so the number claiming it has risen steadily so that now it is claimed by about two-thirds of taxpayers.

The taxpayer's tax-free income[2] is thus normally the sum of his exemptions and either the standard deduction or his itemised deductions.[3] Income in excess of this total is subject to the tax rates shown in Table III–4 (for a single person). The marginal rates for a single person rise from 14 per cent of the first $500 of taxable income to 70 per cent of taxable income in excess of $100,000 (but with a maximum rate of 50 per cent on earned income). In sharp contrast to the UK the marginal rates start at a low level and rise smoothly and never by jumps of more than 3 per cent in the ranges of income covering the majority of taxpayers.

In addition a social security contribution is paid at a rate of 5.85 per cent for employed persons (7.95 per cent for the self-employed) on earnings of up to $14,100 per year.[4] This correspondingly raises the marginal rates of tax in the lower income ranges.

The normal tax year for federal individual income tax is from 1 January to 31 December; the deadline for filing one's tax return is usually the 15 April following the end of the tax year. The filing unit is either the individual or the husband and wife jointly.

The husband and wife have complete choice over whether to file jointly or separately and will generally choose each year that arrangement which minimises their tax liability. Usually it will pay to file jointly; but separate filing may be more advantageous, for example, where husband and wife both have about equal taxable incomes, and where the wife has medical expenses in excess of 3 per cent of her own gross income (and hence deductible if she files separately), but where the husband's and wife's medical expenses are less than 3 per cent of their combined gross income (and hence not deductible if they file jointly).

Since there is a marked contrast with the UK it is worth dwelling on the relative treatment of single and married taxpayers in the USA. The principle underlying their relative treatment is that of 'income splitting' between husband

---

[2] Some types of tax-free income such as social security benefits, public assistance, unemployment compensation, state and local government bond interest, etc. are not required to be reported on returns.

[3] There are also 'adjustments to income', which are akin to itemised deductions but are available even to those who elect the standard deduction (e.g. moving expenses, and payments to pension plans).

[4] US Government employees and a few other categories of employees are excluded. The ceiling of $14,100 was raised to $15,300 in 1976.

Table III–4 The Federal Tax Schedule for a Single Taxpayer, USA, 1975

Taxable Income $	Marginal Tax Rate %	Tax Bill at Start of 'Slice' of Income $	Effective Tax Rate at Start of 'Slice' %
0–500	14	0	0
500–1,000	15	70	14.0
1,000–1,500	16	145	14.5
1,500–2,000	17	225	15.0
2,000–4,000	19	310	15.5
4,000–6,000	21	690	17.25
6,000–8,000	24	1,110	18.5
8,000–10,000	25	1,590	19.9
10,000–12,000	27	2,090	20.9
12,000–14,000	29	2,630	21.9
14,000–16,000	31	3,210	22.9
16,000–18,000	34	3,830	23.9
18,000–20,000	36	4,510	25.1
20,000–22,000	38	5,230	26.2
22,000–26,000	40	5,990	27.2
26,000–32,000	45	7,590	29.2
32,000–38,000	50	10,290	32.2
38,000–44,000	55	13,290	35.0
44,000–50,000	60	16,590	37.7
50,000–60,000	62	20,190	40.4
60,000–70,000	64	26,390	44.0
70,000–80,000	66	32,790	46.8
80,000–90,000	68	39,390	49.2
90,000–100,000	69	46,190	51.3
100,000 and over	70	53,090	53.1

SOURCE: *Your Federal Income Tax, 1975.*
NOTE: The figures exclude rebates paid under the 1975 Tax Reduction Act.

and wife, whereby income is treated as if divided equally between them and each is then taxed as a single individual.

The effect of income splitting is to make the tax structure less progressive for married couples. In the USA a single person pays marginal rates of 14 per cent, 15 per cent, 16 per cent and 17 per cent on the first four $500 segments of his taxable income. A married couple with $2,000 of taxable income splits it into two halves of $1,000 and applies the first two tax rates to each half. The more progressive is the marginal tax structure the greater the benefit of income splitting to married couples.

Income splitting applies in this form to couples with combined taxable incomes below $8,000. For incomes above this a modified version applies resulting from political pressure in the late 1960s to ease the tax burden on single taxpayers. These pressures led to the adoption of a new tax schedule under which a single person's tax rate never exceeded that of a married couple by more than 20 per cent.

A third rate schedule lies midway between that for single persons and that for married couples. This applies to unmarried heads of household, broadly defined as unmarried persons supporting one or more dependant relatives (e.g. a divorced or widowed person with children, or a child supporting an aged parent).[5]

Thus there are three tax schedules—that for single persons shown in Table III–4, that for married couples, based on a modified version of income splitting, and that for unmarried heads of household. It is up to the taxpayer when completing his return to select the table appropriate to his filing status.

Withholding

The amount of tax withheld by employers depends on (a) the number of exemptions claimed by the taxpayer, (b) his earnings, and (c) whether or not he is married. The employee obtains from his employer a withholding exemption certificate which he completes and returns to his employer. This tells the employer how many exemptions are being claimed and the taxpayer's claimed marital status.

Thus, if a taxpayer has a wife and two children, he is, in principle, entitled to four exemptions. If the taxpayer has only one job or if married and his spouse does not have a job, he may claim an additional withholding 'allowance' equal to the value of one exemption. However, if he wishes more tax to be withheld (e.g. anticipating tax liability for income on which tax is not withheld) he may claim fewer (or even zero) exemptions. Conversely, if he anticipates a large personal deduction at the end of the year (e.g. a large medical bill) then he can claim (say) six exemptions. This latter procedure is explicitly legal, with the sole proviso that the taxpayer may incur a penalty if at the end of the tax year he has substantially underpaid his true liability.

There is, in any case, no burden on the employer of checking the veracity of employee claims—if a taxpayer claims more exemptions than his entitlement it is the tax administration, not his employer who has to check this. Many recurring and predictable deductions are thus dealt with by claiming extra exemptions. The employer needs to know only how many exemptions are being claimed, not why. Such flexibility over the number of exemptions claimed is in striking contrast to the UK coding procedure described in Chapter II.

To a surprisingly large extent taxpayers take active steps to ensure that they are over-withheld. A study by the Internal Revenue Service (IRS) in 1969, confirmed by a later survey by the US Treasury found that no fewer than 50 per cent of employees did not claim during the year all the exemptions to which they were entitled. One reason why taxpayers like to be over-withheld is that they can avoid the need to file estimated tax returns (discussed below) during the year on non-employment income. Another reason is that people find that

---

[5] For a more detailed discussion of the tax treatment of the family see J. A. Pechman, *Federal Tax Policy,* Revised Edition, The Brookings Institution, Washington DC, 1971, pp. 86 *et sequ.*

this is a convenient way to save, even if the real rate of return is zero or negative.[6]

As a practical matter under-withholding is wildly unpopular. It appears that the dollar which is withheld from a pay cheque and hence never received by the taxpayer is perceived as being smaller than the dollar included in a cheque sent to the IRS at the end of the tax year. The tax administration, too, is not unhappy about over-withholding, which reduces the problem of collecting underpaid tax.

Table III–5 A Stylised Version of US Withholding at Different Income Levels

The Tax System:
Tax free exemption: $750
Standard deduction: $2,000
(The standard deduction is incorporated in the withholding table as a deduction from tax at an assumed rate of 18% = $2,000 × 0.18 = $360 per year = $30 per month.)
Tax function: 12% of income between $750 and $5,750
24% of income between $5,750 and $10,750

	dollars						
1. Annual gross income	0	750	1,750	2,750	5,750	6,750	10,750
2. Tax at 12%	0	0	120	240	600	600	600
3. Tax at 24%	0	0	0	0	0	240	1,200
4. Total tax ((2) + (3))	0	0	120	240	600	840	1,800
5. Notional monthly withholding (excluding the standard deduction): (4) ÷ 12	0	0	10	20	50	70	150
6. Standard deduction as tax allowance	30	30	30	30	30	30	30
7. Actual monthly withholding including the standard deduction: (5)—(6), or 0	0	0	0	0	20	40	120
8. True value of monthly standard deduction = 1/12($2,000 × marginal tax rate)	0	0	20	20	20	30[a]	40
9. True monthly liability = (5)—(8), or 0	0	0	0	0	30	40	110
10. Amount overwithheld = (7)—(9)	0	0	0	0	−10	0	10

a At an income of $6,750 the marginal tax rate is 24% for income between $5,750 and $6,750, and 12% for income below $5,750. At this income level $1,000 of the $2,000 deduction is evaluated at 12% and the remainder at 24%.

[6] In 1975 total refunds in the US were $26.5 billion. Let us assume that the overpayment of tax accrued evenly between January and December 1974 and that all refunds were paid at the end of February 1975. Thus on average the refund was owed to the taxpayer for eight months and so on average interest was foregone on 8/12 x $26.5 billion = $17.67 billion. At a rate of interest of 5% this means that taxpayers gave up nearly $900 million by foregoing the interest on overwithheld tax. This is equivalent to an extra 1% rate of income tax.

The method of relating tax withheld to earnings is illustrated in Table III–5 in terms of a stylised version of US income tax. Table III–5 is constructed for an able-bodied, single employee under 65 with no dependants (hence entitled to one exemption of $750) and entitled (by assumption though not in reality) to a standard deduction of $2,000 independent of the level of his income. The first $5,000 of his taxable income is taxed at 12 per cent (again by assumption only) and the next $5,000 at 24 per cent.

Line (1) of Table III–5 gives the various levels of annual gross income under consideration. Line (2) shows the tax liability on this income at the 12 per cent rate, and line (3) liability at the 24 per cent rate. Line (4) shows total tax liability given that one exemption is being claimed, but ignoring the standard deduction. Continuing for the moment to ignore the standard deduction, line (5) shows the monthly amount which would be withheld at the level of income in line (1). The principle is that each month is taxed as though earnings during the month were one-twelfth of earnings during the year. As a logical proposition it can be shown[7] that such a system, when combined with marginal tax rates that rise with income, will withhold accurately if earnings are constant throughout the year but will over-withhold if earnings fluctuate sufficiently so that in at least one month the individual is in a different marginal tax bracket. It should be noted that this over-withholding holds for fluctuations of income in either direction, and this is true both of the US withholding system and of our stylised version of it.

If the standard deduction is now brought into the picture matters are further complicated. If the standard deduction were, in fact, at a flat rate then it could simply be regarded as an additional exemption, and in our example, income would become taxable only when gross earnings exceeded £2,750. But subject to a minimum and a maximum the standard deduction is actually a percentage of gross income (as opposed to taxable earnings) and therefore there exists no simple relationship between taxable income and the size of the standard deduction. For this reason for withholding purposes the standard deduction is evaluated at an *average* rate of tax (18 per cent in our example) and tax liability reduced accordingly.

Thus, in Table III–5 line (6) shows the *monthly* value of the standard deduction of $2,000 evaluated at 18 per cent, and line (7) shows the resulting monthly withholding. Line (8) shows the true value of the standard deduction (i.e. evaluating $2,000 at the individual's *marginal* tax rate rather than at an average rate) and line (9) shows the taxpayer's true monthly liability given his income in line (1).

The comparison of line (7) (the amount withheld) with line (9) (true liability) shows that a result of treating the standard deduction this way is that, other things being equal, those with low incomes will tend to be under-withheld and with high incomes over-withheld. It is, of course, both possible and legitimate

[7] See the numerical example on page 67, below.

for an acute taxpayer broadly to compensate both for this and for any incorrect withholding due to fluctuations in income by an appropriate adjustment of the number of exemptions he claims.

A further aspect of withholding concerns the taxpayer's marital status. A taxpayer and his wife have the choice of filing a joint tax return or filing separately. In either case, the husband and wife are allowed one exemption each so that the total exemption for a married couple is twice that for a single person. If the same were true of the standard deduction then the tax-free income of a couple would simply be twice that of an individual. But, as is shown in Table III–3, the maximum standard deduction for an individual is $2,300 and for a couple is $2,600.[8]

The problem that emerges can be summarised as follows: if the withholding table incorporated the full single person's standard deduction (as is the case with our example in Table III–5) then, if only one spouse works, there is no problem; but if both spouses work, they will be withheld on the basis of two standard deductions and hence will pay too little tax. Conversely, this situation is avoided for two-earner couples if the withholding table incorporates only half the married person's standard deduction, but in that case a couple only one of whom works will be over-withheld. For this reason there are two withholding tables, one for single persons, incorporating the single person's standard deduction, and one for married couples, which incorporates slightly over half the married couples' standard deduction. This still results in single-earner couples being over-withheld and two-earner couples under-withheld, but is a workable compromise. The whole problem results purely because the married couple's standard deduction is not exactly twice that of a single person.

The scope of withholding, by and large, is limited to employment earnings. Certain annuities may have tax withheld at source, but this is voluntary. Interest receipts, dividends, rents, royalties, etc. are not taxed at source. Nor are any checks made on the tax situation of a US citizen leaving the country.[9]

Despite these omissions, the net effect of taxation at source in the USA bearing in mind both the nature of the system, and the propensity of earners to under-declare their exemptions during the year, is to over-withhold by a substantial amount. From Table III–6 it can be seen that (1973 figures) some 64.2 million returns out of a total of 80.7 million, or nearly 80 per cent, claimed a refund. Approximately 17.5 per cent of returns submitted an additional payment, while some 2 per cent neither owed money nor claimed a refund. Overpaid taxes came to some $24.9 billion or over 20 per cent of total liability. Such over-withholding meets with the approval alike of taxpayer and tax administration.

Since non-cumulative withholding is so different from the UK system it is worth explaining in some detail how it leads so easily to over-withholding.

---

[8] These limits were raised in 1976.

[9] A non-resident alien leaving the USA must obtain a 'Sailing Permit' stating that he has no unpaid US tax liability.

Table III–6 Tax Withheld, Refunds and Overpayments, USA, 1973

	Number of returns millions	Amount $ thousand million
Total number of returns and total tax liability	80.7	111.2
Tax overpaid	64.2	24.9
Returns paid in full	2.3	—
Tax underpaid	14.2	12.8

SOURCE: *Statistics of Income, 1973, Individual Income Tax Returns,* US Department of Treasury, Internal Revenue Service, Tables 1.4, 3.11 and 3.12.

Table III–7 is constructed on the same lines as Table II–4, and refers to a hypothetical tax structure under which £520 per year (and hence £10 per week) is tax free and thereafter income is taxed at 30 per cent. Under cumulative withholding cumulative free pay (column (4)) is deducted from cumulative gross pay (column (3)) to obtain cumulative taxable pay (column (5)), cumulative tax due (column (6)), and hence actual tax due (column (7)).

The first three lines of Table III–7 are identical to Table II–4 for the case of cumulative withholding. Columns (8) and (9) show the case of non-cumulative withholding, under which *weekly* free pay (£10) is deducted from *weekly* gross pay (column (2)) to give weekly taxable pay (column (8)) and hence weekly tax due (column (9)). In week 1 gross pay is £40, hence with a non-cumulative system taxable pay is £30 and tax due £9; in week 2 gross pay is £50, taxable pay £40 and tax due £12; in week 3 gross pay is zero and hence taxable pay and tax are zero.

This immediately brings out the contrast between the two methods of withholding; one calculates taxable pay as the difference between cumulative gross pay and cumulative free pay, while the other does the same thing in terms of weekly gross pay and weekly free pay. Hence when earnings drop to zero cumulative taxable pay declines (because free pay continues to accumulate) and hence a refund is paid, while under a non-cumulative system weekly taxable pay can drop only to zero but cannot be negative, and so no refund is paid. The result is that at the end of week 3 total tax liability is £18 (i.e. £60 taxed at 30 per cent); with cumulative withholding this is the amount that has been deducted; with a non-cumulative system the taxpayer has had £21 deducted from his pay. The conclusion is that non-cumulative withholding deducts too much tax if income falls sufficiently to move the individual into a different tax bracket (in this case from the 30 per cent to the 0 per cent bracket).

The second half of the table shows what happens if income rises from zero in week 1 to £40 in week 2. By week 2 cumulative free pay is £20 so cumulative taxable pay is £20 and tax due is £6 (column (6)). Under the non-cumulative system in week 2 weekly free pay of £10 (and *not* cumulative free pay of £20) is deducted from gross pay. Thus under non-cumulation taxable pay is £30 (£40 *minus* £10), not £20 (£40 *minus* £20); hence tax is £9, not £6, and again tax has been over-deducted.

Table III–7 Non-Cumulation and Overwithholding

		Cumulative Withholding					Non-cumulative Withholding	
Week	Gross Pay	Cumulative Pay	Cumulative Free Pay	Cumulative Taxable Pay	Cumulative Tax due	Actual Tax Due	Weekly Taxable Pay	Weekly Tax
(1)	(2)	(3)	(4)	(5)	(6)	(7)	(8)	(9)
Fall in Income								
1	40	40	10	30	9	9	30	9
2	50	90	20	70	21	12	40	12
3	0	90	30	60	18	−3	0	0
Rise in Income								
1	0	0	10	0	0	0	0	0
2	40	40	20	20	6	6	30	9
3	50	90	30	60	18	12	40	12

NOTE: The income tax in question is levied at a rate of 30% above the tax free allowance of £520 per year.

Hence non-cumulation plus a structure of rising marginal tax rates leads to over-withholding for any fluctuation of income in either direction which moves the taxpayer into a different tax bracket. This is true regardless of whether progressivity results from steadily rising marginal rates or from a single tax rate combined with some tax-free allowance. Table III–7 illustrates the latter case. With multiple tax rates consider the case of two individuals whose annual incomes almost border on some higher rate of tax. The first individual earns the same amount in each pay period, pays tax at the lower rate in each period, and has the correct amount of tax withheld during the year. The second has a fluctuating income. In low earning periods his marginal rate of tax is the lower rate, but in the higher earning periods he is subject to higher rates of tax. As a result tax is deducted from his income at a higher average rate than for the first individual and hence tax has been over-withheld at the end of the year. The same result occurs if the second individual has an income that is steadily rising or steadily falling.

In comparison with cumulative withholding a non-cumulative system will have a deflationary macro-economic impact at the time during the year when too much tax is being deducted; and then an expansionary effect when refunds are issued. Thus Australia has known booms in the sales of consumer durables just after refunds were issued. In general, however, such seasonal effects do not cause stabilisation problems in those countries which have non-cumulative withholding. As has already been stated, such countries are in the overwhelming majority.

The Self-Employed and Estimated Tax

We turn now from the employed to the self-employed, and to those employed persons with substantial non-employment income.[10] In contrast to the UK, the aim is to tax such income on a current basis by a mechanism of estimated tax payments.

The operation of estimated tax is as follows: those individuals with substantial non-employment income have to file by 15 April (but separate from the tax return relating to the previous year) a declaration of estimated income (other than employment income subject to withholding) for the current year. Tax liability on this income is calculated by the taxpayer and is paid in four quarterly instalments, the first of which is due at the same time as the tax return for the previous year.

The procedure is facilitated by estimated tax 'kits' which give the taxpayer a form on which he works out his liability, together with four quarterly filing slips with the taxpayer's name, address, and social security number already printed on them by computer. At the end of each quarter the taxpayer simply has to fill in the figure for the tax due and post the filing slip plus cheque

[10] The estimated tax system also applies to partnerships which are regarded not as legal entities but simply as an income conduit. Partners are therefore taxed in basically the same way as other self-employed persons.

to the tax authorities (in a pre-printed return envelope).

If his circumstances change, the taxpayer may file an amended declaration of estimated income at the end of any quarter. Amendments may be made in either direction.

Since guessing one's future income is a difficult exercise the estimated tax system has a number of simplifications. The most important of these concern the conditions the taxpayer has to meet if he is to avoid a penalty. If he has under-estimated his income, but pays all additional tax due at filing time with his tax return, no penalty will be imposed (a) if his estimated tax for the year was an amount equal to his previous year's actual tax liability, or (b) if estimated tax paid was at least 80 per cent of his true liability.

The result of this system is that many people declaring estimated tax will simply use the previous year's actual non-employment income as an estimate of the current year's income, since this will ensure they will not be liable for the estimated tax penalty however high their current income.[11]

Many employees with only small sums of non-employment income (e.g. bank deposit interest) avoid the system of estimated tax altogether by ensuring that they are over-withheld on their employment income (e.g. by claiming fewer exemptions during the year). This greatly reduces the number of people making estimated tax payments.

If estimated tax is paid late a non-deductible penalty[12] is applied. Since the rate charged is lower than relevant market rates, estimated tax is frequently paid late on non-employment income on the grounds that it is cheaper to borrow from the government than from a bank. This penalty rate (which is the same as the interest charge applied to all overdue tax payments) is the average level of the prime rate, and may be revised every two years.

The avoidance of estimated tax penalties by taking last year's actual income as an estimate of this year's can be justified on the grounds of convenience. But the higher the rate of inflation the greater the tendency for such a system to approximate to taxation in arrears. It is therefore possible that equity might be better served by levying tax in arrears on income from self-employment, if nothing else, and applying a mandatory interest charge to enhance equity with wage earners. Either system is compatible with self-assessment.

End-Year Adjustments

Since both the withholding system and the mechanism of estimated tax are designed to collect true liability only approximately, it is not surprising (see Table III–6) that only 2–3 per cent of returns filed require no end-year adjustment. From Table III–6, in 1973 80.7 million returns were filed, of which 64.2 million required refunds. The vast bulk of returns are filed between the begin-

[11] It is noteworthy that with taxation on a current year basis there are no complications over opening and closing years—over the lifetime of a business tax will be paid on the business's total profits over its life. This is another sharp contrast with the UK.

[12] It was 9% in 1975 and 7% in 1976.

ning of February and 15 April (the last day for filing if interest and penalties are to be avoided); the time stream of these returns has two peaks, one in late February, the other in the first half of April. The earlier peak mainly consists of those claiming refunds. By 1 June the vast bulk of returns has received initial processing and necessary refunds have been issued. From this date the IRS has to pay interest on any unpaid refunds on a return filed on time.

The mechanism for such an operation is of necessity large and complex. The process starts with employers issuing a form W2 for each employee. This form gives the employee's name, address, and social security number, together with his gross earnings in that employment, total tax withheld and social security contributions withheld. The employee receives two or more copies of the W2, one for his own records and one to submit to the IRS with his tax return, and extra copies to attach to State and City tax returns. A further copy goes directly from the employer to the IRS.

Other income, such as dividends, interest, annuities, and miscellaneous fees also generate information returns (called form 1099) one going to the recipient, the other to the IRS. It is mandatory to issue a W2 to all individuals whom a firm has employed at any time during the year, and mandatory also to issue 1099s for all interest and dividend payments of over $10 and all fees over $600 per year. All information returns, both W2 and 1099 have to be (and usually are) issued by the 31 January after the end of the tax year on 31 December.

These information returns are an important source of information for the taxpayer in completing his return (details of which are discussed further below). The completed return is sent to the IRS in a pre-printed return envelope. If the taxpayer's calculations show that he owes tax he encloses a cheque for the full amount owing. If he is due for a refund this fact, and the amount he calculates is owing is entered on the return.

The IRS normally receives the return between mid-February and the mid-April filing deadline, and the return is immediately transcribed onto magnetic tape so as to be accessible to computer analysis. This is the most labour-intensive part of the system. The return is received by the IRS, and after initial checking for completeness (e.g. no missing signature or social security number) is issued to an operator with a keyboard and cathode tube display. The operator's function is simply to type onto magnetic tape the contents of the return in a pre-determined order. At peak filing time hundreds of temporary data-entry operators work simultaneously in shifts round the clock.

The return data is then run through a computer for what is basically an arithmetical check. All returns filed are subjected to this procedure. The arithmetical and internal consistency of the return is checked: for example, if the taxpayer declares that he is married a check is made also to ensure that he has used the married person's tax table, not that for single people. If the return is not correct it is returned to a data entry operator and transcribed again—the purpose of this procedure is to guard against apparent arithmetic errors being caused simply by typing errors at the data entry stage. If the return remains incorrect the second time round it is then forwarded to the 'error resolution' side of the operation (discussed later in this chapter).

If the return is arithmetically correct it is then transcribed automatically onto another tape and forwarded to the national computer centre which enters the data on the so-called Individual Master File—a tape containing all individual tax return accounts (around 84 million in 1974). At this stage if a refund is due (and if there are no tax debts from prior years) it is issued automatically—i.e. in the process for checking the arithmetic there is an automated provision for making out refund cheques which are then issued by another office of the US Treasury. In the great majority of cases the taxpayer receives his refund within four weeks of filing his return.

The process of arithmetical checking and the issuing of refund cheques and acceptance of additional tax payments is thus very speedy. But (and this is a crucial difference from the UK tradition) such a settlement is merely on an interim basis. Once the initial end-year adjustments have been made (say around June) use is made of the return data in the Individual Master File to select by a 'scoring' system discussed below a sample of returns for audit procedures. Thus acceptance by the IRS of a cheque with the return or the issue of a refund in no way prevents them from later demanding additional tax after audit. The various audit procedures are discussed in more detail below.

Staffing and Costs

Measured in terms of numbers of employees, total IRS personnel in 1974 came to 82,266[13] of which 71,734 were permanent and 10,532 were temporary (the vast bulk being keyboard operators employed from January to April). Of this total the largest categories were data processing (23,694 employees) and audit (27,411).

In broad terms IRS personnel can be divided into two categories. On the one hand there are those with relatively few skills who deal with the routine aspects of the tax system, such as transcribing returns onto the computer and corresponding with the taxpayer over minor matters such as an unsigned tax return. On the other, there are the highly trained and highly skilled people who deal with the audit investigation and enforcement side of the operation and the overall administration of the system. For instance, the Revenue Agents who conduct the more serious audits all have a university degree specialising in accounting, plus two to three years on-the-job training. The bimodal distribution of skills shows up clearly in Figure III–1 which summarises the distribution of salaries within the IRS.

The IRS total in 1975 of some 82,000 employees for approximately 84 million individual income tax returns and a total for all taxes of some 125 million returns compares with an Inland Revenue establishment in that year

---

[13] These and subsequent figures, are drawn from *Report of the Commissioner of IRS,* 1975, Table 25, p. 147.

Figure III–1 IRS Personnel by Level of Earnings, 1974

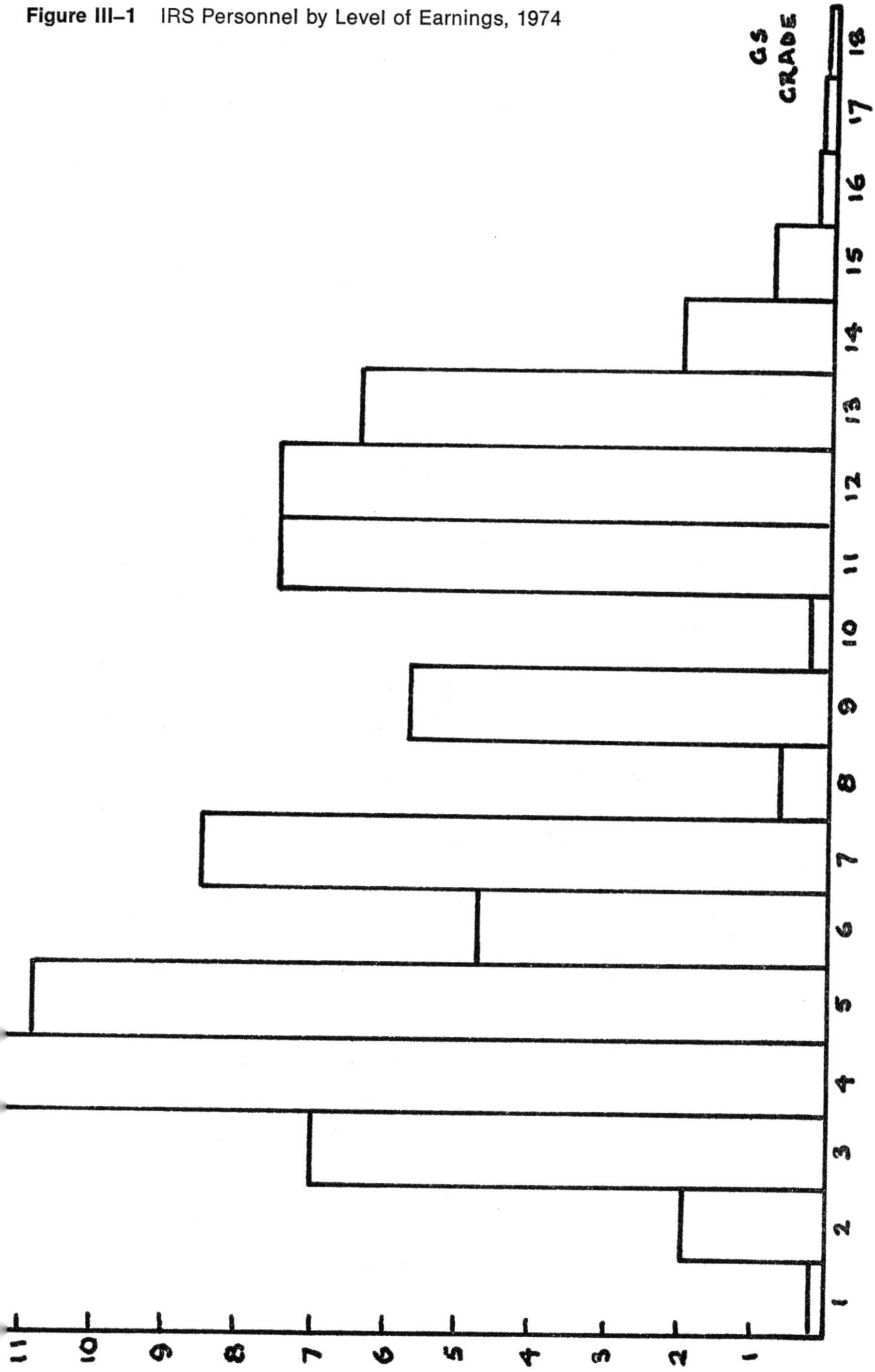

of around 74,000[14] employees for about 20 million[15] taxpayers. As emphasised elsewhere in this book, direct comparison of these figures gives only part of the story because no account is taken of the private compliance costs both of firms and individuals. But it is, nevertheless, instructive to try to see where the IRS manpower savings come.

The most obvious source of difference is that self-assessment places many more compliance costs on the private sector. The majority of US taxpayers receive little personal attention from IRS personnel. Most taxpayers simply file their return with a cheque for the balance due, or claim a refund. Once this is done and any refund has been obtained the account for the year is closed unless the return is one of the approximately 2 per cent subsequently selected for audit. In contrast, in the UK the taxpayer has to contact his inspector during the year in respect of a wide variety of changes in his personal circumstances.

The second obvious difference is that the processing of tax returns is very largely automated, so that the most intensive labour input for a return that is not audited is simply transcribing its contents into the computer. This contrasts with the heavy reliance on manual methods by the Inland Revenue—e.g. coding notices written by hand, and individually typed assessments. The IRS has estimated that at least an additional 12,000 man-years would be needed to process tax returns manually in the absence of an automated data processing system, and there are serious doubts whether a manual system would be feasible at all today given the number of taxpayers and the complexity of the tax structure. That is to say, the IRS personnel is some 13 per cent lower than it would be if there were no computers, though this understates the true degree of dependence of the IRS on automated methods.

The total costs of the IRS operation are summarised in Figure III–2. The most expensive parts of the operation are those with the heaviest concentration of manpower—audit and data processing, which together account for some 60 per cent of total IRS costs. In 1974 total costs were $1.3 billion, or approximately 0.55 per cent of total net collections of $241 billion. This compares with Inland Revenue public costs of collection of approximately 1.75 per cent in 1974/75,[16] but once again the differences in private costs must also be taken into account.

Reform

The general drift of individual income taxation in the USA in recent years has been in the direction of greater complexity, generally in the area of personal deductions, but also in the direction of tax relief for specific classes of taxpayer, such as the retired and low income families.

There appear to be two reasons for this tendency to increase complexity. First, although tax legislation proposals in the USA often originate from the

14 *118th Report of the Commissioners of Her Majesty's Inland Revenue,* Cmnd. 6302, HMSO 1976, para. 130.

15 *Inland Revenue Statistics,* HMSO 1973. See also Chapter IV, Table IV–1.

16 *118th Report of the Commissioners of Inland Revenue, op. cit.* p. 37, para. 173. See also *Developments in the Civil Service since the Fulton Report.* H.C. 368–iv, HMSO 1976.

Figure III–2 IRS Proposed Budget 1976

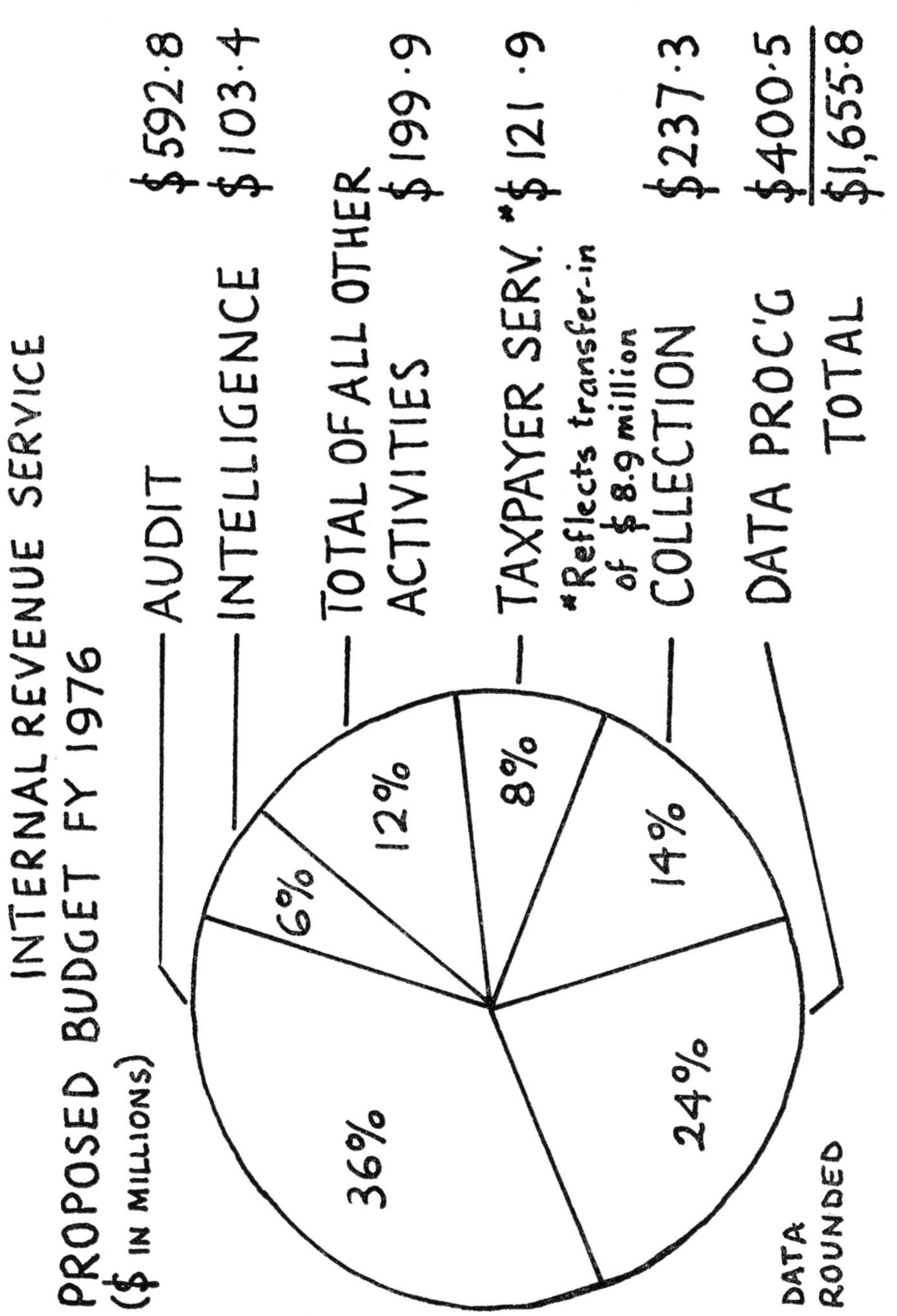

Executive Branch, the legislation which emerges is usually reshaped materially by Congressional committees, with their own political clientele and potential for wide disagreement between them. The multiplicity of deductions is thus the result largely of the political process and the best that can be done is to simplify not the tax system but the tax return (e.g. charitable deductions no longer have to be shown individually). The steady increase in the real value of the standard deduction also helps.

A second source of complexity might well be the computer system itself inasmuch as it enables an arithmetical check to be made of 100 per cent of returns, as compared to the 20 per cent or so of returns whose arithmetic was checked in the pre-computer days. To some extent, increased complexity leads to the sort of errors that are easily picked up by computer (e.g. claiming a medical deduction on expenses totalling less than 3 per cent of gross income). Thus it is possible to have a complex system in which a lot of mistakes are made, since these can be picked up and corrected by an automated system which allows the arithmetic of all returns to be checked. To this extent computerisation, if not a cause, is at least a necessary condition for increased complexity.

An obvious area for reform is the number and complexity of personal deductions, and there is considerable sentiment that in designing a new system from scratch there should be no such multiplicity of deductions. But there is very little political pressure for reform in this direction because there is little political gain in it. As one commentator put it, 'simplification has no political oomph, no sex appeal, whereas a bill to help shoe-makers in Brockton, Massachusetts is terribly important.'

An area on which there is wide (but not unanimous) agreement is the desirability of extending withholding to dividends and interest, especially the former. Withholding on interest was thought to be slightly less urgent, inasmuch as the average tax refund is much greater than the tax due on the interest receipts of a typical taxpayer and so withholding tax on interest receipts would tend simply to bring about larger refunds. Such withholding was suggested a number of years ago by the US Treasury, but the payers of dividends and interest persuaded Congress not to adopt the proposal. This matter was under discussion again in late 1976.

Indexation of the tax system has few strong proponents. A not untypical view was of disliking 'today's arithmetic substituting for tomorrow's judgement.'

2 An Outline of the Canadian Tax System

Allowances, Deductions and the Tax Structure

The Canadian system of personal income tax, like that in the USA, has both exemptions and deductions, though the latter are generally much smaller and of less importance than in the USA both politically and in terms of their effect on the structure of income tax. A key difference from the US system (and from most others) is that as a result of a reform in 1973 both the exemptions and the rate bands of Canadian income tax are indexed. Thus the magnitudes given below for the exemptions and the rate bands apply in nominal terms only in 1975, while remaining constant in real terms over a longer period.

The major exemptions are for the taxpayer and his wife and children. Where the wife and children have no income these exemptions in 1975 were $1,878 for the husband (or for a single individual), plus $1,644 for his wife, plus $646 per child aged sixteen or over during the tax year, plus $353 per child under sixteen. The exemptions for the wife and children are progressively withdrawn if they have more than a small amount of income.

The total value of exemptions claimed is shown in Table III–8 along with the total value of deductions. What emerges clearly is the importance of exemptions ($28 billion) relative to deductions ($11 billion); this contrasts with the US situation shown in Table III–1 where total exemptions come to $161 billion, while deductions (including the standard deduction) total $196 billion.

Table III–8 Exemptions, Deductions and Tax Liability, Canada, 1974

	Number millions	Amount $ thousand million
Total number of returns and total income, all returns	11.5	94.3
Taxable returns and total income, taxable returns	8.9	89.2
Total exemptions		27.9
Total deductions		10.9
Taxable income		50.4
Total tax liability		13.7

SOURCE: *Preliminary Taxation Statistics, 1974*, Revenue Canada, Taxation, Table B, page 9.

Canada has also two deductions which can be claimed independently of actual expenditure. These are the general expense deduction of 3 per cent of employment earnings up to a maximum deduction of $150, and the standard deduction for medical and charitable donations of $100. This latter is not intended to deal with large medical bills or regular church donations, both of which can be itemised, but simply to avoid the need to itemise an occasional donation to the Salvation Army or treatment for a sprained ankle.

Table 111–9 lists the various deductions. In descending order of importance in 1974 they were for Registered Pension Plan contributions, Retirement Saving Plan Premiums, the General Expense Allowance (as discussed above), the standard deduction (as discussed above), Canada Pension Plan contributions, Unemployment Insurance Premiums, expenses of employment, charitable donations, union and professional dues, tuition fees, medical claims, and child care expenses. The major deductions were obviously for pension provision. In addition in 1975 a new deduction became available to encourage people to save to buy a house, called the Registered Home Ownership Plan. Under this scheme savings for house purchase could, if they met certain conditions be tax-

Table III–9 Deductions, Canada, 1974

	Amount $ million
Registered Pension Plan Contributions	1,305
Retirement Saving Plan Premiums	1,237
General Expense Allowance	1,132
Standard deductions	1,050
Canada Pension Plan or QPP Contributions	797
Unemployment Insurance Premiums	664
Expenses of employment other than general expense allowance	532
Charitable donations	437
Union and professional dues	311
Tuition fees	239
Medical claims	118
Child care expenses	105
Other deductions	952
Total deductions	10,894

SOURCE: *Preliminary Taxation Statistics, 1974,* Revenue Canada, Taxation, Table B, page 9.

free (i.e. both the principal and the interest), and hence deductible for tax purposes.

In addition to exemptions and deductions Canada also has a family allowance. The amount involved varies by province—in Ontario the family allowance is $20 per child per month. The allowance is paid to the mother, but is taxable in the hands of the parent claiming the exemption for the child, usually the father.

Once the individual has exhausted his tax-free income he is subjected to marginal tax rates (see Table III–10) which rise smoothly from 9 per cent on the first $587 of taxable income to 47 per cent of taxable income in excess of $70,440. In the USA state income taxes are low and do not significantly alter the picture given by the federal income tax. This is not the case in Canada where a true picture is gained only by looking at the combined federal/provincial tax.

Table III–10 The Federal Tax Schedule for a Single Taxpayer, Canada, 1974

Taxable Income $	Marginal Tax Rate %	Tax Bill at Start of 'Slice' of Income $	Effective Tax Rate at Start of 'Slice' %
0–587	9	0	0
587–1,174	18	53	9.0
1,174–2,348	19	158	13.5
2,348–3,522	20	382	16.3
3,522–5,870	21	616	17.5
5,870–8,218	23	1,109	18.9
8,218–10,566	25	1,649	20.1
10,566–12,914	27	2,236	21.2
12,914–16,436	31	2,870	22.2
16,436–28,176	35	3,962	24.1
28,176–45,786	39	8,071	28.6
45,786–70,440	43	14,939	32.6
70,440 and over	47	25,540	36.3

SOURCE: Canadian Income Tax Package, 1975.

With the exception of Quebec which administers its own provincial tax both the federal and the provincial income tax are collected simultaneously by the federal government on the basis of a single tax return. The provincial tax is simply a proportion of the federal tax, varying in 1975 from a low of 30.5 per cent for Ontario to a high of 42.5 per cent in Manitoba. Taking as an example the 40 per cent rate of Saskatchewan the effect of this 40 per cent surcharge on the federal tax is simply to multiply by a factor of 1.4 both the tax bill column and the marginal rate column in Table III–10. Thus the combined marginal rate of tax on the first $587 of taxable income is 9 per cent $\times$ 1.4 = 12.6 per cent, while the top combined rate is 65.8 per cent. Once the provincial tax rates are included, there is not a great deal of difference between the US and Canadian tax schedules.

Finally, Canada Pension Plan contributions at a rate of 1.8 per cent for employed persons (3.6 per cent for the self-employed) are paid on earnings up to $7,400 per year; unemployment insurance is also payable at the rate of 1.4 per cent, again subject to a ceiling. Since these contributions are deductible for income tax the effective rates of contribution are below the nominal rates. Such contributions raise slightly the marginal rates of tax at the lower levels of income.

The latest date for filing in Canada is the 30 April following the end of the tax year (from 1 January to 31 December). The filing unit is the individual, both for single and for married persons. Where both have income, husband and wife have each to file a return. Income splitting is not permitted and stringent rules exist (and are enforced) to make sure that the partner with the higher income does not transfer income to the poorer partner. If the wife has more than a certain amount of income ($2,000 in 1974) the husband loses the additional personal allowances he receives as a married man; and in such a situation a married couple will pay exactly the same tax as two single individuals with the same total income.

Withholding

The employee obtains a self-coding form (the so-called 'Employee's Deduction Return') from his employer to whom he returns it when completed, and on the basis of which the employer withholds tax. The code, the calculation of which is the responibility of the taxpayer, takes into account the employee's status (e.g. married, disabled), the number of his dependants, and the income of the dependants (since the exemption for dependants is withdrawn as their income rises). The degree of detail appears to be scarcely less than is found in the UK and yet, apparently, causes no problems.

There is no onus on the employer to check the veracity of the employee's claims. Where no code is submitted the employer withholds as though the employee were single. Changes in code are dealt with in exactly the same way as its initial calculation i.e. the employee simply gives his employer an amended tax deduction return.

The method of calculating how much tax to withhold each month is basically the same as that discussed above in Table III–5. The withholding tables are calculated so that a typical family with no fluctuations in income will have tax withheld accurately. However, the logic of non-cumulative withholding combined with rising marginal tax rates again makes it inevitable that fluctuations in income will result in too much tax being deducted.

Thus the average refund in respect of the tax year 1974 was $240 and Table III–11 shows that some 8.4 million returns out of a total of 11.1 million, or some 75 per cent claimed a refund. About 1 million returns, or some 10 per cent, remitted additional tax with the return. About 13.5 per cent of returns neither claimed a refund nor paid additional tax (in contrast to under 3 per cent in the USA); this is largely due to the fact that personal deductions (which can normally be dealt with only at the end of the tax year) are of considerably less significance in Canada.[17]

Table III–11 Tax Withheld, Refunds and Overpayments, Canada, 1973

	Number of Returns millions	Amount $ thousand million
Total number of returns and total tax liability	11.1	11.4
Tax overpaid	8.4	1.6
Returns paid in full	1.5	—
Tax underpaid	1.1	0.8

SOURCE: *Taxation Statistics, 1975,* Revenue Canada, Taxation, Table 3, page 226.

Though over-withholding is generally popular the taxpayer can prevent over-deduction of tax by application to the tax authorities. For instance, where hardship could occur (e.g. starting work in mid-year, or regular alimony payments) the taxpayer can ask the tax administration to instruct his employer to use a larger code number than would normally be possible under the self-coding process. This is the Canadian alternative to the option of the US taxpayer to claim more exemptions than would be accounted for solely by his family responsibilities. However, the Canadian taxpayer does have the freedom to claim a *smaller* exemption than he is entitled to. For instance, someone with additional income might well prefer to be fully taxed on a current withholding basis and so omit his wife and children in filling in his tax deduction return (in which he calculates his code for submission to his employer).

The scope of withholding in Canada is slightly larger than in the USA inasmuch as Social Security benefits are generally taxable and (in striking con-

[17] Deductions are even less important in the UK. In 1972/73 the major deductions (interest payments, superannuation contributions and life assurance premia) totalled £1,691 million, while the personal allowances totalled £23,023 million. See *Report of the Commissioners of Inland Revenue,* 1975, *op. cit.,* p. 56.

trast to the UK) are withheld at source.[18] Dividends, interest and Family Allowances are not withheld at source. Since 1974 the first $1,000 of interest is normally allowable as a deduction and is hence effectively free of tax liability. This provision was extended to dividends in 1975. These deductions were meant to be an offset to inflation, though a side-effect may have been to legalise a lot of petty evasion. Despite these gaps over 90 per cent of total liability for personal income tax is withheld at source. Table III–11 shows that total underpayments ($800 million) are only about 7 per cent of total tax liability.

The Self-Employed and Estimated Tax

Like the USA, Canada has a system whereby tax may be paid on a current basis on non-employment income.[19] Tax is paid in quarterly instalments, the calculation being based either on the previous year's actual income or on the current year's expected income. If the former basis is chosen no penalties can be imposed for underpayment of tax. Unlike the USA however, where instalment payments of tax on non-withheld income are obligatory, the system in Canada is entirely voluntary, except that a 6 per cent rate of interest is applied if tax is not paid in instalments. The taxpayer therefore has the choice of paying tax in instalments during the tax year, or tax plus 6 per cent at filing time.

Payment of estimated tax is via an instalment account, which the tax authorities open for any individual paying estimated tax. The individual simply pays into a bank a cheque with a remittance form. These remittance forms are received individually by the taxpayer (i.e. not four at a time, or a whole year's supply, as in the USA) together with a receipt for his last estimated tax payment (no such receipts are issued in the USA).

Tax due is calculated on the assumption that the income flows completely evenly throughout the year. This rules out paying all one's tax in the last instalment, but is unfortunate for those with seasonal income flows mainly at the end of the tax year. As in the USA many people avoid the need for filing an estimated tax return by arranging to be over-withheld on their employment earnings. Many others, in contrast, make use of their legal entitlement to defer any payment until filing time in the belief that they are borrowing money at 6 per cent, in contrast to commercial lending rates of between two and four times this level. This view, in fact, exaggerates the difference since the 6 per cent per annum interest is chargeable on the whole of the deferred tax even though

---

[18] The payers of benefit under Canada Pension Plan, Old Age Security and Unemployment Insurance withhold tax in the normal way—i.e. non-cumulatively—and as though the benefit being paid was the recipient's sole source of income. If the recipient has other sources of income this method will withhold too little tax. The taxpayer can pay the balance due at the end of the tax year or he can request the payer to withhold more tax.

[19] As in the USA, income from a partnership is treated in essentially the same way as income from other self-employment.

most of the liability has been outstanding for less than a year. The true annual rate of interest is closer to 10 per cent.[20]

End-Year Adjustments

Table III–11 shows that nearly $1\frac{1}{2}$ million returns, or some 14 per cent of the total require no end-of-year adjustments—a figure considerably higher than in the USA. The difference is probably explained by the fact that Canada has fewer personal deductions than the US tax system,[21] and this makes it easier to withhold accurately on those with non-fluctuating incomes.

Nevertheless, in 1973 8.4 million returns, or some 75 per cent, claimed refunds out of a total of 11.1 million, the bulk of the claims coming in a peak around early March. The mechanism for processing end-year adjustments is similar to arrangements in the USA. By 28 February all employers should have issued form T4 to all those employed at any time during the previous tax year. This form fulfils the same role as the W2 in the USA, and contains the employee's name, address and Social Insurance number, together with gross earnings in that employment, and total income tax, Canada Pension Plan contributions and Unemployment Insurance contributions withheld. The employee receives two copies of the T4, one for his records and one to submit to the tax authorities with his return. An additional copy goes directly from the employer to the tax authorities.

Information returns are issued also for some other types of income—T5As for Family Allowances, T5s for dividends and T600s for bank deposit interest, one copy going to the taxpayer and another to the tax authorities. It is mandatory to issue such information returns for dividends or bank deposit interest in excess of $10, though it is possible that this ceiling might be raised in the future since most dividends and interest receipts below $1,000 per year are tax-free. Using these information returns the taxpayer completes his return, calculates his tax liability and sends the return to the tax authorities either with a cheque for the balance due or with a claim for a refund.

Returns are normally received in the months of March and April prior to the

[20] Instalments of one quarter of annual tax liability are payable on 30 April (one year before the filing date), 31 July (nine months before filing), 31 October (six months before filing), and 31 January (three months before filing). Alternatively the whole liability can be discharged on filing day together with the 6% interest charge. For an annual liability of $100 the taxpayer can pay four instalments of $25 or can pay $106 on filing day. If he chooses the latter then the $25 instalment due on:

30 April	remains unpaid for 1 year
31 July	„ „ „ $\frac{3}{4}$ year
31 October	„ „ „ $\frac{1}{2}$ year
31 January	„ „ „ $\frac{1}{4}$ year

Let r = the *quarterly* rate of interest. Then

$$25(1+r)^4 + 25(1+r)^3 + 25(1+r)^2 + 25(1+r) = 106 \qquad (1)$$

so:

$$(1+r)^4 + (1+r)^3 + (1+r)^2 + (1+r) = \frac{106}{25}$$

implying a quarterly rate of interest of approximately 2.4% and an annual rate of approximately 10%, i.e. inserting r = .024 in equation (1),

$$25(1.0995) + 25(1.0737) + 25(1.0486) + 25(1.024) = 106.15$$

[21] See p. 78 *supra*.

filing deadline on 30 April. After initial checking for surface errors (e.g. a missing signature) the return is typed on to punch cards and thence on to magnetic tape. All returns are thus put on to tape, and are then processed by computer to check for arithmetic errors. A computer printout is generated for each return—an assessment in the case of those that are correct and a tentative indication of the problem area for returns with errors.

An assessment is issued for each return—in the case where a return has no arithmetical errors and where a cheque was enclosed for the full amount of tax due, the assessment will simply be for the amount of $0. If the taxpayer is claiming a refund it will be issued automatically at this stage for returns which pass the arithmetical check. Generally, the taxpayer will receive his refund within a month of filing.

Again like the USA, and unlike the UK, such a settlement is made only on an interim basis. Once all returns have been given an initial processing a selection is made of returns for more detailed audit, at which stage the taxpayer can be assessed for additional tax. Audit procedures are discussed below.

Staff and Costs

In 1975 the Canadian federal tax authorities employed 12,278 people in permanent positions, and in addition about 7,000 keypunch operators in the period from January to the end of April. In this total the largest single categories are enforcement and data processing.

Inspection of the salaries of permanent and temporary employees shows a broadly bimodal distribution similar to that found in the USA. Again, personnel can be split into two broad categories—the relatively unskilled operatives who do the routine work following pre-ordained procedures, and the skilled and frequently highly skilled personnel (e.g. in audit) who deal with the supervision and investigatory side of the operation. For instance, all fully fledged audit personnel have university qualifications in accounting.

Thus Canada uses an average of 14,600 people to deal with approximately 11 million returns—or about 500 returns per employee, in comparison to slightly over 1,000 in the US and fewer than 300 taxpayers per employee in the UK. As stated earlier, a comparison of these figures without consideration of private sector costs is incomplete—but they do give some measure of the extent to which the costs of tax administration can be moved out of the public sector.

As was suggested for the USA the probable reasons why the costs of tax administration are so low in Canada relative to the UK are (a) that during the year the taxpayer has little contact with the tax authorities, and (b) at filing time the bulk of the work is automated, personal attention being devoted only to incorrect returns or those that are audited.

The result is that the public costs of collecting income tax in Canada are only some 0.9 per cent of total revenue collected, or approximately $100 million. Of this total, the largest single items of expenditure are on data processing and enforcement.

Reform

The major event in the reform of the Canadian taxation system was the Royal Commission Report of 1966.[22] This led two and a half years later to a White Paper[23] in which the federal government watered down substantially the proposals in the Report. Legislation resulted in 1971 and the reformed system came into effect on 1 January 1973. Among the proposals of the Royal Commission which did not reach the legislative stage were the integration of personal and corporate taxation, the treatment of capital gains as ordinary income, a maximum marginal rate of personal income tax of about 50 per cent, and a federal estate and gift tax. Two of the more substantial reforms were the introduction of capital gains taxation and the broadening of income averaging provisions.[24]

In addition to reforms arising out of the Royal Commission other changes have also had a substantial impact on tax administration. First, after very little discussion indexation was introduced in 1973; under this both the allowances and the rate bands of personal income tax were tied to movements in retail prices. Second, personal deductions were extended in 1975 by allowing the deductibility of savings held in Registered Home Ownership Plans.

While both these moves can be defended on many grounds, they have the administrative disadvantage that they complicate the tax system in a fairly major way. The extension of personal deductions reduces the probability that non-cumulative withholding will deduct the correct amount of tax even for those whose incomes do not fluctuate. The indexing of personal allowances also introduces complexity inasmuch as indexed magnitudes will only by accident be round numbers. Thus in 1975 the personal allowances for a man, his wife, an older and a younger child were $1,876, $1,644, $646 and $353, respectively, not numbers particularly conducive to accurate arithmetic.

The broadening of income averaging provisions also decreases the probability of correct withholding. With general averaging an individual whose income rises by more than 10 per cent (in nominal terms) between one year and the next can average his income and hence his tax burden. In fact this averaging is done automatically as part of the computer check on the arithmetic validity of returns—again it decreases the probability (a) of the correct amount of tax being withheld and (b) that the return itself will be correct (since the return will generally show calculations without any averaging).

[22] *Report of Royal Commission on Taxation* (Carter Commission), Queen's Printer, Ottawa, 1966.

[23] *Proposals for Tax Reform,* Queen's Printer, Ottawa, November 1969.

[24] For a discussion of these reforms see M. Bucovetsky and R. M. Bird, 'Tax Reform in Canada: A Progress Report', *National Tax Journal,* March 1972, and the references cited therein.

There is no evidence of any pressure within Canada either for simplification or for major reform in any other direction. Withholding on dividends and interest, so strongly advocated in the USA is of much less relevance in Canada where, as we have seen, the first $1,000 of such income is generally free of tax.

Major reform has also come at a provincial level. Ontario has introduced tax credits that correspond closely to a universal negative income tax. The gross credit is based on the property tax and sales tax paid by the individual. The net credit is the gross credit *less* 2 per cent of gross income, so that the net amount received declines as income rises and is eventually reduced to zero. Various other provinces have now also introduced a property tax credit. It should be noted that these credits are paid even if the taxpayer has no income tax liability, and that tenants as well as owner-occupiers are eligible for the credits.

Under a federal scheme retirement pensioners receive in addition a guaranteed income which pays the difference between a benchmark level of income and whatever the individual receives in federal pension plus any supplementary payment. These credits apply universally to the elderly and could in principle lead to universal filing, since the only way to claim them is to file a tax return, and those likely to benefit most are precisely those who would not otherwise have to file a return.

In terms of the UK generally and the recent Tax-Credit proposals[25] what is particularly interesting is that Ontario feels able to offer not only a universal tax credit, but a tapered credit that declines to zero as income rises.

3 An Outline of the Swedish Tax System[26]

Allowances, Deductions and the Tax Structure

One of the main contrasts between the Swedish personal tax system and those of North America and the UK is the extensive role of local taxation.

In Sweden local income tax is levied at a single rate, currently averaging just over 25 per cent, and takes a larger proportion of most taxpayers' income than the more progressive national income tax. The result of the two taxes is that an average wage earner in Sweden faces a marginal tax rate of between 55 and 65 per cent. The administration of the two taxes is almost entirely integrated, with both subject to nearly the same rules. Only one tax return is used for both the income taxes and for the net wealth tax. As the rates of local income tax vary from 21.6 per cent to 29 per cent, people may attempt to avoid tax by registering in an area with a low rate. The normal rule is that a person is registered as living in the area in which he sleeps, but should two local authorities disagree over where a person actually resides there are about 25 registration inspectors who adjudicate.

The main allowances against taxable income include a personal allowance

[25] *Proposals for a Tax-Credit System, op. cit.*

[26] For a more extensive discussion see: Simon James 'The Swedish Personal Taxation System' *British Tax Review,* No. 6, 1975.

of SKr 4,500 (about £560)—which declines as income rises beyond SKr 30,000 (roughly £3,750) by one-fifth of the excess until it disappears on income of over SKr 52,000 (approx. £6,500). There is also a special allowance for children under 16 years if both spouses have earned income, designed to compensate in part for the cost of child care. It is given to the spouse with the lower income, at a rate of 25 per cent of that income up to a maximum allowance of SKr 2,000 (around £250). A child's income, earned or unearned, is not aggregated with the income of its parents.

There are two categories of deduction. 'Source' deductions are those expenses incurred in the earning or collection of income; they may be deducted to give a net income from each source. For example, in contrast to British practice, travel expenses to and from work and the extra costs of living while working away from home are both deductible. Second, there are 'general' deductions which may be deducted from the taxpayer's net income, e.g. pension contributions and certain insurance premia.

Capital gains are taxed on the same basis and at the same rates as income, thus reducing the incentive to transform income into capital gains. However, capital gains are deflated by an official price index before being subject to tax. The entire gain from selling property such as buildings is included in taxable income, unless the property has been held for more than two years in which case only 75 per cent is included. There is some relief for home-owners who are entitled to a deduction of SKr 3,000 (approx. £375) for every year they own the house. The entire gain from selling financial assets is also included as taxable income if the period of ownership is less than two years. However, the proportion counted as income varies inversely with the period of ownership so that none of the gain is taxable if the property is held for more than five years.

The Swedish wealth tax is levied on residents possessing net wealth (i.e. assets minus debts) in excess of SKr 200,000 (about £25,000). Taxable assets include most kinds of property, but certain items (household goods, books, paintings, stamps and some personal insurance) are exempt. The administration of the wealth tax is fully integrated with that of the national and local income taxes. A person required to file an income tax return must state on it the amount of his net wealth and must also list his taxable assets and their value. In contrast to the income taxes where spouses are taxed separately, a couple's assets, together with those of children under 20 years old, are aggregated for the purposes of the wealth tax and taxed at the same rates as those used in assessing individuals. There is an overriding limit of 85 per cent of a taxpayer's total income that can be paid in both income and wealth taxes.[27]

In order to match current payments of tax with liability as closely as possible there is a system of preliminary tax which takes two forms. 'A-Tax' is withheld on wages and salaries. 'B-Tax' is paid on an estimated basis by a taxpayer with income from sources not subject to withholding that exceeds 25 per cent of his

---

[27] For further details see Simon James, *op. cit.*

Withholding and A-Tax

As in North America, tax is withheld from employment incomes on a non-cumulative basis. There are only four codes in Sweden: married, single, and with and without children. The amount withheld is designed to cover both national and local liability. At the beginning of the calendar year, which is also the fiscal year, each A-taxpayer receives the table appropriate to his circumstances (i.e. single, married, etc.) that shows the actual amount of A-tax to be withheld. He is also sent a notice of demand which must be handed over to his employer. If the taxpayer fails to present such a demand, or a certificate showing that he is not liable to A-tax, withholding must take place at the highest rate fixed by the relevant table plus 10 per cent. It the employee has income from other sources, such as part-time employment, he may ask his main employer to deduct extra tax, and employers must comply with such a request. Alternatively the A-taxpayer may make extra payments of tax directly to the tax administration.

In the January of 'assessment year' (the year following that in which the income is received) the employer returns the notice of demand to the employee with a statement on the back specifying the amount of tax withheld (i.e. equivalent to a W2 or T4 in North America). By 15 February the taxpayer has to file a return, on which he calculates his final tax liability. No money is due with the return, but if on the basis of the calculation his final tax liability significantly exceeds his preliminary tax the individual has until 30 April to make additional payments and so wipe out the deficiency. Otherwise he has to pay a penalty interest charge. In November or December of the assessment year each taxpayer receives a further notice of demand showing how much tax, if any, is still due. If tax has been overwithheld a money order for the difference is enclosed. If some tax remains to be paid the notice must be passed immediately to the employer who then collects it by extra withholding during the period January to April of the year following the assessment year. The process of final settlement is thus considerably longer than in North America.

Two other substantial differences from North America are also noteworthy: first, withholding on employment income is as directed by the tax authorities, in contrast to the self-coding procedures in the USA and Canada; and assessments issued by the authorities continue to play a major role even though the system is basically one of self-assessment.

The Self-Employed and B-Tax

A person is subject to B-Tax if more than a quarter of his income (together with that of his wife) comes from sources other than employment. An individual may also choose the B-tax system rather than A-tax if he has more than one employer and prefers not to regard any one of them as the main employer who must withhold sufficient tax to cover all the others.

In the same way as A-taxpayers, B-taxpayers receive a notice of demand early in the year, but for B-tax it states specific amounts of preliminary tax that must be paid in equal instalments every two months throughout the year. The level of these instalments is based on the income received two years previously. So, for example, B-tax liability for 1976 is based on the assessment for 1975 which in turn is based on the income of 1974. However if, for example, the taxpayer's income in 1976 is more than 20 per cent higher than his income in 1974, and the absolute difference is at least SKr 600 (about £75), then he has to file a current estimate of income and wealth by 1 December 1976. As with the A-tax system, if the taxpayer finds that he has extra tax to pay when he calculates his liability he may make further payments before 30 April of the assessment year (1977, in our example). If there is still tax due at the end of the assessment year, it must be paid in two equal instalments in March and May of the following year (1978). This procedure is enforced with penalties that are both severe and automatic. Failure to pay one of the instalments on time results in a penalty of 4 per cent of the tax due.

End-Year Adjustments

As in Canada and the USA the combined effects of non-cumulative withholding and estimated tax payments lead to a large number of end-year adjustments. Of the five million or so income taxpayers in Sweden approximately three million (mainly employees) pay too much preliminary tax, two million (including most of those with non-employment income) do not pay enough, and about 10,000 cases are exactly right. The adjustments are normally handled by computer. The average discrepancy is around SKr 500 (approximately £65), and in total SKr 4 billion (about £500 million) is involved.

It is very much more difficult to estimate the costs of collection and assessment of income taxes in Sweden than in Canada, the United States or the United Kingdom. The agencies responsible for taxation in Sweden are involved in many activities other than tax administration. The National Tax Board is responsible also for civil registration, general elections, and controlling the production and sale of alcohol. Much of the work of assessment is performed by part-time laymen and the extensive computer facilities are used by many other public bodies. It is therefore not easy even approximately to apportion the costs to specific functions (but see Chapter IV, Table IV–1).

4 Completing the Tax Return

The Acquisition of Tax Forms

Completion of a tax return consists logically of the following steps:

(a) the acquisition of the necessary forms, chosen appropriately for the tax unit and the type of income,

(b) the calculation of the relevant income total or totals,

(c) the calculation of total tax-free income (i.e. total exemptions and total deductions), and

(d) the calculation of tax due.

In both the USA and Canada the most common form of tax return consists of a main section which everyone completes, plus supplementary schedules (e.g. for capital gains) which are used by taxpayers only as required. In the USA there is also the so-called 'short form', a much simpler tax return which may be used by those taxpayers who take the standard deduction and who have only employment earnings plus small amounts of interest and dividend income. Taxpayers with such simple affairs have the option of using either the short or the long form. Everyone else has to use the long form.

In both the USA and Canada each taxpayer will normally receive by post at the end of the tax year a tax return package containing:

(a) the same type of tax return form as filed in the previous year (in duplicate) with the taxpayer's name, address, and social security number pre-printed by computer,

(b) tax tables enabling calculation of final tax liability,

(c) a pre-addressed (but not postage paid) return envelope,

(d) assorted advice on how to complete the tax return (this aspect will be discussed further below).

For new taxpayers (school leavers, immigrants) or those who do not receive a tax return for other reasons (changed address) returns and ancillary documentation may be obtained from local tax offices and post offices. In the USA some 65 per cent of taxpayers normally use pre-addressed returns.

The Calculation of Gross Income

A key difference between the UK and most other industrialised countries including the USA, Canada and Sweden is that the UK is almost alone in dividing income into the various schedules. In North America and Sweden returns and tax liability relate entirely to total income.

For most people the main source of information on their gross income is the information return (e.g. the W2 in the USA and T4 in Canada). For employment earnings this will be issued by their employer(s) shortly after the end of the tax year. Unlike the UK where the P60 gives a cumulative total for the whole year, these information returns give details only of income paid by the employer issuing them. Thus someone who has had three jobs during one year will have three information returns, and total employment earnings for the year will be the sum of three gross earnings figures. Copies of these information returns have generally to be sent to the tax authorities for checking purposes (discussed in more detail below).

Information returns are issued also for most kinds of unearned income. Dividends and interest are covered by so-called 1099s in the USA and by T5s and T600s, respectively, in Canada. Thus, shortly after the end of the tax year the taxpayer will receive from his bank an information return showing how much interest he was paid during the year. Similarly, General Motors will issue such a statement to each of its shareholders showing dividend payments during the year.

Thus, in striking contrast to the variegated pattern in the UK, most income in North America is covered by information returns. These facilitate the accuracy of tax returns in two ways. First, and most obviously, taxpayers have accurate and timely information about their income. For most taxpayers, calculating their gross income is simply a matter of adding up the income reported in their information returns. Second, accurate reporting is enhanced also because once an information return has been issued to the taxpayer (and a copy to the tax administration) he will be very wary about not reporting that income. The threat of random cross-matching of the information return issued by the payer with the tax return submitted by the payee is a powerful discouragement to the non-reporting of income, even though such cross-matching occurs only on a small scale.[28]

The main types of income not covered by information returns are self-employment incomes and casual earnings. In the latter case there is no systematic way of reporting casual income. The onus is on the taxpayer to make sure that it is all reported, but of course the compliance record for such earners (e.g. gardeners, home help, etc.) is far from perfect. This will be taken up further below.

In the case of the self-employed, their gross income will be their trading profits. These are calculated on a separate schedule of the tax return. Like casual earnings there is no method of systematically reporting self-employment earnings, and the onus is on the taxpayer to keep good records.

The Calculation of Total Tax-Free Income

The calculation of tax free income is for most people a question of calculating the value of the exemptions and the deductions to which they are entitled. The simplest case of exemptions occurs in the USA where (in most cases) the taxpayer claims one $750 exemption per person in the tax unit. In Canada matters are complicated both by the facts that different family members receive different exemptions and that exemptions for persons other than the household head are progressively withdrawn as the income of that person rises. Such allowances are even more complicated in Sweden. In both North America and Sweden, it is the taxpayer's responsibility to ensure that he claims only the exemptions to which he is entitled. But no supporting evidence is required by the tax authority at filing time, though it may, of course, be demanded during an audit. Thus, if husband and wife are divorced they have to decide which of them will claim the exemptions for the children.

In both the USA and Canada the tax return contains space for the calculation of total exemptions. In particular, in the case of the more complicated Canadian situation space is included for each type of family member; it also allows for the calculation of the reduction in the exemption due to (say) the fact that the wife has income in her own right.

[28] With the exception of the T4 cross-matching programme in Canada discussed below.

In the case of deductions the matter is simple if a standard deduction is taken, in which case the relevant tax-free income is either a flat amount or a simple percentage of gross income. If deductions are itemised the taxpayer will be involved in a much greater burden of record keeping (medical bills, details of expenditure on child-care, etc.), and frequently also a much greater burden of calculation (e.g. where expenditures are deductible only if they exceed a minimum percentage of total income, or where only a fixed percentage of expenditure is deductible).

In the case of itemised deductions the taxpayer does not usually have to submit supporting evidence at the time of filing, though in Canada receipts have to be submitted for contributions to Registered Retirement Savings Plans, Registered Home Ownership Plans and charities. In any case the taxpayer has to be prepared to back up his claim should he be audited. Itemising one's deductions can thus frequently end up as an exercise in the collection of receipts.

If deductions remain relatively simple and clear-cut no serious problem arises. But if, as in the US, they breed and multiply both in number and in complexity, then a sizeable burden of record-keeping and calculation is imposed on the taxpayer, as well as a feeling of discontent if he takes the standard deduction to save effort, but suspects that he might pay less tax by itemising. Furthermore, it is here that a major 'grey area' of tax law can arise. If, for instance, not only payments to registered medical practitioners and payments for medically prescribed drugs are deductible, but also 'related expenditures', then people will try to deduct diet food on the grounds that their psychiatrist recommended it.

A relatively strong case can be made for the view that deductions, if they become too broad-ranging, can interfere with the smooth operation of a self-assessment system (or, for that matter, any income tax system).

The Calculation and Remittance of Tax Payable

Having completed the parts of the tax return dealing with the calculation of gross income and total exemptions and deductions, all that remains is the now relatively simple task of calculating tax liability. Taxable income is simply the difference between gross income and total tax-free income. Once tax-free income has been calculated tax liability for the year can simply be read off the tax table supplied with the return. The Canadian table, for instance, shows federal income tax payable for every $10 of taxable income. Thus if a taxpayer has $12,381 of taxable income he will round this down to $12,380 and read off the table (1975 figures) that he has a federal tax liability of $2,509 plus (in Ontario) a provincial tax liability of $831.80.

In the USA the procedure is made even easier for straightforward cases. Tax tables are issued not only in terms of taxable income (see Table III–4) but also in terms of gross income. A taxpayer with gross income below $15,000 and taking a standard deduction selects the tax table appropriate to his circumstances (number of exemptions, marital status, etc.) and simply reads off his tax liability without any need to calculate taxable income. This procedure is not available to those with higher incomes or to those who itemise their deductions.

In some countries (e.g. Canada) it is necessary to calculate not only income subject to income tax, but also income which is liable for social security contributions. In the USA social security contributions are all levied on the same income base. But in Canada the so-called 'Earnings Subject to Contribution' for Canada Pension Plan need not be the same as 'Insurable Earnings' for the purposes of unemployment insurance. These two magnitudes are calculated on a separate part of the Canadian tax return, and the contribution due for pension and for unemployment benefit is then read off a table accompanying that for income tax.

Having calculated one's liability for the various taxes the next step is to compare these figures with the amount of tax actually paid during the year via the withholding and estimated tax systems. If total liability exceeds payments made on a current basis during the tax year additional tax will be due and a cheque for the outstanding balance will normally be enclosed with the completed return. If tax has been overpaid during the year the taxpayer will normally claim a refund. He has the option also of crediting the overpayment against the following year's liability.

Provided sufficient tax has been paid during the year (the definition of 'sufficient' is outlined above on page 68) no interest penalty is payable in respect of any balance due, provided it is paid by the last day for filing; and provided the refund is issued promptly (in the USA within 45 days from the last day for filing) no interest is payable by the tax authorities on overpaid tax.

Unless the taxpayer is subsequently audited (discussed below) the payment of balance due or receipt of a refund closes matters for the tax year in question.

5 Taxpayer Assistance

Assistance from Published Sources

For the vast majority of taxpayers most of the information they need to complete their return is acquired either by word of mouth or from the information supplied with the tax return. This is enhanced by the fact that more and more tax education takes place in schools. In both the USA and Canada and in Sweden a detailed description of the return and the meaning of the items in it are part of the tax return 'kit' sent out automatically to all non-transient taxpayers.

In the USA the Taxpayer Services Program is in charge of all direct assistance to taxpayers. For fiscal year 1975 its budget was $102.9 million, or some 6.5 per cent of total IRS expenditure; its manpower was just over 3,000 or 3.25 per cent of the IRS total. These figures are very narrowly defined, however, and do not include the cost of many publications, nor the help given to many taxpayers by tax officials at times other than filing time. The true proportion of resources going to taxpayer assistance in one form or another is likely to be considerably more than 6.5 per cent.

Most taxpayers turn for help first to the literature which comes with (or as part of) the tax return. In Canada, as a typical example, the tax return is accompanied by a 45 page booklet designed to be easily understood by everyone, but offering insufficient information for complicated situations. The book is divided into sections: the first gives step-by-step details for completing the return; the second gives more detailed information on various types of income, exemptions, and deductions; the last three are entitled 'Problems?', 'What's New in 1975', and 'Questions?'. Finally, the book contains also tax tables for the year in question for federal income tax, provincial income tax, Canada Pension Plan, and unemployment insurance.

Should this prove insufficient the taxpayer can turn to the tax administration or to private advice (discussed in the succeeding two sections). In the USA taxpayers who file the short form (and some who file the long form) need not compute their tax liability. Provided that they complete the first part of the return the IRS will calculate their liability for them and send a bill for the amount due, or send any refund due. But if a man wishes to work out his affairs himself he can turn to more detailed publications supplied by the tax authorities. In the USA there exists the so-called 'Blue Book' (Publication 17) entitled 'Your Federal Income Tax'. This volume has 192 (large) pages and contains a great deal of detailed information. Contrary to past practice it is now issued free, but only on request—the tax return package contains only an abbreviated version.

Unlike the simpler publications the Blue Book contains detailed discussion of the taxation of capital gains and losses and of trading profits and losses. It also contains a list of IRS toll-free telephone numbers, a list of other IRS publications, and a list of tax forms.

Yet more broad-ranging are the information circulars issued by the tax authorities in both the USA and Canada. These can cover such things as appeal rights and audit methods, and also technical matters such as the tax administration's interpretation of a particular point of law. In 1976 there were 88 such circulars listed in the back of the Blue Book. These are only the more important and frequently consulted of such circulars. All are available free on request.

Finally, the tax return is the object of the closest scrutiny. Its design and any changes in it are carefully analysed, including frequently the use of expert psychological assistance. At least one of the present authors finds the US tax return considerably easier to complete than his native UK one.

Assistance through Personal Contact

Compendious and comprehensible though they may be, many people have questions that are not answered in official publications, or simply find it hard to understand written material. For these it is vital to have a mechanism whereby the tax authorities can be approached directly with taxpayer queries. Help of this sort falls into five major categories:

(a) propaganda and use of mass media,
(b) telephone assistance,
(c) face-to-face help in preparing returns,
(d) help prior to preparing a return,
(e) dealing with questions about returns that have already been filed.

Extensive use is made of media propaganda in the USA, Canada and Sweden, including both television 'spots' (i.e. lasting 1–3 minutes) and longer, more ambitious productions. These aim to inform the taxpayer of his rights and obligations. They try to inform him ('hey, did you know that you could deduct your doctor's bill?'), and educate him—e.g. by an animated film of how to complete a tax return. Newspapers are encouraged to print tax features, especially in the months preceding filing time. There is also some propaganda, including film, on the consequences of cheating.

More specifically, in both the USA and Canada, taxpayers can telephone the tax authorities free of charge to seek assistance. These free phone networks cover the entire country (in Canada only for part of the year) and are very widely used. In 1975 in the USA there were about 85.5 million individual returns filed. The number of enquiries was 40.6 million of which 29.4 million were by telephone, 11 million were enquiries made in person, and 190,000 were in writing.[29] It is hard to imagine a smoothly running system of self-assessment without this feature.

Face-to-face assistance is provided in the USA in the 58 District Offices and the much larger number of sub-offices. In Canada there are only 28 such offices. The IRS will fill in the tax return for the taxpayer if he provides the appropriate documentation (e.g. a W2) and earns below approximately $20,000 per year and takes a standard deduction. Such cases can be accommodated on the short tax return. The Canadian tax authorities do not officially offer such a service of filling in tax returns—they set out only to answer questions. In fact, Canadian tax officials frequently tell people not to worry about the arithmetic since the computer will check it anyway. But a blind eye is turned in cases such as the aged and mentally handicapped, whose returns are often unofficially filled in at a local tax office. In both countries the fact that the return has been completed by the authorities in no way precludes a later audit.

In addition to advice and assistance given by employees of the tax administration, the tax authorities in both countries run schemes to train people like senior citizens (e.g. a retired accountant, or trade union member) to help others with their tax returns. Such people could help fellow residents in an old people's home, or fellow union members. In the case of the USA this

[29] *Report of the Commissioner of IRS, 1975,* pp. 6 and 13. See Chapter II, p. 43, for the contrast with the UK.

scheme (the Volunteer Income Tax Assistance Program—VITA) is now quite large (some 800,000 US taxpayers were assisted by VITA in 1975).

Another example of outside help to which the tax authorities give their blessing are the self-help areas provided around filing time in many of the US District Offices. Here people can sweat through their return asking for help from others in the same position, or from tax office officials.

Help prior to tackling the tax return can be obtained from any tax office, but more long range help is available from the central tax authorities in the form of advance rulings. In the USA, Canada and Sweden a taxpayer may apply to the tax authorities for an advance ruling on the tax implications of a proposed transaction. This service is of assistance not only to the taxpayer, but also to the tax authorities, who thereby know what people are getting up to, and can, if necessary take steps to have any loophole plugged.[30]

In the USA and Canada, such rulings are binding (by custom, not law) on the tax authorities, but only for the person to whom the advice has been given. If of sufficient importance they may later be published in more general form. In the USA the Freedom of Information Act has greatly reduced the power of the federal bureaucracy to preserve the secrecy of its methods and documents, and this has brought into question the confidentiality of such advance rulings. This matter is as yet unresolved.

Advance rulings are issued free in the USA. In Canada the minimum fee is $150 plus an additional fee depending on the time taken in producing the ruling. In Sweden the fee ranges from £25 to £125 depending on the time required.

Finally, there is the question of taxpayer queries once the return has been filed. If a taxpayer does not understand why he has been billed for additional tax plus an interest penalty he can, of course, seek help from his local tax office in person, by telephone, or in writing. With the advent of computers the tax authorities can rapidly (i.e. within a matter of days rather than weeks) acquire the details of the return and issue a reply.

But in the USA it is now possible to deal instantly by telephone with many post-filing queries. The role of computers in tax administration will be discussed in more detail below, but it is useful briefly to anticipate some of these sections here. In the USA data from all returns are put onto magnetic tape and hence can be checked by computer and retrieved at need. But data concerning 'problem' returns (e.g. those on which money is still owed) are stored also on disc, whence they can be retrieved much more rapidly. In the US disc system the taxpayer's social security number is typed into a terminal in a tax office and (provided his return data is in the disc system) the return will be flashed onto a screen within seconds.

This system (called the Integrated Data Retrieval System—IDRS) not only retrieves tax return data within seconds, but also allows them to be adjusted

---

[30] The IRS will not rule on a proposed transaction if it appears to be solely a tax avoidance scheme.

(e.g. incorrect data cancelled and new data entered). An example of the capabilities of IDRS is instructive. Taxpayer Smith files his tax return on 10 April with a cheque for $89.67, this being his calculation of his outstanding tax liability. Five weeks later he receives a letter from the IRS saying that he has failed to pay tax on time, and still owes $89.67 on which a late-payment interest penalty is now due. Smith telephones the IRS (free, even if long distance) and tells the IRS official that he has paid already.

The official will be seated at a keyboard with a screen at his desk. He punches in Smith's social security number (or his name and address) and his return appears on the screen. This shows an unpaid liability of $89.67. Smith says that he has the cancelled cheque. This suggests that the cheque and the return parted company prematurely during the processing of the return, so the keyboard operator 'requests' the computer to flash up on the screen all unidentified cheques for $89.67. There are six such cheques of which one is 'Smith, 10 April 1975, $89.67'. The operator then cross-references (all via the keyboard) the now identified cheque with the tax return. The matter is now cleared up during the course of one telephone call, and the computer can even be told (still via the keyboard) to send out a letter to Smith cancelling the delinquency notice and the late-payment penalty.

Assistance in the Private Sector

In the USA, Canada and Sweden, just as in the UK, those with complicated tax affairs frequently make use of a lawyer or accountant. This is likely to be the case under any system of assessment, and will therefore not be discussed further.

Of much more relevance is the fact that under self-assessment a great many people with relatively *simple* tax affairs may want help, may be unprepared for a variety of reasons to obtain it from the tax authorities, and may be willing to pay a modest amount for a service that will complete their return for them. Such a tax assistance industry flourishes, especially in the USA.

In neither the USA nor Canada are tax advisers required to be licenced, and lurid tales are told of fly-by-night operators in department stores and of massage parlours offering tax advice as part of their service. But the general feeling on the part of senior tax officials in the USA was that such cases were infrequent, and that not only did the tax advisory industry run reasonably well, but that it was in fact a necessary part of the tax system, since otherwise either the tax administration would be inundated with requests for help, or the accuracy of returns would decline drastically (if nothing else, tax preparers generally ensure that numbers are entered into the correct place on the tax return). Canadian tax officials were less happy about cheap tax preparation, but have less experience of it than in the USA since this service is a relatively recent phenomenon in Canada.

Certainly the use of such services is widespread—in the USA it is estimated that in 1974 some 45 per cent of returns filed had been completed by a commercial tax preparer, though some of these were by highly qualified accountants. In Canada the comparable figure is around 15 per cent. The average payment for the service in the USA in 1974 was around $20, giving an estimated expenditure on such services of $760 million. If we were to double this figure (because just under half of taxpayers use the service) we should obtain a very crude minimum estimate of the private compliance costs for individuals of federal income tax of about $1.5 billion, a sum approximately equal to the public costs of the IRS.[31]

By far the largest of such tax preparing firms is H & R Block (henceforth HRB) who operate on a franchise basis and have some 7,000 offices throughout the USA. In the year to 30 April 1975 the firm had a turnover of $114 million and after-tax profits of $17.5 million resulting from the preparation of approximately 8.6 million returns, or somewhat over 10 per cent of all individual income tax returns. The firm has recently extended its operation also to Canada. For a charge from $5 upwards HRB undertake to complete any tax return, whether individual, partnership, or corporate, though the vast bulk of their work deals with the first category.

The crucial questions with any operation such as this concern the quality of the work done, which in turn depends on the training and supervision of staff. There is no formal check by the US or Canadian tax authorities on the performance of firms such as HRB (at least, none of which there is public knowledge), but the casual opinions of tax officials on the quality of their work have already been mentioned.

In the absence of any licencing of tax practitioners the quality of training and supervision will clearly vary from company to company. HRB is relatively thorough in this respect. It runs its own training school, which is available to all comers on a commercial basis. There are two courses, one basic, one advanced, at $75 and $120, respectively, running from mid-September to the end of December. In 1974 classes were held in 2,200 locations throughout the USA, involving 42,000 students. Such classes are conducted simultaneously in all locations so that a businessman going from New York to Los Angeles for a fortnight need not miss his classes. Of the 42,000 students some 25,000 are employed by HRB, 95 per cent of them on a seasonal basis. An important point is that all HRB personnel have to take this course each year, the basic course if they are new and the advanced course otherwise. Even old-stagers take the advanced course each year to keep them up to date.

Once he has completed the course a new employee is assigned to an office under the supervision of a manager. HRB's method of operation is that the taxpayer will come to the shop with his tax return and such details as are necessary to complete it. He will talk to the tax preparer, who will then complete not the tax return but an HRB facsimile. The taxpayer is then told to come back in five days for his completed return. In the meantime the HRB

---

31 See Chapter IV, Table IV–1, for further discussion and for comparison with the UK.

copy is checked by the company's internal checking staff. Those returns prepared by new recruits are subjected to closer scrutiny, and (at least in principle) further education takes place if the mistakes are systematic.

HRB will pay any interest penalty that results from an error of theirs, and also offer to assist free of charge any client who is audited. This gives them an incentive to complete the return correctly the first time, since any further involvement will cost them money. To this extent at least quality of work and profitability coincide. Perhaps a more serious potential source of difficulty is the fact that HRB retain their internal facsimile of the client's tax return, and this could easily result in violations of privacy. To some extent federal regulations guard against this, and HRB's internal security appears to be effective. But a potential problem area remains.

It is very probable that such an organisation would rapidly develop if self-assessment were introduced in the UK. It is hard to be dogmatic about whether this would be a problem or not. The evidence from North America is anecdotal rather than systematic, but suggests that this need not be regarded as a major disadvantage of self-assessment, especially if appropriate licencing arrangements exist from the start.

In addition to assistance from the tax administration and from private firms it is possible to aid taxpayers also as part of a government's welfare programme, for instance the Community Income Tax Service (CITS) of the provincial government in Manitoba, which describes itself thus:

'The CITS's program offers two basic services to its users, assistance in preparation of tax returns, and a short-term loan service based on the calculated tax refund. Both services are intended primarily for those with annual incomes of less than $8,000 . . . The income tax assistance service is free for persons with no taxable income, for the remainder a sliding fee of $1 to $7 is charged . . .[32]

CITS is now well-established and likely to spread. The initial impetus to its formation was to give poor taxpayers an alternative to the so-called tax discounting firms who completed clients' tax returns and then issued them with their refunds immediately; but the price of such 'instant cash' was a loss of 40 to 70 per cent of the actual value of the tax refund. In the UK such a community service could be organised either by local authorities or by an institution such as the Co-operative movement.

Taxpayer Attitudes

The effectiveness of self-assessment depends not only on the quality of the assistance available to the taxpayer, but also on his attitudes to the structure and administration of taxation in general, and on self-assessment in particular. Though the tax authorities in both the USA and Canada are very much aware

[32] Community Income Tax Service, *Annual Report 1976*, Winnipeg, Manitoba.

of this, little systematic information on taxpayer attitudes is available.[33] What follows is therefore of necessity somewhat anecdotal.

Looking first at the specifics of self-assessment, the necessity of filing an annual return is accepted as part of the way of life—'one of the rites of Spring' as one tax official put it. It is clear that the refund of over-withheld tax which most people receive goes a long way towards removing the sting of having to file a tax return.

There is very little direct defiance—even at the height of the turmoil over the Viet Nam war, only a handful of US taxpayers refused to pay income tax. One senior official described the US system as 'voluntary compliance—with a little bit of help.' By the 'little bit of help' he was referring less to taxpayer assistance than to the big stick of enforcement, discussed below. What is certainly true is that to a large extent the effectiveness of self-assessment is enhanced by taxpayer fears of the enforcement powers of the tax authorities. Such fears are greater in the USA than in Canada—but in Canada too the tax administration has wide powers (discussed below) and public knowledge of these powers aids compliance.

The main complaint of taxpayers is over the complexity of the system. But it is likely that there would be complaints however simple the system, since complaints come even from those in the very simplest financial circumstances who can use the US short form.

More interesting, perhaps, is the fact that when, due to miscalculation, tax was recently under-withheld in the USA so that most taxpayers had to pay additional tax at filing time there was a storm of protest. In both the USA and Canada the evidence strongly supports the view that over-withholding is generally popular, while under-withholding is wildly unpopular, and this appears to be the case also in other countries such as Australia.

6 Enforcement: Checking

The Role of Computers in Checking Returns

Enforcement activities may conveniently be divided into three aspects:

(a) checking returns—i.e. verifying that the return is internally correct, but not checking the accuracy of the figures on which the return is based (e.g. no attempt is made to verify that charitable donations claimed were actually made),

(b) auditing returns—i.e. checking on a sample basis that the data on which the return is based are accurate, and

(c) collection—i.e. the process of ensuring that all tax assessed is actually collected.

These three aspects of enforcement are the subject of this section and the following one.

---

[33] A small counter-example is the *Taxpayer Opinion Survey,* IRS Memorandum, April 1975.

Computer techniques lie at the heart of the process of checking returns in North America, and it is worth briefly outlining the system. The description will be in terms of the USA—the Canadian system is broadly similar and any significant differences will be mentioned. Returns are first scanned manually for obvious errors (e.g. unsigned, or with social security number missing). Returns that pass this stage are transcribed onto magnetic tape by what is essentially a typing operation. For most returns this is by far the most labour-intensive part of tax administration. The tape is then run through a small computer for a thorough check of its arithmetic, including checks for obvious mistakes like declaring that one is married and filing jointly, but claiming only one exemption. If the return is not arithmetically correct it is re-typed onto tape to check that there was not a manual typing error. If it is still incorrect it goes to an 'error resolution' side of the operation, which may involve contacting the taxpayer to see whether the discrepancy can be cleared up without auditing the return.

If the return is arithmetically correct a refund will be issued if one is due, and the return will be transferred to another tape and forwarded to the national computer center where it is entered on the Individual Master File (IMF). The IMF has a file on each taxpaying individual, containing fixed items like name, address, and social security number, plus his returns for the previous 3–6 years depending on the type of taxpayer and type of return. The master file is a key element in the audit process (see the following section), and is used also for research purposes. It is updated each week.

These procedures are slightly modified in Canada inasmuch as the tax authorities have the power unilaterally to correct certain types of mistakes. Thus, for instance, overpaid Social Insurance contributions are automatically refunded, as is any tax overpaid because the taxpayer has not made use of the income averaging provisions. Such returns in Canada are corrected automatically and added to the master file in corrected form.

A record like the IMF is very compendious, but retrieving information from it is relatively slow in computer terms—to retrieve a given tax return could take from 10–30 minutes, since the correct tape has to be found, and has then to be mounted on the tape drive and searched for the correct return. The analogy is with finding the third movement of Brahms' second piano concerto recorded on a cassette tape. One has first to find the right cassette and then spin it until the start of the third movement.

While this is adequate for most purposes it is far easier to deal with taxpayer queries if instant access can be gained to his return. Thus all 'problem' returns on the IMF (i.e. all those on which tax is still owed) are stored not only on tape, but also on disc. The analogy with disc storage is a jukebox—one simply presses the button with the record's code number, and the record plays almost immediately. In the disc system the code number is the taxpayer's social security number, and the return is typically flashed onto the screen in seconds. This is the Integrated Data Retrieval System (IDRS) discussed above.

Canada has no system equivalent to this.

In both the USA and Canada, the IMF is used also for mundane tasks like pre-printing returns and estimated tax returns with the taxpayer's name, address, and social security number. Additionally, in the US system, the IMF can be used automatically to stop a tax refund if the taxpayer still has tax debts outstanding. Thus in many cases the 1974 tax rebate[34] of between $100 and $200 was automatically stopped either because the taxpayer had unpaid income tax from previous years or because a cross reference into the Business Master File showed that he had unpaid corporate tax liability.

Finally, a word on the extent to which security and confidentiality are both possible and enforced. Each IRS employee who works with the computer has a personal code number. In addition, there is a system of daily passwords. Without the password he cannot operate any of the computer systems; his personal number determines what he may or may not do. Many people are empowered to retrieve data from the system, but fewer are able to enter data. In addition, when IDRS is used the operator's personal number is left on the tax return. This is done so that all later queries can be referred to the same operator. But in addition, the fact that an operator will leave 'foot-prints' in his wake is an additional check against fraud (e.g. cancelling a friend's tax delinquency) and invasion of privacy (e.g. looking at a colleague's tax return).

Thus in the USA all returns have their arithmetic checked by computer. This is the only aspect of the return in which a 100 per cent sample is checked. Canada, in contrast, goes further, firstly by automatically correcting returns in cases where the taxpayer would benefit by income averaging and, secondly, with its programme of cross-matching information returns issued in respect of employment earnings, interest payments and dividends. In the case of employment earnings the T4 (equivalent to the P60 in the UK) sent in by the employee is checked against that submitted by the employer. Additionally, the employer's T4 is cross-checked against the withheld tax he has actually submitted to the tax authorities in the name of the taxpayer. There is thus an automatic guard against (a) the taxpayer entering on the T4 an amount of tax larger than has actually been withheld, and (b) the employer issuing a correct T4 but actually submitting to the tax authorities only a fraction of the tax he has withheld.

Information returns issued in respect of certain types of dividends and interest (T600s and T5s) are also cross-checked, though somewhat less completely. In addition, the Canadian income tax authorities have to produce for the Social Insurance authorities a magnetic tape of all Social Insurance contributions. Since an entry has to be made for every contributor for this purpose the cost of adding additional information from the T4 is low, and it is for this reason that a tape containing records of all T4s is made. It is this tape that enables the T4 matching programme to be carried out. Its companion tape, created by the Social Insurance authorities, contains details of all Social

[34] This was a tax cut legislated by the US Congress in 1975 (the Tax Reduction Act of 1975).

Insurance *benefits* paid during the year. This tape is used by the tax authorities to make sure that all Social Insurance benefits (which are generally taxable in Canada) have been declared in the tax return.

To a large extent, therefore, it is possible to check automatically those types of income that are quantitatively the most important. The key to doing so is to make sure that the taxpayer has an identifying number (in North America his social security number) and that all information returns contain that number.[35] If, in addition, organisations issuing information returns can supply copies to the tax authorities on magnetic tape (as is done already in North America by large firms and major banks) cross-checking is made even easier.

Problems with Self-Assessment

Of the many problems involved in tax administration three are particularly relevant to a system of self-assessment:

(a) errors in tax returns,

(b) delays in payment and loss of revenue, and

(c) the peak load on the tax authorities at filing time.

A recent survey in the USA showed that approximately 54 per cent of non-business tax returns were correct to within one dollar of tax and 72 per cent to within \$25. In Canada some 50 per cent of returns require a tax change, though about 20 per cent are due to income averaging[36] which the tax authorities explicitly say they will check on the taxpayer's behalf. Thus some 30 per cent of Canadian returns contain a genuine arithmetic error.

In the USA a recent study by the US Treasury suggests that only half of those who would benefit by income averaging actually make use of this option. Further difficulties arise from the complications of the system of personal deductions.

In both countries mistakes multiply for taxpayers with capital gains and income from annuities. In the USA, for instance, audit of a random sample of returns[37] showed that 31 per cent of all returns had errors in the calculation of adjusted gross income (i.e. gross income after adjustment for capital gains, excludable income from annuities, etc.),[38] 42 per cent had errors in calculating deductions,[39] and only 0.4 per cent had errors in calculating exemptions.[40]

---

35 In Canada there has been talk of starting a new 'foolproof' system of identification numbers to prevent people having more than one number. In a recent Canadian fraud case a man was reported to have twelve social insurance numbers. Sweden goes even further. All Swedish citizens and immigrants are given a National Registration number which is used throughout their life for all official purposes—see Simon James, *op. cit.*

36 Under which those whose incomes change drastically from year to year may obtain tax relief by averaging their income over several years.

37 Taxpayer Compliance Measurement Program, *Summary Results: Individual Returns, Tax Year 1969.*

38 Representing 67% of the errors in dollar terms in computing taxable income.

39 Representing 24% of the errors in dollar terms in computing taxable income.

40 Representing 9% of the errors in dollar terms in computing taxable income. The percentages cited in the text are not additive, as some returns contained errors in two or more of these categories.

When the sample was restricted to the simpler returns (non-business income below $10,000) the number of errors associated with adjusted gross income, deductions and exemptions rose to 34 per cent, 59 per cent and 6 per cent, respectively.[41]

There is one interesting example of the dog that did *not* bark—in the USA there is a widespread belief that errors would multiply greatly if the basic exemption were not a flat rate one. Yet Canada has sliding-scale exemptions that vary with family member and this seems to cause no problems there—certainly none which the computer checking system is unable to handle.

Turning to delays in payment and lost revenue, punctuality in filing returns is high in both the USA and Canada. The IRS estimate that 96 per cent of individual returns are filed by the due date, 99 per cent by one month later and virtually 100 per cent by two months later. In the case of late returns, a late filing penalty of 5 per cent per month is levied on outstanding tax (plus the interest charge which is adjusted every two years), though in both the USA and Canada there is flexibility in its application provided the taxpayer shows 'reasonable cause' for being late (e.g. being involved in a serious motor accident seven days before the latest filing date).

There are two aspects to lost revenue: (a) what percentage of tax is never assessed, and (b) what percentage of tax assessed is never collected. Anticipating the more detailed discussion of the following section, figures on these matters are both scant and only partly matters of public record. Both the USA and Canada estimate that they assess somewhere in the region of 95 per cent of total liability. An additional loss, though, is that not all tax which is assessed can be collected, as will be discussed further below. Both countries write off some 1.5–2 per cent of total assessed liability.

A final problem of self-assessment is the peak load that occurs during the filing period. In the USA and Canada thousands of extra keypunchers are employed in the first third of the year. Returns have to be fed rapidly into the computer because they have to be subjected to at least an arithmetic check before a refund is issued, and taxpayers are impatient to receive their refunds. It is therefore important that the arithmetical checking and the issuing of

---

41 The IRS estimate that the eight most frequent mistakes by US taxpayers in filing their federal income tax return are:

1. Failure to sign the return (or absence of one of the spouses' signature on joint returns);
2. Failure to indicate the payers of dividends or interest whenever the latter exceed a given annual ceiling;
3. Failure to correct errors appearing on the label sent by the IRS with the taxpayer's address and social security number;
4. Failure to attach the W2 withholding form, supplied by the employer, to the annual return;
5. Failure to claim all of the exemptions to which they are entitled;
6. Failure to credit the amount of US $30 against the assessed tax, which may be credited for the taxpayer and for each dependant;
7. Errors in the arithmetical calculations made on the return;
8. Not benefiting from the 'earned income credit' as authorised by law.

US News and World Report, 8 March 1976.

refunds be speedy though the various types of audit can wait until the main filing peak is over.

One alternative to this peak is to announce in advance that returns must be filed by (say) mid-April, but that no refunds will be issued until mid-October. This is the method used in New Zealand; the difficulties with such an arrangement are both political and economic—it is possible that a large injection of spending power shortly before Christmas might be rather destabilising. Another possibility is staggered filing, though this has been investigated extensively in the USA and Canada and rejected as impractical. The consensus is that it is best simply to accept the need for a tax system geared to a very uneven work load, though this can be linked equally well to the rapid one-year cycle in the USA and Canada, or to the more leisurely two-year Swedish cycle.

7 Enforcement: Auditing

The Selection of Returns for Audit

Both the USA and Canada investigate tax returns only on a sample basis, normally selecting only 2–5 per cent of individual income tax returns for audit. The effectiveness of such investigations, both in terms of the extra revenue they raise directly and, far more importantly, the revenue they raise indirectly by deterring tax evasion, is greater the more they focus on evaders. Thus it is useful to audit more intensively those groups that evade most, rather than simply to take a random sample of all returns. In Canada returns are explicitly divided into audit classes (e.g. taxpayers with employment income only, the self-employed, taxpayers with unearned income above a specified amount, taxpayers with capital gains, etc.), and also divided up by size of total income, this procedure being done mainly by computer. The selection of returns from a given audit class is usually manual, relying on supervisors with skill, experience and local knowledge.

The probability of a return being selected for audit depends greatly on its audit class. Taxpayers with low income, all from employment, have a low probability of being audited, while the probability of being audited increases for returns containing multiple sources of income, itemised deductions, self-employment income, or substantial property income. Thus a taxpayer with his own business, a salary of $60,000, assorted directors' fees and $5,000 per year in dividends has a very high probability of being audited in any one year.

In contrast, the USA now has a system of selection for audit that is mainly computerised. The method of selection is somewhat technical, but is nevertheless worth delving into; it is a good example of the sophisticated techniques made practicable by automatic data processing systems.

The start of the US system of audit selection is the Taxpayer's Compliance Measurement Program (TCMP). Returns are divided into ten audit classes and TCMP then takes a random sample of returns from each class and audits them thoroughly. Thus, for returns in the sample the IRS knows (a) the amounts entered by the taxpayer on the return, item by item, (b) the amounts as determined after audit, and (c) the difference between the two for each item on the return—the so-called 'tax change'.

The application of the statistical technique of discriminant function analysis to these tax changes reveals which items on the tax return are associated with the greatest tax error. For example, the probability of error in the entry for wage income of someone earning $10,000 per year will be low, whereas the probability of a significant error in the entry for capital gains of a self-employed professional with an income of $100,000 per year is likely to be high. These probabilities are what the IRS call 'DIF coefficients', and a knowledge of these probabilities by item on the tax return and by gross income enables the IRS to estimate for each return the probability that it will require a significant 'tax change'.

Turning now to the question of the selection of returns for audit the procedure is as follows: all returns are checked arithmetically and at the same time have the DIF coefficients applied to them to come up with a 'DIF score' which shows the estimated probability of the return containing one or more errors. The returns are then ranked according to their probability of error, and the 2 per cent or thereabouts with the highest probability of error are selected for audit, essentially on the basis of this mechanical process.

The result is that audit is applied to fewer than 1 per cent of incomes below $5,000 but to 60–70 per cent of those between $50,000 and $70,000.[42] In the late 1960s something like 40–45 per cent of audits led to no change in the tax bill—i.e. the IRS aim was not very good. As a result of the development of the computer criteria this figure was down to 23 per cent in 1975—i.e. of every 100 returns audited 77 required a tax change, a much higher figure than would result from auditing a random sample.

The results of the audit programmes described above may briefly be summarised on the basis of a 1969 study by the IRS which was confidential at the time, but which since the passing of the Freedom of Information Act is now in the public domain.

Table III–12 shows that in 1969 some 92.7 per cent of total tax liability was offered voluntarily, though with wide variation between income types. Thus the voluntary compliance level by those filing the short return (the 1040A) is 96.3 per cent (largely because this group has little opportunity to evade), while that for those with low business income (i.e. the low income self-employed) declare voluntarily only 68.7 per cent of their tax liability. In general, compliance is lowest where the opportunity to evade is greatest; thus there are problems with agricultural workers and domestic employees.[43]

[42] i.e. such cases are likely to be audited approximately twice every three years.
[43] Some supporting evidence from non-official sources may be found in H. M. Groves, 'Empirical Studies of Income Tax Compliance', *National Tax Journal,* Volume XI, No. 4, December 1958.

Table III–12 An Analysis of Voluntary Compliance, USA, 1965 and 1969

Audit Class	Voluntary Compliance Level % 1965	Voluntary Compliance Level % 1969	TCMP Man-Hours Per Return[a] 1965	TCMP Man-Hours Per Return[a] 1969	Yield per Manhour, 1969 $
1040A Type	95.8	96.3	2	3	113
Low Nonbusiness	92.4	89.6	3	4	78
Medium Nonbusiness	96.6	96.1	4	5	83
High Nonbusiness	95.8	94.1	16	19	238
Low Business	78.0	68.7	13	14	54
Medium Business	90.7	87.8	15	16	51
High Business	93.3	91.2	20	25	134
TOTAL	93.8	92.7	4	5	88

SOURCE: *Taxpayer Compliance Measurement Program Summary Results, Individual Returns, Tax Year 1969*, page 9.

a TCMP (Taxpayer Compliance Measurement Program) is a detailed quantitative study of taxpayer compliance conducted on a sample basis.

The aggregate figure of 92.7 per cent compliance implies that 7.3 per cent of income tax liability is not declared voluntarily. In recent years about one-third of this amount has been collected by the audit programme (i.e. an audit of approximately 2 per cent of returns has collected about 33 per cent of outstanding tax).

These figures relate only to returns filed and do not include non-filers. But survey evidence indicates that non-filing is small by number and even less by amount, since most non-filers are small wage-earners who would normally have been overwithheld.

Table III–13 shows clearly the extent to which the fear of being audited is based as much on bluff as on the unpleasantness of a thorough audit since the percentage of returns audited is very small and has tended to decline in recent years.

Table III–13 Number of Audits, USA, 1965–75

Year	Number of Audit Examinations thousands	Number of Returns Filed thousands	Percent Coverage
1965	3,092	65,072	4.8
1966	3,092	66,894	4.6
1967	2,768	69,452	4.0
1968	2,563	72,094	3.6
1969	2,196	73,760	3.0
1970	1,672	76,024	2.2
1971	1,346	77,143	1.7
1972	1,343	75,267	1.8
1973	1,409	79,545	1.8
1974	1,767	83,029	2.1
1975	1,955	85,519	2.3

SOURCE: *Ibid.*, page 8, and *Annual Report of the Commissioner of Internal Revenue, op. cit.*, various years.

The Simpler Types of Audit

The simplest of all the verification actions is not really an audit at all, but part of the checking procedure. In the USA this is called a 'math verification' or 'error resolution'. This occurs, for example, if a taxpayer has put the correct numbers in the correct places, but has simply added them up wrongly, or has made inconsistent entries. This is not a matter of falsification or evasion, nor a problem of enforcement, and one letter to the taxpayer normally closes the matter.

The Canadian tax authorities have wider powers than the IRS to alter their returns unilaterally, and in the case mentioned above they would simply correct the return and inform the taxpayer of the results.

The simplest audit proper is the so-called correspondence audit, which generally deals with items which appear on their face to be 'unallowable'; e.g. a casualty loss deduction not reduced by the $100 floor. An exchange of correspondence usually resolves such apparent errors with no further ado.

Returns containing items which experience has shown to be frequently in error are checked by the so-called office audit which generally deals with the following types of problems: itemised deductions, exemptions (e.g. a divorced couple each claiming exemptions for the children), small businesses (cafés, petrol stations), business expenses for the self-employed (car, travel, entertainment), capital gains, annuities.[44]

The taxpayer is invited to the tax office and the audit is conducted not by a fully fledged accountant (as would be the case with a more thorough audit) but by someone with less training, since an office audit is mainly a matter of simple verification. The taxpayer is told in advance which areas of his tax return are in question, and is invited to bring corroborating evidence (e.g. cancelled cheques for claimed charitable donations). If satisfactory evidence is supplied the audit is finished quickly. A great deal of common sense is applied in simple cases (e.g. if a hotel bill is supplied for a claimed business trip it will normally be assumed that a meal was bought also). The audit deals not only with straightforward verification (e.g. was the money actually spent?), but also with more technical matters (e.g. is the deduction legal?).

Once the audit is concluded the auditor writes a report on any tax adjustment. The taxpayer can pay additional tax on the spot, can be billed for it later or can appeal. If the auditor suspects fraud no additional tax is levied at the time, but the auditor will write a report which is passed to higher authority for a decision as to whether to prosecute.

---

[44] When a return of employment income is submitted without a W2 and without explanation for its absence the IRS will write to the taxpayer requesting the missing W2(s). This is the 'error resolution' aspect of audit, and the IRS estimate that approximately 500,000 such letters were sent in 1975. If the taxpayer has been unable to obtain a W2 the IRS will contact his employers to try to obtain it. Where all efforts to obtain a W2 fail the IRS will not pay any refund to the taxpayer unless there is some evidence to corroborate his figure (e.g. his payslips). Thus a simple audit is the usual response to the relatively unusual event of missing W2's.

In Canada the auditing of individual income includes not only the auditing of the tax returns, but also the auditing of the withholding of tax at source by employers. The so-called 'payroll audit' deals with the policing of the way employers turn over to the tax authorities the full amount of the tax and social insurance contributions they have withheld from employees. In 1974 payroll audit collected $50 million in taxes withheld by employers but not handed over. The whole operation is now computerised including the selection of employers for payroll audit. The purpose of such an operation is twofold:

(a) to collect unpaid revenue, and

(b) to deter potential delinquents by publicity and fines on the small percentage audited.

Employers are picked out for audit either if they are late with their monthly remittance of withheld tax, or if, at the end of the year, the totals declared on the T4s (equivalent to P60s in the UK) they issue do not match up with their remittances to the tax authorities. Both cases are automatically picked out by computer.

More Complicated Audits

Field audits are conducted by fully fledged accountants. They apply only in complicated situations such as partnerships and unincorporated businesses, and deal not simply with verification, but with the entire method of account keeping. In extremely complicated larger cases a team of three to five auditors may work on the case. Returns are generally assigned to auditors on the basis of their experience.

While an office audit normally concentrates on two or three specific items, a field audit can be far more general. The auditor usually develops and follows an audit plan but can (and does) follow wherever he feels it would be worthwhile to check. He is free not only in respect of what he investigates, but also where he goes—e.g. the taxpayer's firm, his warehouse, his home.

Very frequently in the USA (though less so in Canada) if a field audit is instituted it will look at more than one year's return—sometimes (but rarely) as many as four years' returns. If the agent suspects fraud he first gives the taxpayer a chance to explain. If no satisfactory explanation is forthcoming the interview is ended immediately and the agent writes a report which is evaluated for possible prosecution.

There is a variety of safeguards. The agent's report on tax changes is subject to two internal reviews which form a sort of quality control on audits. A second safeguard is the appeals procedure.

If fraud is suspected the audit section will collaborate in building up a case for prosecution with a branch of tax administration which deals solely with enforcement against criminal tax offences, called Intelligence in the USA and Special Investigation in Canada. What follows describes the Intelligence section of the IRS; it applies, *mutatis mutandis,* to Canada.

Intelligence deals with the criminal activities uncovered by office or field audits, or by informers. It is essentially a criminal department in contrast to audit which deals with civil matters. Thus audit, as a civil department, can operate on the basis that the onus of proof lies on the taxpayer (e.g. to prove that he really did spend $1,000 on medical expenses). Intelligence has to work with the burden of proof the other way round.

The department covers all extremes, from pure accounting to pure detective work. The Revenue Agent (from audit) generally handles the technical/tax side of the investigation, while the Special Agent from Intelligence concentrates on proving criminality. To do this he can look at the broad pattern of an individual's life-style (e.g. can he afford the life-style he is living on the basis of the income he has declared?).

An important source of information is 'tale telling' by members of the public. In the USA it is possible for informers to claim a reward of up to 10 per cent of the tax plus penalty actually collected (not *assessed,* but actually *collected*). Such payments are neither advertised nor volunteered; nor is there any equivalent in Canada, where compensation is paid to an informer only if by giving information he has incurred a financial loss (e.g. lost his job).

Publicity of prosecutions is very important. It is thought (though there is no solid proof) that the successful prosecution of former Vice-President Agnew for tax fraud in 1973 resulted in a large number of new returns being filed. There is a conviction (or a plea of guilty) rate of between 85 per cent and 90 per cent for cases brought to trial in the USA both because IRS cases typically have no single crucial witnesses, and because they are very selective in whom they prosecute. In most cases the taxpayer pleads guilty. In the USA in the year to June 1975 there were 9,268 fraud investigations leading to 1,397 prosecutions. In Canada in the year to 31 March 1975 246 investigations were completed, resulting in $18 million in additional taxes and penalties. Of the 127 prosecutions concluded there were 122 convictions.

In Canada a taxpayer who has committed a tax fraud may 'come clean'. To do so he must disclose the *full* facts (disclosing only part will be interpreted as further fraud), and must do so *before* an investigation into his affairs is started. If he complies with these conditions the individual is allowed to settle his liability simply by paying the tax and late payment interest due. This applies however grave the original fraud, and is justified on the grounds that it encourages compliance. There is a similar practice of non-prosecution in the USA, but the taxpayer must usually pay a civil fraud penalty (described below) of 50 per cent of the outstanding tax. The figures on the number of prosecutions should be set alongside those for the total number of audits. In the USA in 1974 there were some 726,000 field audits, about 1.5 million desk audits and in addition some 1.3 million correspondence audits. In Canada, too, the number of prosecutions is small relatively to the number of audits.

Collection

A taxpayer may under-pay either as the result of an arithmetical mistake revealed at the checking stage, or as determined later by audit. In either case the responsibility for collecting tax falls on the collection division. The US collection activity is outlined below—apart from matters of detail it describes also the Canadian situation.[45]

The collection activity starts by sending one or more (computerised) notices requesting the additional payment. There is a legal obligation to send the first notice; the number sent thereafter depends on the type and amount of tax. For income tax the fourth notice is normally the final one, unless the taxpayer still has tax outstanding from an earlier year, in which case only one notice will be sent.

By no means all demands sent out by collection are enforced. Collection has the discretion of abating a tax demand if the circumstances warrant. For instance, the audit division might query a large medical deduction, but receive no reply from the taxpayer. They would then assess the tax owed on the assumption that the medical deduction was invalid, and pass the case to collection with the amount of tax owed already determined. When a collection officer visited the taxpayer (all notices having been ignored) he would finally be given proof of the medical expense. In such a situation (which occurs frequently) collection activity would normally be suspended while audit reconsidered the claim.

Where a taxpayer claims that he is unable to pay his outstanding tax liability immediately, collection policy is flexible. The first step is for the taxpayer to supply the collection officer with a statement of his financial circumstances. This is analysed carefully and a repayment programme will be worked out in the light of the taxpayer's individual circumstances. Thus, other things being equal, a taxpayer will be given longer to pay if he has a sick child and heavy medical expenses. Similarly, in the case of a self-employed person, an amount can be set aside for 'tools of the trade' provided that in the view of the IRS the business remains viable.

If the collection officer feels that a person cannot pay at the time, action can be suspended until such time as he can pay. The computer, keyed to the taxpayer's social security number will link up with the following year's tax return, and will continue to do so until the Statute of Limitations applies after six years. At this stage the taxpayer will normally waive his rights under the Statute—the alternative being that the IRS would promptly sell all his assets to recover what they could.

There is a tolerance level below which underpaid tax is too small to be worth chasing. In such cases the matter will be suppressed if there is no response to the first notice. However, the tax liability remains in the computer and will automatically be deducted from any refund claimed in a future year. Additionally, if tax is under-paid in a later year, even if only by a small

[45] For a detailed account of collection in the USA, see *Collection of Delinquent Taxes*, US House of Representatives, Committee on Ways and Means, Subcommittee on Oversight, Washington, DC, 1976.

amount, collection activity will be resumed if the combined tax delinquency exceeds this tolerance. The tolerance is smaller for companies than for individuals, because of the tendency for individuals to be over-withheld. In the case of individuals a high percentage of delinquent taxes is paid out of withheld refunds in future years. The tax rebate resulting from the Tax Reduction Act of 1975 wiped out a large number of delinquent accounts.

Another logical duty of the collection side is to deal with all unidentified cheques. Any cheque that goes astray will result in an account not being credited with its payment, and hence being declared delinquent and passed to collection. It is thus the collection side which frequently has to unscramble the cases where a cheque is sent on time, but is lost.

Following the pattern of the audit section, collection is divided into an office and a field activity. Office collection deals with the sending out of the routine notices and the simpler cases, while field collection deals with the larger and more complicated cases where a search for assets and possible seizure may be required.

Powers and Penalties

It is generally accepted that a successful system of self-assessment requires the authorities to have very broad powers of enforcement. In the USA and Canada this is certainly the case. There are three major areas of enforcement powers:

(a) penalties and interest charges for late filing and late payment of tax,

(b) subpoena and summons powers to obtain taxpayer records, and

(c) powers to obtain taxpayer assets by methods such as seizure.

The major civil penalties in the USA are imposed by the IRS by administrative authority without reference to the courts though the taxpayer can, of course, make use both of the tax authorities' internal appeal procedure and, ultimately, an appeal to the courts. These penalties are:

(i) for late filing of a tax return, 5 per cent per month on the delinquent tax up to a maximum of 25 per cent;

(ii) for late payment of tax liability, $\frac{1}{2}$ per cent per month on the delinquent tax up to a maximum of 25 per cent. The late filing plus late payment penalty may not exceed 5 per cent per month. These and the following penalties are in addition to the interest charge (7 per cent in 1976) for late payment of tax. There is no appeal against interest charges;

(iii) for negligence, 25 per cent of the deficiency;

(iv) for civil fraud, 50 per cent of the deficiency. This penalty is levied where there is insufficient evidence to ask a court to impose a criminal conviction. The penalty is also imposed in cases where a criminal conviction has been obtained, in addition to any fines imposed by the court.

Civil penalties in Canada follow a similar pattern—again the tax authorities have wide powers to impose heavy penalties without resort to the courts.

In addition to the interest penalties on the taxpayer, penalties can be imposed also on firms and individuals who fail to turn over promptly to the tax authorities tax which they have withheld from their employees. In the USA a penalty of 100 per cent of the unpaid amount can be imposed personally on the 'responsible officer', whose name can be determined by seeing who usually signs cheques, or by inspecting minutes of committee meetings, etc. This penalty is used only as a collection device; if the tax is later paid by the employer the penalty is abated.

Where the taxpayer refuses to file, or where he refuses to corroborate items on his return with which the tax authorities are not satisfied, it is necessary for the tax authorities to obtain such information as they require without his consent. The task of seeking this information and the power to obtain it is normally within the scope of the audit division. The IRS has very broad subpoena powers—they have the *administrative* authority to demand that a taxpayer submit his bank statements, credit card slips, etc. subject to the Fifth Amendment (that no one may be compelled to testify against himself). If a man refuses, the IRS can then demand the information they seek from his bank, his stockbroker, American Express, etc. (where the Fifth Amendment will not apply). Testimony may be required also from third parties, such as the taxpayer's secretary or accountant. One of the reasons why the IRS alone of American government departments has the power of administrative subpoena is that it deals mainly with financial matters and hence would normally subpoena documents rather than people (so that no considerations of *habeas corpus* arise). Additionally, the sort of evidence usually demanded is easily destroyed.

In Canada, also, there is virtually no limit on the ability of the tax authorities to demand information both from the taxpayer and from third parties. If the taxpayer refuses to co-operate the tax authorities also have the power to issue an arbitrary assessment, which is often used specifically to force out information in just the same way as the Inland Revenue does in the UK.[46]

In both countries, as a last resort, the tax authorities have broad-ranging search powers, applicable both to the taxpayer's home and his place of work. These search powers are normally exercised under court authority, though it is most unusual for this to be withheld.

A further range of powers is required in cases where, his liability having been established by one means or another, the taxpayer refuses to pay. The main powers in the USA are:

(i) an earnings attachment order, whereby an employer pays the IRS a specified sum each month out of the employee's earnings. This is within the administrative power of the IRS;

(ii) seizure of financial property such as a bank account or shares. This can be done by administrative authority;

(iii) a federal tax lien, which prevents the sale of an asset to which it is applied, and

---

[46] See Chapter II, page 40.

(iv) outright seizure and, if necessary, sale of real property. This normally requires court permission.

The Canadian authorities have similar powers.

APPENDIX III–1:

The Introduction of Self-Assessment Abroad

The USA and Canada

In the case of Japan (discussed later in this appendix) the introduction of self-assessment occurred in circumstances which yield observations relevant to the UK situation. The same is not true in the North American case, and so that history is touched on only briefly. In both the USA and Canada income tax, especially federal income tax, became a mass tax only at the start of World War II and self-assessment of the sort that exists today was therefore introduced in the early 1940s. The introduction of self-assessment thus occurred during a popular war, and at a time when the provisions of income tax were considerably simpler than they are today. Both factors greatly aided the successful introduction of self-assessment—in the 1940s tax law was sufficiently simple to make compliance easy and patriotism reduced (at least so it is thought) the number of actual and potential evaders. There do not seem to be any lessons for the UK from this aspect of the North American experience, though it is interesting to speculate on the social and historical reasons which explain why the solutions to broadly similar problems were so different.

Computerisation was introduced into North American tax administration much later than self-assessment, and this phase of the American experience is relevant to the UK. The USA switched to a computerised handling of tax returns in 1962. From its first introduction all types of individual (but not corporate) returns were handled automatically, but in the first few years only the checking operations (i.e. the arithmetical check and the issuing of refunds) were automatic. Since then refinements have been introduced gradually—the use of computers for audit selection (TCMP and the DIF system, as discussed above), and for taxpayer assistance (IDRS as also discussed above), as well as technical refinements such as eliminating punch cards when typing the returns onto tape.

The scale of the system was massive from the start. By 1966 annual expenditure on data processing (both capital and running costs) had reached $155 million. For fiscal year 1976 the budget for data processing was $400 million.

From the first the system proved reliable and never 'went off the air'. Even in the early days it dealt with 40–50 million refunds in 45 days. The fact that it never broke down completely was crucial—a breakdown could have had disastrous effects on taxpayer confidence, since the whole operation was far too large to enable the old manual and the new automatic system to run in parallel for a year while the new system bedded down. There was a complete break in switching from the old to the new system.

In designing such a system the optimal strategy seems to be to introduce above all a *reliable* system, even if it is clumsy at first, and to deal with the refinements later. With computer processes it is crucial not to let the best be the enemy of the good.

Canada was more gradual in phasing in its computers. In the first year (1962) only the simplest (mainly wage and salary income) returns, and then only for the province of Ontario, were processed automatically. By the third year all individual returns were computer processed, while other applications such as the division of returns into audit classes were phased in gradually over a six year period.

By this progressive phasing computerised systems in both countries were introduced (at least in the eyes of the taxpayer) smoothly and with no disasters.

Japan

The introduction of self-assessment in Japan took place in the immediate post-war years in far less favourable circumstances than those prevailing in the UK today. In particular, there were vast increases in the number of taxpayers and tax officials and widespread social, administrative and economic upheaval, and an established system of meeting 'goals' that had created intense hostility between taxpayers and tax officials.[1] Since the existing system was functioning so badly self-assessment was a natural device for the American authorities to introduce. Despite the contrast with current UK circumstances the Japanese experience is of some relevance.

After the war Japan faced hyperinflation, and widespread starvation. The inflation meant that progressive income tax rates and exemptions designed for non-inflationary conditions were applied to greatly inflated nominal incomes.[2] In addition there had been attempts greatly to increase tax revenue to pay for the war and the combined result was that the number of taxpayers rose from 700,000 before the war to around 7 million after it. The 700,000 were used to having their taxes assessed for them by the authorities and the rest were inexperienced in any type of assessment, let alone self-assessment.

The small and medium-sized businesses posed particular problems. During the war their assessments had been on the basis of a standard or average for each type of business rather than by an examination of accounts.[3] Many had no records whatever and those who did keep accounts each had their own system. Furthermore, the extensive land reform of the time had the effect of turning large numbers of tenants who did not pay tax into farmers who did; and then they found themselves in much the same position as the small businessman.

The two main professions to which taxpayers could have looked for assistance were unprepared for the task. There were too few accountants, and those few had little experience in dealing with tax affairs in any detail. The legal

[1] See *Report on Japanese Taxation*. Shoup Mission (GHQ, SCAP, Tokyo, 1949), Vol. II, pp. 212 *et seq.* and Vol. IV, pp. D58 *et seq.* Also Pechman and Vlaizuko, 'Taxation', in H. Patrick and H. Rosovsky (eds.) *Asia's New Giant*. The Brookings Institution, Washington DC 1976.

[2] Taking 1948=100, money wages rose from 17 to 173.3 from the 4th quarter of 1945 to September 1949.

[3] Noburu Tanabe 'Blue Return System in Japan' in P. L. Kelley, *Readings in Income Tax Administration*.

profession had no experience of clients' tax affairs at all. At the same time the tax administration itself was in chaos. To cope with the increased work-load during the war the number of Revenue Service employees had increased from 16,000 to 60,000 over a short period.[4] Seventy per cent of Japanese tax officials had fewer than three years' experience of tax administration at the time of the introduction of self-assessment.

One result of the economic and administrative disorganisation was a growth in tax evasion. Many Japanese had insufficient means to enable them to comply willingly with their liabilities to taxation. Second, rationing led to widespread black markets, the income from which was rarely declared for tax purposes. Third, there was a large element of corruption within the administration itself.

The combined effect of all these factors was that in 1948, after the first year of operation of self-assessment, 70 per cent of taxpayers and 55 per cent of the tax due were reassessed by the authorities. Of the tax finally payable, 40 per cent would not have been paid had there been no official reassessment.[5] However, an intensive and patient educational programme was undertaken and a number of incentives such as an allowance for bad debts were introduced to encourage taxpayers to produce proper accounts. The result was that by 1950 the number of taxpayers reassessed fell to 4 per cent, and only 5 per cent of total tax revenue was involved. In recent years the figures have been 2.5 per cent and 1 per cent respectively.

It is difficult to gauge how far the social and administrative difficulties in Japan in the early post-war years influenced the development of self-assessment. At first sight chaos would appear to be unfavourable to the introduction of a new system. Yet the force of crisis may be greater on occasion than that of inertia. Many of the most radical reforms in tax administration have been successfully implemented during periods of upheaval. The introduction and re-introduction of income tax in the United Kingdom took place during wartime in 1799 and 1803. PAYE with all its complexities arrived during the Second World War. Without elaborating the thesis that self-assessment might have a better chance of a successful introduction during some form of major crisis there appear to be two reasons why this may be the case. First, acceptance in principle of a new system may attract less opposition if the focus of attention is on some other crisis. Second, with taxpayers, tax officials and tax preparers under pressure, it may be easier to implement a new system (initially on a rough and ready basis) than if it were being grafted onto nearly two centuries of established practice.

An interesting comparison between Japan and Britain arises with the figure of 70 per cent of Japanese taxpayers who were reassessed in 1948. A survey undertaken by the Inland Revenue in 1971, but not published (see Appendix IV–1) investigated the possibility of self-coding in the United Kingdom and

[4] Minoru Ohashi *The Evolution of Self-Assessment System in Japan.*
[5] Tanabe *op. cit.*

found that 67 per cent of taxpayers taking part completed the experimental self-coding form incorrectly. Although the sample was confined to employees, these figures seem to indicate that some two-thirds of taxpayers need special attention in an exercise of this kind. If the Japanese experience were to apply to Britain the percentage of taxpayers committing major errors would drop to about 4 per cent within the first three years of self-assessment.

A comparison between what happened in Japan and what might happen in the United Kingdom if self-assessment were to be introduced is obviously difficult. However, there are several factors which suggest that the circumstances would be more favourable to a changeover to self-assessment in Britain. There would not be the same element of antagonism towards a new system introduced by an alien occupying force as was the case in Japan. It may also be asserted with some confidence that evasion and corruption are less prevalent in Britain today than in Japan in 1947. The people who would be subject to self-assessment in Britain are used to the idea of paying income tax. There is an established body of accountants and lawyers with a reasonable degree of experience and competence with British tax affairs; and a large proportion of taxpayers assessed under Schedule D already have their accounts prepared by accountants. Taxpayers, accountants and the Inland Revenue are experienced in dealing with frequent changes in tax administration. The competence of the Inland Revenue staff is high and would be likely to increase if staff numbers were reduced—unlike the Japanese case, where self-assessment was immediately preceded by a vast increase in tax officials, so reducing their average level of competence and experience. All these factors indicate that the introduction of self-assessment in the United Kingdom faces a better chance of initial success than was the case in Japan in 1947.

APPENDIX III–2:

Tax Returns and Explanatory Literature

The evidence that the returns and tax guides issued by the Inland Revenue cause a considerable amount of confusion on the part of taxpayers (and some non-taxpayers) is largely anecdotal, but some has been formally documented. Sandford's study of individual taxpayers[1] discovered that an appreciable proportion (39 out of 235) of those who employed tax advisers gave the complexities of the tax return as one of their reasons for doing so. The comments received from respondents to the survey included: ' "Incomprehensible language . . ." "I am not able to understand the forms . . ." "I had one hell of a job to understand half the questions." "Some say income tax is worse than a foreign language." "Forms differ from year to year; time consuming taking copies of information sent . . ." "Some of the guide notes could be improved and made easier to understand." "Tax assessment forms are written for clerks and accountants." "The correspondence I receive is difficult to understand, the words used not being in any dictionary of mine." ' Sandford also adds 'The number of such quotations with the theme, "the forms are too complicated, the system is too complicated, I do not understand it," could be trebled.'[2] Clearly a large part of the demands made on taxpayers and a large number of the complexities in the tax return literature mainly arise from the underlying complications of the tax system. It may be the case that the Inland Revenue returns are defensible under present circumstances; so this Appendix examines in turn those features of foreign returns and return guides that might be useful in the UK under a different tax régime.

(1) *Short tax returns*: the first simplification is to avoid confronting taxpayers with complexities that are not relevant to their circumstances. In other words, let simple forms apply to those with simple circumstances. At least two countries, the USA and Ireland, have special short forms for those taxpayers with only wage and salary income, and perhaps a small amount of investment income. Of the 83 million income tax returns filed in the USA in 1974 over 22 million individual taxpayers used the Form 1040A[3] (reproduced on pages 118–19). The short return may not be used by individuals receiving more than $400 in dividends or interest during the year. Ireland has a special return, Form 12, for wage and salary earners, but it can also handle interest paid by the Post Office Savings Bank, building societies and banks. The four small pages of the short Form 12 contrast markedly with the six very much larger pages of the more detailed Form 11 which is sent to Irish taxpayers with more complex financial circumstances.

The benefits of a short form are at least twofold. First it is likely that a simpler form can be processed more easily and rapidly by the tax authorities.

[1] Sandford, 1973 *op. cit.*
[2] *Ibid* pp. 137–8.
[3] Commissioner of Internal Revenue, *Annual Report*, 1974, Washington DC, p. 8.

Second, many taxpayers (and some non-taxpayers) are saved from the need to read questions and notes which only increase their confusion. It is true that the more complex standard Inland Revenue returns confront the taxpayer with information he might otherwise have missed, but this benefit should be weighed against the extra work for all taxpayers and against the occasional reaction that if one part of the form is not relevant neither is the rest. How many people for instance, have daughters on whose services they are compelled to depend?[4]

(2) *'Loose-leaf returns'*: a second way of lightening the load on the taxpayer is to break up the tax return into a simple form which is sufficient for individuals with straightforward circumstances, but with extra schedules which are attached to the main form by those with more complicated financial arrangements. This method is used in both the USA and Canada. In the USA the main Form 1040 is sent to taxpayers as part of a 28-page 'package' which also contains extra schedules such as Schedule C (profits from a business or profession), and Schedule G (used for income averaging). An American with dividend or interest income over $400 would use the main Form 1040 and attach to it Schedule B which gives details of dividend and interest income.

(3) *Simplifying tax returns and the tax structure*: self-assessment has considerable relevance to the complexity of tax returns. There is extra work for Americans in that they are obliged to submit not only details of their financial circumstances but also to calculate their total income, total tax due, tax already paid and the value of any refund or balance due. They have to do this every year, though in the USA the tax authorities will (subject to certain income limits) calculate an individual's liability for him if he files the short Form 1040A, or the long Form 1040, and takes the standard deduction.[5]

However, a far more important reason for simplifying the returns is to place the responsibility for the assessment on the taxpayer rather than on the authorities. This means first of all that every effort must be made to ensure that he is able to understand the process sufficiently to perform the operation. Second, he has to be trusted to a certain extent; in the USA only about 2 per cent of returns are examined for errors other than arithmetical slips whereas in the UK all[6] returns are examined and checked with the previous return. It does seem a little excessive that individuals in Britain claiming blind person's relief should be required to state both the local authority with which they are registered and the date of registration every time they file a return. Third, because the Revenue is responsible for the assessment the returns are designed more for its convenience than for that of the taxpayer. For example there is a question on page 1 of both the P1 (1975) and form 11 (1975) asking 'If you or your wife were born before 6 April 1915 please enter date(s) of

[4] Seven questions regarding this allowance appear on the Inland Revenue's form P1 (1974).

[5] See Chapter III, p. 58.

[6] It should be remembered that only about half the taxpayers in the UK make a return in any one year. (See Chapter II, p. 27.)

Figure III–2.1 Short Form 1040A

Short Form 1040A — U.S. Individual Income Tax Return — 1975

Department of the Treasury
Internal Revenue Service

Please print or type

Name (If joint return, give first names and initials of both) | Last name

Present home address (Number and street, including apartment number, or rural route)

City, town or post office, State and ZIP code

Your social security number

Spouse's social security no.

Occupation — Yours ▶ — Spouse's ▶

For Privacy Act Notification, see page 2 of Instructions.

For IRS use only

Requested by Census Bureau for Revenue Sharing ▶

A In what city, town, village, etc., do you live?

B Do you live within the legal limits of the city, town, etc.? ☐ Yes ☐ No ☐ Don't know

C In what county and State do you live? County | State

D In what township do you live? (See page 5.)

Filing Status

1 ☐ Single (*check only ONE box*)

2 ☐ Married filing joint return (even if only one had income)

3 ☐ Married filing separately. If spouse is also filing give spouse's social security number in designated space above and enter full name here ▶

4 ☐ Unmarried Head of Household (See page 4 of Instructions) ▶

5 ☐ Qualifying widow(er) with dependent child (Year spouse died ▶ 19). See page 4 of Instructions.

Exemptions

6a Regular ☐ Yourself ☐ Spouse — Enter number of boxes checked ▶

b First names of your dependent children who lived with you — Enter number ▶

c Number of other dependents (from line 22) . ▶

d Total (add lines 6a, b, and c) . . . . ▶

e Age 65 or over . ☐ Yourself ☐ Spouse — Enter number of boxes checked ▶
Blind . . . . ☐ Yourself ☐ Spouse

7 Total (add lines 6d and e) . . . . ▶

8 Presidential Election Campaign Fund . . ▶ Do you wish to designate $1 of your taxes for this fund? . . Yes No
If joint return, does your spouse wish to designate $1? . . Yes No

Note: If you check the "Yes" box(es) it will not increase your tax or reduce your refund.

Attach Copy B of Forms W-2 and Check or Money Order here

9 Wages, salaries, tips, and other employee compensation (Attach Forms W-2. If unavailable, see page 6 of Instructions) . . . | 9

10a Dividends (if over $400, see Instructions at top of page 3) $........ 10b Less exclusion $........ Balance ▶ | 10c

11 Interest income (if over $400, see Instructions at top of page 3) . . . . | 11

12 Total (add lines 9, 10c, and 11) **(Adjusted Gross Income)** (If less than $8,000, see page 18 of Instructions on "Earned Income Credit.") . . | 12

- **If you want IRS to figure your tax, see page 6 of Instructions.**
- **If line 12 is under $15,000, find tax in Tax Tables (on pages 8–18) and enter on line 13a, on the back.**
- **If line 12 is $15,000 or more, figure your tax using the Tax Computation Worksheet on page 18 of Instructions.**

13a Tax, check if from: ☐ Tax Tables (pages 8–18) OR ☐ Tax Computation Worksheet (page 18) . . . 13a

b Credit for personal exemptions (multiply line 6d by $30) . . . b

14a Balance (subtract line 13b from line 13a). If less than zero, enter zero. . . . 14a

b Credit for contributions to candidates for public office (see page 7 of Instructions) . . . b

15 Income tax (subtract line 14b from line 14a). If less than zero, enter zero. . . . 15

16a Total Federal income tax withheld (attach Forms W–2 to front) . . . 16a

b Excess FICA, RRTA, or FICA/RRTA tax withheld (two or more employers—see page 7 of Instructions) . . . b

c 1975 estimated tax payments (include amount allowed as credit from 1974 return) . c

d Earned income credit . . . d

Pay amount on line 18 in full with this return. Write social security number on check or money order and make payable to Internal Revenue Service.

17 Total (add lines 16a, b, c, and d) . . . 17

18 If line 15 is larger than line 17, enter **BALANCE DUE IRS** . . . ► 18

19 If line 17 is larger than line 15, enter amount **OVERPAID** . . . ► 19

20 Amount of line 19 to be **REFUNDED TO YOU** . . . ► 20

21 Amount of line 19 to be credited on 1976 estimated tax . . . ► 21

If all of overpayment (line 19) is to be refunded (line 20), make no entry on line 21.

Other Dependents

(a) NAME	(b) Relationship	(c) Months lived in your home. If born or died during year, write B or D.	(d) Did dependent have income of $750 or more?	(e) Amount YOU furnished for dependent's support. If 100% write ALL.	(f) Amount furnished by OTHERS including dependent.
				$	$

22 Total number of dependents listed in column (a). Enter here and on line 6c . . . ►

Under penalties of perjury, I declare that I have examined this return, including accompanying schedules and statements, and to the best of my knowledge and belief it is true, correct and complete. Declaration of preparer (other than taxpayer) is based on all information of which preparer has any knowledge.

Sign here

► Your signature — Date

► Spouse's signature (if filing jointly, BOTH must sign even if only one had income)

► Preparer's signature (other than taxpayer) — Date

Address (and ZIP Code)

☆ U.S. GOVERNMENT PRINTING OFFICE : 1975—O-575-059

16—82503-2

birth.' There is a second question on page 6 of the P1 and page 4 of form 11 which read 'If you and/or your wife were born before 6 April 1911, enter "X" here.' Why not just one question?

This leads on to the more general point that in order to make an accurate assessment the Inland Revenue has to extract a large amount of detail that would not be required if the taxpayer were assessing himself. For instance, to claim the allowance for a dependent relative the taxpayer has to provide the name and address of the dependant; the relationship to the dependant; the dependant's annual income (divided into National Insurance pension or benefit, other pension and other income—but excluding voluntary contributions); the amount the taxpayer contributes if the dependant is not resident with him; how much any other relatives contribute; the date of birth of the dependant; and the nature of any infirmity. Whilst these nine questions reflect the complicated restrictions on the allowance, might it not be simpler to trust the taxpayer's judgement as to whether or not he is entitled to the allowance and check just a small sample of claimants rather than all of them?

Self-assessment, with sample rather than universal checking, would make possible many simplifications but one should not neglect the government's propensity to complicate, all the more as self-assessment would permit complications that are not administratively feasible at the moment.

(4) *The use of background information*: as the onus of assessment is currently on the Inland Revenue, there is no obvious need to explain to the taxpayer how administration works nor to encourage his interest and co-operation over and above the requirement to complete a return. If taxpayers were more informed about the process of assessment their voluntary compliance might be secured more easily. The Swedes, for instance, have a section in their guide called *What happens to your tax returns?*[7] a question which if answered in the United Kingdom might do something to encourage a greater spirit of co-operation among taxpayers. In addition the resulting increase in general enlightenment may reduce the extent of taxpayer error or fear, delays in making returns and the number of individuals needing further assistance. Another device which might generate taxpayer interest and hence perhaps compliance is a breakdown of government expenditure. This is done in South Africa and something similar appears on local authority rate demands in the UK.

(5) *Issuing tax returns in duplicate*: in the USA and Canada returns are sent out in duplicate so that the taxpayer is able to keep a copy of the information he files; this facility is useful not only in the event of any enquiry by the revenue authorities, but also in giving the taxpayer guidance when the time comes for him to complete his next return.

(6) *Step-by-step instructions*: in Canada, New Zealand, South Africa and Sweden the instructions for completing the return are laid out in a 'step-by-step'

[7] For example, the section explains who examines the returns, how the taxpayer's final liability is determined and the months during which any adjustments are made.

manner, telling the taxpayer specifically what he has to do. For instance, in several guides one of the earliest instructions ('Getting ready' in the Canadian case) is a list of the items needed to complete a return—dividend slips and so on. The Canadian return guide also manages to separate the notes that are applicable to everyone and those necessary for only a restricted readership. There are 'five pages of very easy instructions' printed on blue paper ('everyone follows the blue') followed by more detailed information further on in the guide for those who need it. The United Kingdom guides in contrast just present a long list of the details concerning each entry on the return.

(7) *A 'What's New' feature*: some people have pointed to the build-up of human capital as individuals become more practised over time at filing tax returns. An excellent aid to this learning process is the *What's New in 1976* feature of the Canadian and Swedish guides which lists those changes in tax law which have affected the return since the previous year. One particular complaint of the taxpaying community in the UK relates not so much to the complexity of the tax system, as to the continual changes, e.g. bank interest being deductible one year and not the next with the details being slightly different each time. A *What's New* feature in British guides would be an easy way of drawing the attention of the taxpaying public to changes in the rules, and might reduce the number of people who think they understand some aspects of the system when in fact their knowledge has become obsolete.

(8) *Sample questions and sample returns*: an often used idea is to list frequently asked questions and their answers. Again, the Canadian guide provides an example. A booklet was published in the United Kingdom in 1942[8] in which such questions were answered and useful examples given. The Inland Revenue continues the practice in some areas, for example with the publication *Paying Tax for the First Time*, but there is no attempt to do so with the notes accompanying the returns. Typical taxpayers' questions and the answers to them appear to be a useful method of disseminating information not contained in the more formal notes, and should be used more widely.

An extension of this type of assistance is to provide a sample tax return which has been completed with an example. Both the New Zealand and Swedish guides provide very helpful examples which show taxpayers which figures are meant to go in which spaces on the return. It is worth noting in passing that the Swedish authorities publish their guide in a number of languages, a facility of considerable help not only to immigrants but also to foreigners who incur some liability to Swedish income tax. The obvious relevance of such a facility in the UK is (Wales apart) for the various immigrant communities.

(9) *Layout and presentation*: the presentation of some of the tax guides used abroad provides something of a contrast to those employed in the UK. A number of countries manage to package their material about as attractively

8 Board of Inland Revenue *Income Tax Quiz for Wage Earners*, London, 1942.

as is possible for tax guides—the Swedish authorities even use a number of cartoons. Instead of large quantities of small, monotonous and closely packed print it might be worthwhile to attempt to produce more palatable and colourful tax literature in the United Kingdom. The private sector takes trouble over the presentation of its products, and presumably the customers appreciate this or the firms would not bother. There is no apparent reason why taxpayers would not appreciate a similar service, which could be provided at very little extra cost. However, the trend in the United Kingdom has been in the opposite direction with the print and size (but not the number of questions) of the P1 (1975) and accompanying notes being even smaller than the P1 (1974) and its notes.

A final point is that it is possible for provision to be made on the return for individuals to be able to calculate their own liability. This feature is not confined to those countries with self-assessment. There is no compulsion on wage and salary earners in Australia, for instance, to assess themselves, yet space, instructions and a tax table are incorporated into the return to enable them to calculate their own tax refund or balance due if they so wish. Such a facility gives the taxpayer a more tangible reason both to complete his return, and to complete it correctly. Furthermore, he has a simple and independent check on the calculations performed by the administration, a privilege which need not be confined only to those employing assistance or subscribing to *Money Which?*

The table below summarises the various taxpayer aids used abroad. It is noteworthy that, as in the comparison of self-assessment features,[9] the UK is very much out of step with other countries. Many of these devices could, of course, be used whether or not self-assessment is introduced in this country.

Table III–2.1 Taxpayer Aids

	Australia	Canada	New Zealand	South Africa	Sweden	USA	UK
1.	X	X	X	√	√	X	X
2.	X	√	√	√	√	√	X
3.	X	√	X	X	√	X	X
4.	X	√	X	X	X	X	X
5.	X	X	√	Partially	√	1040A but not 1040	X
6.	√	√	√	√	√	√	X

KEY:
1. Some explanation of the process of tax administration over and above that necessary for simple compliance, or information about how tax revenues are spent.
2. The return guide adopts a 'step by step' approach to filing, e.g. with a list of documents needed to complete the return.
3. A *What's new in 1976* feature.
4. A list of the most frequently asked questions and their answers.
5. A sample tax return is provided—having been completed with an example.
6. The return allows the taxpayer to calculate his liability.

NOTE:
√ = Aid provided.
X = Aid not provided.

[9] See Chapter IV, p. 153.

APPENDIX III–3

Other Aspects of Tax Administration

The purpose of this Appendix is to discuss some characteristics of relevance from other countries' tax systems, but without remotely attempting to present a complete picture of their operation.[1] It should be emphasised that the details of tax administration have a remarkable tendency to become obsolete rapidly;[2] and that the operation of taxes in different countries often takes place in very different circumstances.

Allowances, Deductions and Tax Structures

Personal allowances for taxpayers and their dependants are to be found in some form in almost every tax system. Normally they consist of specified sums for each category of individual, spouse, child, etc., which may be deducted from gross income. In a few countries these allowances may be reduced if the income of the taxpayer or his dependants exceeds a certain amount.

Special mention might be made of the French *quotient familial* system of operating such allowances. By this method the total net income of a family is divided into a number of parts depending on the taxpayer's status and the number of dependants. The tax attributable to a single part is then multiplied to give the total tax payable. Thus the income of a married couple is divided into two parts, and an extra half part is counted for each dependent child. An extra half is counted where both husband and wife are invalid or disabled and a full part is added for an invalid child. The system also extends to single individuals with responsibilities or handicaps by counting one and a half parts.

Although some deductions such as those for life assurance premia are common, others reflect the special interests or circumstances to be found in various countries. Thus Australian individuals following a profession or trade could claim the costs of metrication and conversion to decimal currency. A clergyman in Ireland, if he uses any part of his home for the purposes of his duty is entitled to a deduction for the rent; and Israel has a deduction for air raid precautions.

A number of countries allow taxpayers a deduction for the costs of completing a tax return. For example, in Australia the fees paid to a registered tax

---

1 For those interested in more detail there are a large number of sources such as: The Board of Inland Revenue, *Income Taxes Outside the United Kingdom*, London, 1973 ed. (8 volumes), supplemented by *Overseas Tax Developments*, plus updated booklets for individual countries (five volumes, looseleaf); Confederation of British Industry, *Taxation in Western Europe*, latest edition; International Bureau of Fiscal Documentation, 'Guides to European Taxation, Volume III Taxation of Private Investment Income', Amsterdam, 1976. Also useful, but frequently dated, is the Harvard Law School's 'World Tax' Series, and recourse can often be made to the literature published by tax administrations for the guidance of taxpayers.

2 Except where otherwise stated the information in this Appendix is correct as of March 1976 in the case of European countries, and December 1975 in other countries.

agent for preparing a tax return are allowable. There is no such deduction for employees (assessed under Schedule E) in the United Kingdom, and theoretically not for the self-employed (Schedule D). However, in the latter case the costs of preparing tax returns are usually allowable in practice as part of the ordinary costs of producing accounts which are then converted into tax returns. Despite the discrepancy in treatment of the two groups of taxpayers the Royal Commission of 1955[3] decided against recommending a general deduction for all individual taxpayers on the ground that 'the existing allowances fell where they were most needed, in the sense that the business account and the maintenance claim are the most onerous to prepare privately and the most likely to require professional assistance in their preparation'.[4] Under a system of self-assessment where all Schedule E as well as Schedule D taxpayers would have to file a return annually[5] a stronger case could be made for some form of deduction for the costs of filing.

The Rates of Tax

There is a sharp contrast between income tax rates in the UK and those found in other countries. The distinctive features of the British income tax include an exceptionally high initial rate of tax, a high maximum rate, and a long

Table III–3.1 Comparative Initial and Maximum Rates of Tax on Earned Income

Country	Income year	Income tax threshold £	Initial rate %	Maximum rate %
Belgium	1975	1,290	14 (14.8)	72 (75.6)
Denmark	1975	1,670	14.4 (35)	39.6 (60.2)
France	1975	3,120	5	53.5
Germany	1975	1,800	22	56
Ireland	1975/76	1,410	26	70
Italy	1976	1,320	10	72
Luxembourg	1975	3,740	18	57
Netherlands	1976	2,300	20	72
UK	1975/76	1,383	35	83
Sweden	1975	1,150	7 (30)	56 (79)
USA	1975	3,430	14	50 (55.5)
Canada	1976	3,350	6 (7.8)	47 (61.3)
Japan	1975	3,000	10 (14)	67.5 (83.5)

SOURCE: *Hansard*, Written answers, 25 March 1976, cols. 247/8.
NOTES:
1. Sterling equivalents are calculated at 8 March 1976 and rounded up to the nearest £10.
2. The figures in brackets show rates inclusive of representative local income tax, or of general additional charge.
3. The figures take account of the deductions available to a married man with two children both under 11 years.
4. Family allowance deduction is subtracted for the UK but the investment income surcharge is omitted.
5. The calculations assume that all income arises from the husband's employment.

[3] Royal Commission on the Taxation of Profits and Income, *Final Report*, Cmd. 9474, HMSO, June 1955.
[4] *Ibid*. para. 929.
[5] In contrast to the present system, see Chapter IV, p. 147.

basic rate band. There are a number of difficulties in comparing tax structures between countries as the relevant rules and circumstances can and do differ considerably. Nevertheless, we can see from Table III–3.1 that the starting rate in the United Kingdom in 1976 (35 per cent) was much higher than the initial rates found in neighbouring countries. Whilst some countries had starting rates of over 20 per cent (Ireland 26 per cent and West Germany 22 per cent) France began at 5 per cent and Canada at 7.8 per cent.

Nor can it be said that Britain's high starting rate does not apply to individuals with comparatively low incomes. If we look at the income tax threshold faced by a family with two children and with all its income arising from the husband's employment the position in March 1976 was that of the countries listed in Table III–3.1 only Belgium, Italy and Sweden had a lower threshold in terms of sterling than the United Kingdom. On the other hand, France, Luxembourg, USA, Canada and Japan each had thresholds more than twice as high as that of the United Kingdom.

The contrast between the maximum rates of income tax in the United Kingdom and other countries was less pronounced for earned incomes, though the 15 per cent investment income surcharge gave Britain its famous marginal rate of 98 per cent on investment income. But confining ourselves to earned incomes, the maximum marginal rate in the UK (83 per cent) was about the same as Japan (83.5 per cent) and only marginally greater than Sweden (79 per cent) and Ireland (70 per cent in 1975/76 but 77 per cent in 1976/77). However a number of countries had maximum rates which were considerably lower, e.g. France (53.5 per cent), West Germany (56 per cent) and the USA (55.5 per cent).

It may be mentioned in passing that one of the highest marginal rates of income tax in fiscal history used to be found in Denmark, where the rates of national income tax went up to 110 per cent. However, income and net wealth taxes paid during the year were deductible in computing taxable income. This arrangement has now been abolished, and replaced with another interesting system. The national income tax in Denmark is now imposed at progressive rates up to a maximum of 44 per cent. But these rates are only notional and tax is actually assessed each year at some percentage of these rates. Thus for 1976 the percentage was 90 so that the maximum rate imposed in practice was only 39.6 per cent.

The third major distinctive feature of the UK rate structure is the very long basic rate band. In 1976/77 this covered the first £5,000 of taxable income and was the marginal rate for most taxpayers. It is not a feature normally found in foreign national income taxes.

Local Income Taxes

A number of countries overseas levy a local income tax, normally at a single rate, though the rate may vary between local authorities. For example, local income tax in Finland is levied at rates of between 13 and 18.5 per cent. In

Norway the rates rise from 18.5 to 22 per cent though nearly all local authorities who impose it do so at the maximum rate, and in Italy local taxes are subject to a minimum of 8.9 per cent and a maximum of 14.7 per cent. Denmark imposes the tax at both the local tax district and the county tax district level at combined rates ranging from 16 to 26 per cent.

In addition to national and local taxes various other charges are made on incomes in many countries. Church taxes are levied in Denmark (rates between 0.4 and 1.8 per cent), Finland (1 to 2 per cent) and West Germany (8 to 9 per cent), though the tax is not payable in Germany if the taxpayer is not a member of any church. Greece imposes a 10 to 15 per cent surcharge on behalf of the Farmer's Social Insurance Organisation, and, of course, some form of social security levy is to be found in many countries.

Capital Gains

Capital gains are taxed in one way or another in many countries, though unlike the United Kingdom which has a separate capital gains tax, the more common approach abroad is to treat gains as income, though they may be subject to different regulations. For instance, under certain circumstances gains from the sale of shares or bonds are treated as income in Austria, Belgium and West Germany.

The idea of separate capital gains taxes appears to be gathering wider support. Ireland introduced a tax applying to capital gains accruing from 6 April 1974. In the budget for 1974/75 it was proposed to introduce a separate capital gains tax in Australia, but this was later dropped because of the difficulties of introducing a comprehensive capital gains tax during a period of inflation; and it was thought that withdrawing the proposal would boost business confidence and stimulate private investment. At the time of writing (mid 1976) France was also considering a capital gains tax.

Withholding at Source

Nearly every country, large or small, industrialised or non-industrialised, has some provision for the withholding of tax at source from wages and salaries. In contrast to the United Kingdom, withholding is almost invariably on a non-cumulative basis with each pay period during the tax year being treated separately, and a final assessment normally raised after the end of the year.[6] There is, however one exception. A cumulative system of Pay-As-You-Earn was introduced in Ireland in 1960. Like the United Kingdom, the changeover came because the existing system of taxing employees was based on pay earned in the preceding tax year. This meant that sometimes tax on relatively high incomes had to be paid out of lower income which often caused difficulties; and, in addition, the tax was payable in two lump sums on 1 January and 1 July, which again caused problems for some people.

---

[6] Cf. Chapter III, p. 68.

The operation of PAYE in Ireland has many similarities with the UK system, but there are a number of differences. In Britain the Inland Revenue sends a taxpayer's code representing his allowances direct to the employer as well as to the employee. In Ireland the authorities send the employee a notice which shows how his allowances have been calculated together with a detachable certificate showing his total allowances, and it is the employee's responsibility to pass this certificate to this employer. When a person leaves a job the certificate is returned to him together with a P45 (which closely resembles its British equivalent, see Chapter II, p. 28), to pass on to his new employer so that cumulation may continue. The certificate of tax-free allowances may be valid either for one year, or indefinitely, in which case it will continue to be used by an employer in succeeding tax years until an amended certificate is issued. The allowances are not expressed in the form of a code as they are in the UK, but as a monetary amount. The main advantage of a code, however, is retained in the Irish system as the employer knows only the total figure and not the individual allowances making up the total.

The calculation of the allowances due in any pay period varies between the two countries. In the UK employers use the free pay tables (Table A) to translate an employee's code into the amount appropriate in any period. In Ireland the job is done by the authorities. Employers are issued with the appropriate deduction card for each employee on which the employee's cumulative allowances are printed. Just as the UK codes each cover bands of £10 for administrative convenience, in Ireland the range of deduction cards is limited and printed in steps of £13 for weekly paid individuals and £12 for monthly paid. The allowances due to any person are rounded up to the nearest deduction card, which results in marginal underwithholding that is collected by adjusting the tax-free allowances for a later year.

Ireland has a system of collecting tax through stamps which has no equivalent in the UK. The Irish stamp book system was designed for employers who have only a small number of employees whose earnings do not normally fluctuate appreciably. The tax-free allowances of the employee are shown by the stamp book and each week, or month, the employer is required to attach to the book income tax stamps to the value of the amount of tax withheld. The stamps are sold at Post Offices.

The tax tables employed in Ireland also differ considerably from those in use in the UK. Table B in the UK is used to calculate tax payable at the basic rate. Table C is used to calculate higher rates, and is broken down into weeks and months so that tax is withheld correctly throughout the year. In Ireland there are two tables: Table A which is designed for those with taxable earnings of no more than £1,550 a year, and Table B for those who earn more. As the first £1,550 of taxable income is subject to a single rate of tax (26 per cent in 1976/77) Table A will withhold the correct amount of tax throughout the year from those whose taxable earnings do not exceed £1,550. But because the tables do not divide the amount to be withheld into pay periods, a person may find his tax payments rising as the year progresses. The reason is that withholding at rates above 26 per cent only begins under Table A when cumulative taxable pay reaches £1,550. Withholding then starts at the next rate (38.5 per cent) until the next rate band is reached and so on. The rates of withholding therefore have a tendency to be higher during the later part of the tax year.

To spread the withholding more evenly throughout the year, Table B is designed for employees with taxable income over £1,550. Taxable earnings up to £3,846 are subject to a rate of 38.5 per cent but an additional allowance of £504 (1976/77) is granted to compensate for the higher withholding on the first £1,550. The result of this procedure is that withholding is less accurate than in the United Kingdom, both during the year and after the end of the tax year. However, the other major feature of cumulation, that rebates will be payable during the tax year for any pay period in which an employee's earnings are less than his allowances, is the same as in the UK.

The Self-Employed and Provisional Tax

A common characteristic abroad is the requirement for taxpayers in receipt of income not subject to withholding to make provisional tax payments on that income during the year in which it is received. The normal rule is that the provisional payments are based on the liability of the previous year, except that where a taxpayer's income falls substantially he is usually permitted to make a revised estimate of his liability and reduce his current payments accordingly. The number of payments during a year varies between countries, e.g. from twice a year in South Africa to six times in Sweden.[7]

Withholding and Investment Income

The taxation of small amounts of investment income can lead to particular problems of tax administration. With a cumulative system of withholding whereby wages and salaries have the correct amount of tax withheld an assessment would not normally be made (see Chapter II, page 27). In the year to 31 March 1975 there were almost 55,000 small cases of under-assessment to tax in the United Kingdom, most of which concerned interest which had been received or credited without deduction of tax and had not been shown on taxpayers' returns.[8] By exempting small amounts of certain types of income the difficulties can be reduced. For instance, in Ireland the first £70 per annum (1975/76) of interest from deposits placed with qualifying Irish banks was exempt. In France resident taxpayers were exempt from tax in 1976 on the first Frs. 3,000 (about £330) of interest payable on most long-term fixed interest securities. And in the UK the first £40 (1976/77) of some savings bank interest is exempt.

In Norway single taxpayers were exempt from both national and local income taxes on the first NKr 1,000 (around £100) of qualifying investment

[7] See also Chapter V, p. 168.
[8] 118th *Report* of the Inland Revenue, Cmnd. 6302, *op. cit.*

income (taxpayers with dependants, NKr 2,000). In Sweden the first SKr 800 (£100) (single individuals) and SKr 1,600 (married couples) of income from capital was exempt from national income tax. Although such exemptions from tax may be granted for a number of other reasons, they have the effect also of considerably easing the burden of tax administration.

A separate method of tackling the problem is to impose a withholding tax on investment income at some flat rate, which can then become the taxpayer's final liability, regardless of the marginal rate applied to any other income he may have. For example, in Italy there is a withholding tax of 10 per cent on all types of dividends distributed to residents which may be credited against the individual income tax and any excess refunded. However, taxpayers have the option of having a 30 per cent tax withheld which then constitutes a final tax on that income. In Greece the withholding tax on dividends (of 33 per cent in 1976 if the shares were quoted on the Athens stock exchange, 41 per cent otherwise) is normally a final tax, though the taxpayer may opt for liability to income tax and receive a credit for the tax withheld.

This method is also widely used in the taxation of investment income for taxpayers resident in many other countries. Thus in Sweden and Australia where dividends and interest payable to residents are not subject to withholding, there was a 30 per cent withholding tax on payments to non-residents. In Sweden this applied to dividends and in Australia to both interest and dividends. Like other countries operating such a tax, the Australian and Swedish withholding taxes are subject to double taxation agreements.

Leaving aside Australia and North America, withholding of tax from dividends and/or interest payable to residents is quite widespread, particularly in Europe, and appears to be spreading. In Europe withholding taxes of between 20 and 30 per cent normally apply to dividends distributed to residents in the Benelux countries, Austria and West Germany. Italy has a basic withholding tax of 10 per cent (subject to the option mentioned above), Denmark one of 30 per cent, and some of these countries also have provisions for withholding on interest payments. In Finland there is 'progressive withholding' whereby tax is applied to dividends at a rate of 15 per cent on the first FMk 500 (£75) paid by a company to any one shareholder and 30 per cent on any excess. Withholding at the flat rate of 30 per cent is applied also to interest payments. In Greece tax is withheld on most types of interest payment at the progressive rates of the income tax up to a maximum marginal rate of 60 per cent.

Outside Europe withholding on investment income applies both in large industrialised nations such as Japan (generally 20 per cent on dividends and interest), and in smaller countries such as Hong Kong (at the 'standard rate'[9] on interest).

---

[9] The standard rate in Hong Kong bears no resemblance to the old standard rate or the present basic rate applying in the United Kingdom.

Chapter IV

The Arguments for and Against Self-Assessment

In this chapter we shall examine the arguments for and against introducing a self-assessment system into the UK. The aim is not in any sense to set out a detailed programme but to forge a link between the description of existing systems set out in the two preceding chapters and the specific proposals in the two that follow.

Initially, we shall sketch in the general features of any likely system of self-assessment and the probable background to its operation. We shall then consider the advantages and disadvantages likely to flow from such a development in the context of both self-employed and employed people. Then we shall show that a number of arguments frequently aired on this subject are fallacious or lacking in substance or both. Finally, we shall attempt an overall summary. An experiment in self-coding is described in the Appendix.

1 The General Nature of the Changes

A number of aspects of self-assessment have emerged in the preceding chapters and if we are going to discuss the pros and cons we must obviously single out the distinguishing features in any change of system. They may be listed as follows:

Taxpayer declaration of numbers of dependants,
Simplification of allowances, deductions, etc.,
Estimation of income, calculation of tax liabilities and payments on account during the year (if withholding does not apply),
Employer etc., deductions (if withholding does apply),
Completion of annual returns of total income by all taxpayers or near-taxpayers together with payments of final instalments of taxes due or claims for refunds,
Suitable official procedures for checking returns and taxes paid,

Penalty provisions for delinquent and dishonest taxpayers,
Provision of adequate guidance to taxpayers.

We shall explore all of these characteristics of self-assessment in much greater detail in the following pages. At this stage we must point to another change which really would be inevitable if there were to be a widespread move towards self-assessment of employees in this country: the supersession of the present cumulative withholding system by a non-cumulative one. The interrelation between self-assessment and non-cumulative withholding is as follows. First, it seems likely that taxpayer comprehension of non-cumulative withholding would be somewhat greater than with our present system[1,2] and if one is going to thrust the burden of assessment on to the taxpayer this is important enough in itself. But it is even more important that a non-cumulative system of tax withholding will, for the reasons explained in Chapter III p. 64 tend to lead to over-deductions in the course of the year for most people (e.g. two-thirds of Swedish, five-sixths of US and four-fifths of Canadian taxpayers). This is critical for the successful working and effective policing of any self-assessment system covering employees. Without the prospect of a tax refund as compensation for completing one's return, administration of a self-assessment system for employees would be a nightmare. There is also the further advantage that overwithholding in the case of wage and salary earners is a very useful means, even if only a rough and ready one, of offsetting under-payment or non-payment of tax on their non-wage income during the course of the tax year. It is conceivable that self-assessment could operate side by side with a cumulative system designed to over-deduct during the course of a year but this would be even more incomprehensible to taxpayers than the present cumulative system.

But it should not be thought that it is just a matter of non-cumulative withholding being a pre-condition for self-assessment. It is also highly desirable (though not inescapably necessary) to have some self-assessment if one has non-cumulative withholding. Overpayment of tax by most wage and salary earners in the course of a year would by itself make a sharp contrast with the traditional UK system by which many other types of income (principally, but not exclusively, Schedule D income) have normally paid tax in arrears. To get away from such an arrangement involves some sort of pay-as-you-go system

---

1 C. V. Brown ('Misconceptions about Income Tax Incentives' *Scottish Journal of Political Economy,* February 1968) showed some years ago that there was very little knowledge among a sample of people interviewed about the structure of tax rates on earned income. Understanding could conceivably be even less with a non-cumulative system but this seems very unlikely. See also C. V. Brown and E. Levin 'The Effects of Income Taxation on Overtime: The Results of a National Survey' *Economic Journal,* December 1974. The Inland Revenue itself is on record as saying that the tax-payer does not understand the present system (Select Committee on Tax-Credit, Session 1972–73, Volume II. *Evidence* H.C. 341–II HMSO, 1973, p. 463).

2 This point has added force since employee national insurance contributions became entirely earnings related in 1975. A man now suffers two sets of deductions from his pay each week, one on a non-cumulative and the other on a cumulative basis. This seems to be a sure recipe for misunderstanding.

and this in turn involves in practice some sort of self-assessment and payment of provisional tax on account on the part of self-employed people. It can also be argued that self-assessment is desirable for wage-earners when non-cumulative withholding applies. But the experience of countries which practise the latter without the former makes it difficult to maintain this argument through thick and thin. So we may conclude that there is a two-way relationship: self-assessment by wage and salary earners really does imply non-cumulative withholding and the latter in turn is greatly facilitated if self-assessment applies, at least to some forms of income.

The next topic is tax-credits. Although the Conservative Government's 1972 proposals[3] embraced both non-cumulation and tax-credits for many people[4] it does not follow that the latter must accompany the former. This can be seen straightaway from the fact that all countries (other than the UK and Ireland) which have a withholding system operate it on a non-cumulative basis, even though tax-credits are very often non-existent or at most only a minor element in the system. The substitution of tax-credits for allowances or exemptions reduces the propensity of the non-cumulative system to over-withhold in that tax can then be negative and not just zero (e.g. when a man is sick and away from work). It therefore reduces the number of people due for refunds at the end of the tax year. So it clearly has administrative merits quite apart from all the social welfare aspects. But in our context, we can by-pass the arguments about tax-credits on the grounds that their introduction is not *essential* (as distinct from *convenient*) for the working of a self-assessment system. We shall therefore proceed on this assumption.

Other aspects of the area of potential reform may be noted more briefly. First, we shall assume that the coverage of tax withholding remains at least the same as at present. In sharp contrast to many other countries (Japan being an exception)[5] the UK withholds tax on all dividends and on much interest as well as on wage and salary incomes. This provision is clearly not a *sine qua non* for the operation of self-assessment but as it exists already there would be no point in changing it. Second, we shall assume that capital gains as well as other forms of income will fall within the self-assessment provisions, though postponing the details until Chapter V. Third, it was proposed in the tax-credit discussions of 1972–73 that various simplifications should be made in tax assessment, specifically that a standard deduction be made for the small expenses claimed by 11½ million people and that mortgage interest (affecting 5 million taxpayers) and life assurance premia (affecting 14 million taxpayers) be paid net of basic rate tax (with direct recoupment of the balance by the recipients from the tax authorities); and withholding of tax on interest income should be extended to cover at least some of the cases (e.g. bank interest) where this does not occur at present. Although, as we shall try to show, the

---

[3] *Proposals for a Tax-Credit System*, Cmnd. 5116, HMSO, 1972, *op. cit.*
[4] Though not for self-employed.
[5] See Chapter III, Appendix III–3, p. 129.

case for self-assessment does not stand or fall with such changes, they would certainly help and so we shall assume that they are as possible and practicable in the future as they were in 1973 and should be part of the background against which self-assessment can be judged. In similar vein, we shall also take into account the tax-free child endowment plan which starts to replace family allowances and income tax children's allowances in April 1977.[6]

There are many other contentious issues; one is the indexation of tax allowances and tax bracket limits; another is the relative treatments of married couples and single individuals i.e. the case for separate assessments in one form or another; still another is the appropriate computation of profits under Schedule D. However, it does not seem necessary or desirable to come to grips with any of these subjects here. If we are sure, as we can be on the basis of foreign experience, that a self-assessment system can work, whatever the background in matters such as these, we need not spend more time on them here.

One other subject is important. The time period of any changeover could not be short and many issues of a temporary nature would arise, such as the application of self-assessment to some types of income but not to others. In this chapter we shall concern ourselves mainly with the advantages and disadvantages of self-assessment once this temporary adjustment phase is over and the plateau stage has been reached. Of course, this does not mean that the short-term costs of changeover can be neglected but rather that we shall try to avoid bemusement by them.

If we are concentrating mainly on the longer term we must not assume that general economic conditions will remain as they are to-day, but keep at the back of our minds some of the likely relevant developments. We shall come to this subject in more detail in Chapter V but some of the important relevant points may be mentioned now. One is the general capacity of the population to cope with self-assessment. On the one hand, there is some expectation of an increase in the ratio of older to younger people[7] and this would be a disadvantageous change; on the other hand, one would hope that general levels of literacy and numeracy would tend to rise rather than fall and that people would learn to cope with these matters over the life-cycle. Another general development to take into account is the composition and character of incomes. One obvious point is the likelihood of more people having 'mixed' incomes (i.e. some combination of work and property incomes) whether in the sense

---

6 The case for such simplifying changes was argued forcibly by the Inland Revenue before the General Sub-Committee of the Expenditure Committee on 24 May 1976. It was estimated that child payment direct to the mother, abolition of minor personal allowances and deduction at source for life assurance and mortgage interest relief would save some 4,500 staff; and even this may be an underestimate. See 'Developments in the Civil Service Since the Fulton Report', evidence by the Inland Revenue to the General Sub-Committee of the House of Commons Expenditure Committee, H.C.–368–iv, 1976.

7 In 1974, the proportion of the population over retiring age was 16.9%. It is estimated that in 1991 the ratio will be between 16.8% and 17.8%, depending on the basis of the projection. (*Variant Population Projections,* Office of Population Censuses and Surveys, HMSO 1975.)

of enjoying both simultaneously or at different stages of the life cycle. Over recent years, there is clear evidence of the growth of mixed incomes;[8] the further development of pension provisions, over and above the state basic pension, is just one reason why we should expect this trend to continue in the future. Another striking development in recent years has been the growth in the relative number of Schedule D incomes. Although some of the advantages of this Schedule might well disappear under a self-assessment régime, it would be surprising if the upward trend of recent years[9] were to disappear altogether.

Then there is the question of administrative capacity. Although the Inland Revenue has an extensive programme of computerisation on hand,[10] it remains to be seen whether the public costs of income tax administration can be kept down in the years ahead any more successfully than in the recent past. It was stated in May 1976 that the ratio of Inland Revenue administration costs to all taxes collected had risen to 1.75 per cent (compared with 1.45 per cent in 1969/70 and some 0.5 per cent in the USA). Those figures relate to all taxes and not just income tax, but they are clearly dominated by the latter. This outcome should not surprise us. It is simply one manifestation of the working of the relative price affect i.e. that the costs of services tend to rise relatively to the cost of goods through time as the scope for productivity increases is less in the former case. The likely future increase in relative costs of labour-intensive services is clearly a major consideration to keep in mind throughout our discussion.

This listing of future relevant developments is obviously no more than illustrative and we shall return to the subject in more detail in Chapter V.[11] It is simply meant to emphasise that the background against which the arguments for and against self-assessment have to be judged is not that existing to-day but that which may be expected to emerge over the next few years.

2 Advantages and Disadvantages of a Self-Assessment System

The Force of Tradition

Any proposal for self-assessment is bound to be confronted with the inertia argument: that in the UK people have traditionally had their tax computations and assessment done for them by the Inland Revenue and that the present system of withholding has itself been with us for over 30 years. It can also be said that the Royal Commission of the 1950s broadly endorsed the present system as satisfactory.[12] No doubt, the Inland Revenue Staff Federation would

[8] e.g. the number of cases with investment income was 6.2 million in 1972/73 whereas it was 4.3 million in 1967/68.

[9] The number of Schedule D assessments (Cases I and II) was 1.9 million in 1967 and 2.4 million in 1972. See Chapter II, p. 34.

[10] See Chapter II, p. 22.

[11] See Chapter V, p. 161.

[12] Royal Commission of Taxation of Profits and Income, especially *Second Report* Cmd. 9105, HMSO, 1954). It might be noted however that one of the well-known members of that body, Lord Kaldor, has expressed rather different views in recent years. Cf. 'A Critique of the Green Paper Proposals' in Select Committee on Tax Credit, Session 1972/73, Volume II, *Evidence,* HC 341–II HMSO 1973 for a general endorsement of the system of non-cumulative withholding, coupled with self-assessment.

start with a bias against a change towards self-assessment.[13] And the more euphoric apologists for the present system would no doubt start to talk about the importance of preserving the tradition of 'your friendly helpful Income Tax Inspector' and the dangers of opening up the possibilities of a relationship which is basically more of an adversary character. Even without the euphoria,[14] one can point to other ways in which broad principles of self-assessment have been whittled away in recent years e.g. the systems of issuing automatic reminders when television or car licences fall due rather than making it the responsibility of the individual to remember such matters himself.[15] Stripped of any rhetoric, there clearly is here a case which the proponents of change must meet: if the present system is well-known and understood then why change it, even though it may have some imperfections?

There are a number of responses to this challenge. The most obvious is that if one took the argument too literally, there would never be any change of any sort. It can also be said that there are counter-illustrations about the prevalence of the self-assessment principle e.g. traders subject to VAT must compute and pay their tax liability each quarter, the Wealth Tax proposals specifically called for self-assessment for that tax[16] and the Customs declaration procedure at UK ports and airports now embodies the same general principle in that the passenger takes the initiative in declaring dutiable goods. Another example is the income declaration accompanying applications for grants to University students. Going further afield, the self-service principle is to be found everywhere nowadays in the form of supermarket shopping. And in answer to the traditional Cornford principle of unripe time,[17] one must point out that the most important development in income tax machinery in modern times in this country—we refer, of course, to PAYE—was planned in the middle of the greatest war in history and was in operation well before that war ended. If the strong opposition at the time had been taken over-seriously, this change would never have come about.

An example of another major income tax innovation introduced under most unpropitious conditions was that of self-assessment in Japan—put into effect in 1948, only three years after the end of a war and whilst the country was still under foreign occupation and military government.

So although one must give due weight to the important truth in the inertia

---

[13] See *Select Committee on a Wealth Tax,* Session 1974/75, HC 696–IV, Vol. IV, Appendix 7.

[14] And this is certainly by no means justified. For an example of the way in which University teachers' book allowances had not been given in full see Chapter II, p. 15.
It should also be remembered that some 50% of taxpayers in England and Wales are no longer assessed in the tax district in which they reside and that in any event tax inspectors move from one district to another after short periods of sojourn.

[15] By analogy, it can also be argued that the cumulative basis for tax has received a powerful boost with the introduction of Capital Transfer Tax.

[16] e.g. *Wealth Tax* (Cmnd. 5704, HMSO, London 1974) p. 19. Also *Select Committee on a Wealth Tax, op. cit.,* Vol. I.

[17] F. M. Cornford *Microcosmographia Academica,* 6th edition, London 1966.

proposition—that one must demonstrate that the benefits of change outweigh the initial as well as the continuing costs—it must not be elevated into a principle of overriding importance.

General Arguments for Self-Assessment

The argument differs according to whether we are considering Schedule D Cases I and II or Schedule E taxpayers (other categories are considered in Chapter V, but are largely ignored here for the sake of simplicity). With Schedule D, the basic consideration is that of equity. The system of paying tax in arrears in many cases confers a benefit compared to Schedule E concurrent tax payment. Schedule D payers have a relative advantage in times of rising incomes, whether due to nominal or real changes. On the other hand, Schedule D payers would, as now, all be looked at individually and so the scope for administrative savings is minimal. With Schedule E it is the other way round. It might be thought inequitable to introduce a system which in many cases collects more tax than is due in the course of the fiscal year even though refunds are made later. On the other hand, there are potential savings in public administration costs in this case though it would, of course, be a matter for discussion whether these should be offset to any extent by, say, a restriction of the width of the basic band to secure greater equity between low and medium incomes.

As the nature of the argument differs so much in the two cases, we must clearly take them separately. So we shall start with Schedule D and then proceed to Schedule E. Subsequently, we shall be concerned with aspects of self-assessment which are more or less common to both cases.

The Schedule D Arguments

We start with the central proposition that if taxes on wages and salaries are collected concurrently with income (and *a fortiori* if they were collected in advance as would inevitably be so for many wage and salary earners if a non-cumulative withholding system were in operation) there is a degree of inequity if taxes on other forms of income are levied at the same rates but normally paid[18] in arrears,[19] as with Schedule D, Cases I and II. This is particularly obvious at a time of rapid inflation when tax bills in respect of income of year 1 are liable to be paid in the depreciated £'s of year 2, but it is, of course, a more general proposition in so far as the level of real profits rises year by year in a growing economy.

In principle, the introduction of some elements of self-assessment can go a long way towards correcting any such inequities. If a taxpayer has to make

[18] Apart from special cases such as opening and closing years of business activity.

[19] Entirely independently of whether the same nominal rate of tax is or is not the same true rate, because, as in the UK, expenses deduction rules differ. It should also be understood that one argument sometimes advanced—that Schedule D income is liable to fluctuate over time more than Schedule E income and is therefore penalised by a progressive system—points towards a system of income averaging rather the deferral of tax payments.

quarterly estimates of his current income from profits, dividends, interest etc. and pay tax to the authorities on each occasion, this would amount to something like comparability with tax burdens on wage and salary earners. In practice, when there is a system of estimated or provisional tax of this kind, the result falls short of the above, in that people are usually given the option of assessing their tax liabilities on the basis of preceding year or current year income. Thus in the USA the usual rule that taxes paid on account must amount to at least 80 per cent of total tax liability for the year is waived if tax is paid quarterly on the basis of preceding year income.[20] There are similar escape clauses in Canada and Australia. It is only when income is falling that there will be a tax instalment payment on the basis of current income.

US-type self-assessment is nevertheless more consistent in its treatment of non-wage and salary incomes than the UK where the following average lags between receipt of income and tax payment on that income prevail:[21]

Furnished rents:	9 months
Unfurnished rents:	3 months
Dividends and interest taxed at source:	9 months
Interest not taxed at source:	15 months (if not coded out)
Schedule D Cases I & II	21 months (if accounts made up to 31 December)
Capital Gains	9 months

It should be understood that when basic rate tax deductions are made at source (e.g. as is effectively the case with dividends) it is only the liability to higher rate tax which is postponed in this way. More generally, it might be said that the apparent differentiation in favour of non-wage and salary income is offset in a variety of ways. One is deduction of basic rate tax at source in some cases; another is direct collection on a quarterly basis;[22] another is the liability to the investment income surcharge on investment income; another is the recent imposition of additional (class 4) National Insurance contributions on Schedule D (i.e. preceding year) earnings, though it may be that there are grounds for arguing that the latter is a means of bringing about equity of

---

[20] Even if the rule were not waived, people could still defer the greater part of their tax instalment payments until the later quarters and so be in a better position than wage-earners paying tax concurrently with income. This opportunity is not open to Canadian taxpayers. See Chapter III, p. 79.

[21] Assuming a constant flow of income throughout the year. This means that if tax on the whole of the year's income were payable in October, the average of the lags, positive and negative, between income receipt and tax payment would be 0 months; if tax is payable in January (as with unfurnished rents) the average lag is three months and so on.

[22] See Chapter II, p. 31. This makes for an element of deferral in tax payments on some Schedule E-type incomes.

National Insurance treatment rather than one of correcting for income tax disparities.[23,24]

But this is clearly a patchwork solution with the gains from tax deferral being more or less arbitrarily distributed among non-wage and salary earners rather than harmonised, or still less, eliminated. A system which relies partly on deduction at source and partly on a miscellany of other measures cannot be expected to do otherwise. Even though the US system has plenty of defects, such as limited deductibility at source and intensive, and for that matter obtrusive, investigations into profits, it is inherently more equitable both within the profits and interest etc. class of income and between that class as a whole and the wage and salary class taken together. And it could clearly operate more effectively still[25] if there were a greater measure of withholding at source on dividends, interest and the like—a situation which has long existed in the UK.

There is another consideration which is even more important here than in the wage and salary income case: the improvement in taxpayer understanding of the system. It can be argued that if wage-earners have to fill in a tax return at the end of every year and compute their residual tax liability, net of tax withheld by employers, there will be some gain in taxpayer understanding and comprehension, especially compared to once every *five* years.[26] If a man has substantial investment income and has to compute his tax due on four or even five occasions each year and not just one, there is likely to be a still greater gain in understanding and perhaps even in resistance to tax levels or tax increases when people realise the full demands of the tax authorities each year. Quick completion of returns by taxpayers at the end of the year is in turn dependent on quick notification by income payers of sums disbursed during the preceding year. It is noteworthy that in the USA this operation is altogether more expeditious and comprehensive than in the UK for non-wage incomes. In so far as this is a spin-off from the need for rapid completion of forms in the USA it could be said to be another valuable by-product of the system.

The Schedule E Arguments

It is convenient to distinguish matters relating to coding from those relating to assessment, even though, and we shall see, there are many points of contact.

---

[23] The answer depends on the contentious question of the incidence of employer National Insurance contributions. Without developing that argument here it should be noted that a by-product of current year assessment for Schedule D would be that the base for self-employed National Insurance contributions would also become a current year one thus obviating the need for the present miscegenation of flat-rate and earnings-related principles.

[24] It will be noted that we do not include in our list the system of coding small investment income out of PAYE. This is for the reason that such entries are normally on the basis of preceding, rather than current, year income.

[25] In that e.g. self-coding errors are then of less importance.

[26] There are also further points such as a wider range of choice among local income tax systems. See Chapter II, p. 50.

CODING AND WITHHOLDING PROCEDURES

In the UK, the Inland Revenue supplies employers with the information needed to enable them to withhold the appropriate amount of tax from employees. Although the necessary information must be supplied at some stage by the employee to the tax authorities, he in no way enters into the system of informing employers, changes in employment apart. As we have seen,[27] the coding notice may embody not only the personal circumstances of an employee and his family but also various other 'positive' items such as miscellaneous expenses, mortgage interest and life assurance premia together with 'negative' entries to take care of other income (e.g. interest, state retirement pensions) receivable without deduction of tax at source or to recoup tax unpaid in earlier years (after allowing for any changes in tax rates).

Changes in coding may be necessary in the course of a year even though an individual remains in the same employment. This could be due to either a change in personal circumstances, such as marriage, or to a change in the scale or scope of allowances—though, as we have seen, it is often possible for the authorities to avoid new coding notices by a system of transforming the value of any given coding supplied to an employer.[28] Changes in tax rates can always be taken care of by supplying new withholding tables to employers without the necessity of altering coding notices to employees. Finally, if an employee changes his job the tripartite P45 issued by the old employer informs the old tax office and (via the employee) the new employer and the new tax office of his tax position to date and the basis for withholding in the future.

The advantages and disadvantages of this system are well known. First, it is reasonably comprehensive in the sense of encompassing all the information necessary for tax deductions for a great number of employees. Second, partly because it is so comprehensive but also because the procedure is uniform and standardised, the coding can correspond exactly to the circumstances of the taxpayer as supplied by him. The mistakes which could arise if coding were in the hands of the individual rather than performed at official level were brought out very vividly in an experiment in self-coding described below.[29] Third, it is now an established pattern for large employers to send employee names on magnetic tape to the Revenue so that the appropriate coding can be entered; this clearly saves time and trouble. Fourth, the P45 system has some merits, to which we shall return later. Lastly, the width of the band of income taxed at the basic rate makes it possible to achieve reasonable accuracy of deduction, even when a man has more than one source of earnings.

As for disadvantages, the most obvious is the work burden imposed on the tax authorities. It is estimated that some 25 million coding notices are issued

---

[27] Cf. Chapter II, p. 27.
[28] Cf. Chapter II, p. 28.
[29] Cf. p. 155. Also *Select Committee on Tax-Credit,* Vol. II, *op. cit.* p. 240 for an account of the experiment.

each year,[30] all being hand-written except those from the East Kilbride Computer Centre. Although no figures would appear to exist of the exact numbers of Inland Revenue personnel engaged in these matters, it would seem that some 4,000 of the 35,000 people engaged on PAYE are involved. There are also others employed in the process of taking account of P45s and transferring taxpayers' files from one income tax district to another. It is an integral part of the present system that when there is a job change, the Revenue must note the name of the new employer on the taxpayer's records and transfer those records to the district dealing with the new employer. At the employer level, there is the disadvantage that if the previous employer has failed to issue a P45 or if the employee has lost it, tax will then have to be deducted on a Week 1 (i.e. non-cumulative) basis, hardly a situation calculated to improve industrial relations. There are also other matters connected with the P45 procedure to which we shall return in the context of cumulation and non-cumulation.[31] As far as the employee is concerned, there are very real problems of comprehension in that his particular coding may be derived from a whole series of entries, some increasing and some reducing his total of free pay.[32] There are also particular problems of retired employees.[33]

The coding system could readily be made less elaborate and so presumably more comprehensible by reducing the number of items taken into account (as in Canada).[34] In so far as it was possible to adjust at other points in the system (e.g. as suggested in the tax-credit scheme in respect of life assurance, mortgage interest, superannuation contributions, small expenses and interest received) this would still allow tax deductions to match tax liabilities exactly over the year. But in so far as coding simplification went further than this it would be bound to add to the burden of tax collection at other points in the system e.g. by the need to raise special assessments or at the very least by end-year adjustments.

There can be no question that the US system is in this general respect very much simpler than the British. The tax authorities there play no part in informing the employer about the number of exemptions to take into account in withholding tax. It is a matter for the employee to decide in the light of his family circumstances and according to whether tax is likely to be overdeducted in the course of the year (a case for enlarging the number of exemptions

---

30 Estimated numbers in 1973/74, 1974/75 and 1975/76 were 21½ million, 28 million and 24 million.

31 It is extremely difficult to quantify the burden of work on employers. Cf. *Select Committee on Tax-Credit*, Vol. II, *op. cit.*, p. 283 for the views of the CBI.

32 Table II–6 suggests that there are as many enquiries in total to the tax authorities in the UK as in the USA—i.e. that the average UK taxpayer makes four times as many enquiries as his US counterpart. While due caution has to be exercised because Inland Revenue data on enquiries is not systematic it can, nevertheless, be stated with some assurance that even under the present system considerable resources have to be devoted to taxpayer assistance. Hence a change to self-assessment might make less difference in this respect than would appear at first sight.

33 See below p. 142.

34 See Chapter III, p. 77.

claimed) or under-deducted (a case for reducing the number, at any rate if there is any danger of the total of tax deducted being less than the critical 80 per cent of total liability).[35] The translation of exemptions into withholding is also simpler.[36] The greater degree of simplification is also brought out in the annual returns completed by taxpayers. Thus whereas 45 questions are necessary to determine eligibility for personal allowances in the UK, only 11 are necessary in the US.

The price paid for this simple system of basing tax withholding on the number of exemptions claimed (plus the standard deduction) is a greater degree of approximation in the sums withheld, with a consequential need for many more end-year adjustments than in the UK. Although, as we shall see, the figures are complicated by the differing effects of cumulative and non-cumulative withholding in the UK and the USA, it should be noted that some 10 million taxpayers in the USA (16 per cent of the total) are underwithheld in the course of a year. Non-cumulation cannot play much of a role in this respect and so it seems likely that this is an indication of the inaccuracies of the system in one direction—probably due to the restricted range of withholding in the USA. This in turn leads to problems of tax recovery in such cases, given that there is no means of instructing employers to withhold more tax in the year following, as in the UK.

At the same time, it should be noted that a US-type tax system *could,* if the authorities wanted, be operated in such a way that if the level of allowances were raised (or tax rates reduced) in mid-year the benefit to taxpayers need only start then and need not be accompanied by refunds in respect of the first half of the year. However, that is more a matter of non-cumulation than of self-coding and so we shall not pursue it further at this stage.

It is sometimes argued that it is not a matter of an all-or-nothing choice between coding which is imposed from above and self-coding. In the tax credit scheme it was suggested that a credit card should be issued to an employee by the authorities each year, lodged with the first employer, transferred to other employers as job changes took place and finally collected by the last employer at the end of the year. This can be thought of as a half-way house in that the scheme envisaged non-cumulative withholding but not self-assessment. However, the employers' organisations strongly objected to a tripartite system whereby the Revenue, employers and employees would all be involved.[37] As a result, the proposal was withdrawn and so it would seem that the effective choice (at any rate for the great majority of cases) is between the Revenue–employer combination (as in the UK to-day) and the employer–

---

[35] Cf. Chapter III, p. 68.
[36] Cf. Chapter III, p. 61.
[37] Cf. *Select Committee on Tax-Credit,* Vol. III, *op. cit.,* pp. 48–55.

employee combination (as in the USA to-day).[38]

CUMULATIVE AND NON-CUMULATIVE WITHHOLDING

We have argued previously that any change to self-assessment for wage and salary earners would imply a change to non-cumulative withholding. The *modus operandi* of the cumulative withholding system peculiar to the UK and Ireland (at least among industrialised countries) and of the non-cumulative systems found elsewhere has already been explained[39] and so it will be sufficient here to bring out the essential differences.

The first is that cumulative withholding offers the possibility that for a large number of taxpayers the amount of tax paid in the course of the year will exactly match tax liabilities accruing during the year. For this result to hold, the wage-earner's exact personal circumstances must be reported to the authorities; appropriate coding allowances must be made for subsidiary sources of income and outgoings on such items as life assurance and mortgage interest. Provided these conditions are satisfied, the intra-year tax instalments will exactly meet the tax due over the year as a whole, a result which is far less likely to obtain in the non-cumulative case.

A second characteristic of the cumulative system is that the employer takes on responsibility not only for tax collection but also for tax refunds. If an employee is away sick, for instance, and the cumulative total of free pay builds up during this period by more than the cumulative total of actual pay, the employer is responsible for making the necessary tax refund. If the reason for a refund is unemployment rather than sickness the tax office is then responsible and so the employer no longer comes into the picture and his role is to that extent limited. However, the situation is entirely different from the non-cumulative case where an employer may collect positive tax or zero tax but never negative tax.

A third way in which the two withholding systems differ is the necessity in one case to maintain a cumulative record of pay and tax in each and every case, however many times employees may change their places of work in the course of the year. This leads to the P45 system in the UK, whereby a tripartite form has to be issued by employers on each of the 10–11 million occasions[40]

[38] It is sometimes argued that UK workers could not possibly cope with such matters as self-coding. Two comments are worth making. The first is that, as the Select Committee on Tax-Credit said to the TUC representatives, there never is the slightest difficulty in filling in complicated betting slips. The second is that it is perfectly true that retired people often encounter difficulty in coping with their tax affairs, especially with direct collection. Sandford found this to be so in the case of people writing to the Westminster Press Enquiry Bureau (*Hidden Costs of Tax Collection*, IFS, 1973, p. 81), but may not a major reason for this be precisely that everything has been done for such people by their tax offices during their working lives? Benefits to retired people—and to the Inland Revenue—must always be placed in this context.

[39] See Chapter II, p. 25 and Chapter III, p. 63.

[40] On the basis of *Inland Revenue Statistics 1973* it can be seen that there were 37.0 million PAYE deduction cards in 1970/71 whilst the estimated number of employees and pensioners covered by PAYE was 24.2 million. More computerisation covering large numbers of workers would, as at East Kilbride, reduce the amount of P45 work for the authorities.

in which individuals change their jobs each year as well as a P60 certificate in respect of each employee on the books at the end of the year. Where tax deductions in any one pay period depend solely on the pay during that period and not on a man's previous history during the tax year, there is no need for this kind of documentation to pass from one employer to another. All that is required is that a 'leaving certificate' should be issued by the employer to the employee recording total tax in any one job, i.e. the P45 and P60 procedures converge and there is no need for paper to flow from employer to employer. Nor does the employer need to keep a weekly or monthly, as distinct from an annual, cumulative total of wages paid, although he may, of course, find it convenient to do so.

Such are the major ways in which the withholding process differs under the two systems. Let us now look at the consequences for the different parties involved—the employee, the employer and the government.

It might at first sight be thought that cumulative withholding has decisive advantages for the *employee.* In very many cases, he will meet his tax obligations, large or small, as he goes along and so will be relieved of any need to meet tax bills at the end of the year; and this in turn makes it possible, as in the UK, to relieve many people of the need to make annual declarations of income, claims for allowances etc.[41] Everything exactly matches over the year as a whole. Furthermore, if, for whatever reason, there is a spell of low or zero earnings, this will attract a tax refund, provided of course that the low earning period is not at the very beginning of the tax year before any tax has been paid. It can be argued[42] that it is a sensible system which produces tax refunds in a time of adversity. On the other hand, there can be no denying the evidence to be found in all the countries we have investigated that a withholding system generating lump sum refunds after the end of the tax year is extremely popular. Forced saving in this form is, apparently, a masochistic act which appeals to people; otherwise, it is argued, they would 'never' accumulate the funds needed for holidays, major consumer durable expenditures or even other tax payments. Nor is the 'help in adversity' argument quite as convincing as it may appear at first sight. The difficulty is that the extent of any tax refund depends, *inter alia,* on the time of year in which sickness or unemployment occurs. But this puts social policy in a dilemma. If unemployment or sickness benefits are adequate without tax refunds, some people will do rather well if tax refunds are available. If, on the other hand benefits are insufficient, those unlucky enough to be unemployed or sick at the very beginning of the tax year for instance, will, do badly.[43] So the payment of tax refunds during the year is by

---

[41] Many PAYE taxpayers are not required to complete a tax return form more than once in three years (five years in future).

[42] Cf. A. B. Atkinson *The Tax Credit Scheme and Redistribution of Income* (Institute for Fiscal Studies, London, 1973) p. 45.

[43] The same point would apply to self-employed people who are ill and drawing sickness benefit.

no means an unambiguous blessing from this point of view.[44]

It has been claimed that the TUC expressed hostility before the Select Committee on Tax-Credit to the idea of refunding excess tax payments after the end of the fiscal year. Two observations can be made on this proposition. First, a careful reading of the evidence seems to suggest that the hostility was less than complete depending on e.g. whether non-cumulation was tied to a progressive tax rate structure etc. (*op. cit.*, Vol. II, p. 267). Second, a non-cumulative system could be expected to generate a refund for many people in mid-summer, given our present fiscal year; judging by the appeal of the special tax relief in 1976, which *inter alia* did precisely that, such a move would not be unpopular.

Turning to *employers,* it would seem indisputable that cumulative withholding places a relatively greater burden of work on them. The first reason is that the mechanism of the withholding system tends to be more complex in this case, though no doubt familiarity breeds appropriate procedures. The second and more important reason is the P45 procedure. It is simply unnecessary to have this system in the non-cumulative case. As we have seen, the Inland Revenue manpower bill for this exercise (including the associated movement of files) is very substantial. Given that both the old and the new employer is involved on each occasion, this must be a rock-bottom estimate of the corresponding load imposed on the private sector. At the same time, one must recognise that this is a gross and not a net imposition due to cumulative withholding. Even though the UK employer must send a deduction card or equivalent in respect of every employment during the year he need only send in a P60 to the tax authorities in respect of employees on his books at the end of the tax year. In the USA, the corresponding form, W2, must be sent by any one employer in respect of each employee, even if his employment ceased well before the end of the tax year. So it is not the amount of paperwork flowing from employers to the authorities which is so different but rather the exchanges between employers.[45]

Finally, we may note the point that Sweden did at one time consider the introduction of a PAYE Scheme on UK lines but rejected it on the grounds of the administrative load it would impose on employers.

We now come to the *government* side of things. From its point of view, there is a major administrative gain in a cumulative system: the minimisation of the number of tax adjustments at the end of the year (only about 4 million i.e. 16 per cent of all PAYE cases). This could even outweigh the net addi-

[44] It should also be noted that in the US system over-withholding applies to a relatively greater extent to upper than to lower income groups (Cf. Chapter III, p. 63).

[45] It was estimated in 1972 that firms 'employ perhaps as many again' to run PAYE as the Inland Revenue employees required to administer it. *Proposals for a Tax-Credit System, op. cit.*, para. 2.

If the system of shifting files from one Inland Revenue district to another were to be abolished, this need not lead to any additional work for employers in that they could send all their returns to one office and the Revenue would be responsible for cross-matching.

tional burden of the P45 system resulting from job changes. Against this, there are a number of very severe disadvantages. The first is that the tax rate structure has to be very lop-sided with the basic rate covering a wide band of incomes. It is perfectly true that the UK ran a limited system of reduced rates for many years; and that to-day the tax tables can cope with withholding at higher rates of tax as well as basic rate. Nevertheless, there are inescapable problems when people have multiple sources of earned income and in the case of investment income; the cumulative system will not then give an absolutely correct answer unless (and perhaps not even if) the number of rates is severely restricted.

It is an old question[46] whether this structure helps or hinders work incentives—the answer could readily enough go either way, depending on the number and relative reactions of people on the horizontal and vertical parts of the step progression. But what is much less disputable is that the equity implications are very odd indeed; it is exceedingly curious that the same marginal tax rate should apply whether an individual's taxable income from employment is £1 or £5,000 in the UK to-day. A second point is that the cumulative withholding system (in conjunction with elaborate coding) makes it very difficult to change tax rates more than once a year, at any rate in an upwards direction. For instance, if tax rates are raised the withholding tables have to be revised in such a way that the new rates apply to the total of incomes earned over the year and not just to incomes received in the period following the change. This is not necessarily so with a non-cumulative system. And so we clearly have a constraint on the freedom of a government to pursue flexibility in its fiscal policy, as shown by the differing history of the USA and the UK (in this particular respect) during the post-war period.[47] Of course, it can be argued that it is desirable to clip the wings of government in this regard but this particular way of doing so would seem to be a rather roundabout one.

Even more serious are the implications of cumulative withholding for the social security system: in a nutshell, it bedevils it. This is for two separate reasons. The first is the element of luck in whether a tax refund is due to an individual at the time he becomes sick or unemployed, depending as it does on the time of year; the second is the impossibility, or at any rate very great difficulty, of taxing short term social security benefits under a cumulative system and of preserving a rational relationship to earnings. Although that was the original system in 1948 the legislation had to be changed in 1949 because of the extreme difficulty of integrating such benefits into a cumulative with-

---

[46] Cf. A. R. Prest *Public Finance in Theory and Practice,* Fifth Edition, (Weidenfeld and Nicolson, 1975), p. 271.

[47] Thus for instance, the USA levied a 10% income surcharge in July, 1968; there is no example of a rise in income tax rates in the course of a fiscal year in this country during the post-war period.

holding system.[48] The result is that we now have an anarchical relationship between earned income receipts net of tax and social security payments. For instance, a Parliamentary answer on 10 November 1975[49] showed that if a man became sick or unemployed after being employed from April to December, then over a wide range of family circumstances (e.g. up to four children) and weekly income (up to £65 before tax) many people were better off when not at work. So there is clearly an incentive not to work at those times of the year when cash refunds of tax paid earlier will be forthcoming.[50] The abysmal nature of the situation is shown by the following extract from the Parliamentary answer:

> 'income tax refund while unemployed has been treated as *capital* for purposes of entitlement to free welfare milk and taken into account as *income* for free school meals, rent rebates and rate rebates'[51] (our italics)

If the supporters of cumulative withholding have friends of this sort, they are in no need of enemies.[52]

Another consideration is that the inability to tax short-term benefits means that, as a consequence, employee national insurance contributions are not deductible for income tax (strictly, the argument only carries any weight for the element of contribution corresponding to non-taxable benefit but it has been extended, by a sleight of hand, to the whole of the contribution). Furthermore this spills over into the self-employment field where the contributions are also non-deductible. This in turn engenders feelings of discrimination relatively to employed workers where at any rate the *employer* share of the total contribution is deductible against his tax liabilities.

A topic related to the above is the uncovenanted benefits to strikers.

---

48 See *Select Committee on Tax-Credit,* Session 1972/73, Vol. II Evidence HC 341–II, HMSO, 1973, p. 416.

The argument as set out by Sir Stafford Cripps in his Budget Speech on 6 April 1949 (*Hansard* Cols. 2090–91) was as follows:

> 'National Insurance benefits and contributions . . . it was considered a necessary counterpart of the allowance of relief in respect of the contributions that all benefits of an income nature should be charged to tax. Some of these benefits, however namely unemployment, sickness and maternity benefits are purely occasional and the taxation of these occasional benefits is a great trouble both to the Inland Revenue and to the recipients and cannot, of course, be allowed for in PAYE tables. I propose therefore that, in future unemployment, sickness and maternity benefits should be exempted from tax but that relief should not be allowed in respect of that part of the contributions relating to these occasional benefits.'

49 Hansard (Commons), 10 November 1975, Cols. 540–546.

50 It might be argued that the prospect of tax refunds after the end of the year could have the same disincentive affects in the non-cumulative case; but the rate of discount is likely to be sufficiently high to rule this out in most cases.

51 *Ibid* Col. 542.

52 As another example, take the utterly anomalous position with many types of industrial injury benefits. When questioned why mobility allowance to severely injured people was taxable whereas attendance allowance was not, the Government's answer was that the former, in contrast to the latter, was mainly paid to people at work and that if a benefit was taxed low income people gained relatively to higher income people. (*Hansard,* Written Answers, Col. 828, 19 December 1975).

Neither reason carries the slightest conviction. If the principle is to tax people at work then e.g. disability pensions of such people should be taxed; if the principle is to claw back from higher incomes then why are any of these benefits tax-free?

Provided they choose the right time of year they get a tax refund which may well make nonsense of the standard requirement that only dependants of those on strike can claim social security benefits. Given that the amount of tax available for refund is likely to be at a maximum in those months (January and February) in which certain industries are likely to have maximum bargaining power, one must conclude that it would have been difficult to devise a system which was more calculated to be disruptive.[53]

One other fiscal point needs to be made about the government and non-cumulative withholding. If it were desired at some stage to introduce some form of negative income tax, whether in the guise of a tax-credit or otherwise, the natural accompaniment would be non-cumulative withholding. Negative income taxation must be related to short periods in that one is by definition dealing with poor families without much in the way of resources to tide them over a longer period of time. It is therefore sensible to have a tax withholding system which also operates on a short period basis rather than on cumulative totals. Recent experience in Canada with Ontario tax-credits shows how such a system can work.[54]

So much for the various arguments for and against cumulative withholding. There is no need to summarise them. Suffice it to say that there are overwhelming reasons why no other country in the world (Ireland apart) has seen fit to copy the UK system.[55]

Form Completion, Checking and Penalty Systems

One difference between a self-assessment system and the current UK one comes in the need for annual completion of income tax returns. When the allowances applicable are checked by the authorities before coding and the withholding system is such as to render possible an exact match at the year-end between taxes paid and due, it is possible to dispense with annual returns for many people.[56] Conversely, with self-coding and non-cumulative withholding it is necessary for everyone except those clearly below the tax threshold to make annual returns. So the vast majority of the 80 million or more taxpayers in the USA do have to file returns.

There are arguments for and against near-universal filing. The major[57] argument in favour is the educative one: that if people have to complete a return they are likely to have a greater knowledge of the tax process and of the demands on them by the Treasury. But to the extent that individuals hand

[53] See Chapter II, p. 30.

[54] See Chapter III, p. 83. Similarly, it might be rather difficult to operate a quotient or income-splitting arrangement for families under a cumulative system which does not always match up returns of earned income by husbands and wives.

[55] This simple point was completely ignored by the British Computer Society whilst defending the cumulative principle in its evidence to the Select Committee on Tax-Credit (*op. cit.*, Vol. II p. 437). Some of the other propositions put forward (e.g. that non-cumulation has been proved unworkable in this country or that only cumulation can deal with higher rates of tax) were just plain wrong.

[56] Nevertheless, the authorities review every case every year themselves. See select Committee on Tax-Credit, Vol. II, *op. cit.*, p. 5.

[57] Cf. Chapter III, p. 92.

such matters over to tax preparers and advisers this argument is weakened. If form-filing has to be completed by a certain date after the end of a common tax year, the implication is that records of payments made to individuals must be despatched quickly by employers and others. This really does seem to be the case in the USA and Canada and is in sharp contrast to the UK where the process is both half-hearted (other than for wages) and dilatory. Another problem is the peak load one. If the vast majority of taxpayers have to complete returns and if the completion date is a common one this imposes a peak load on tax authorities, postal services and tax preparers and advisers. This obviously leads to organisational difficulties but nevertheless other countries manage to surmount them by suitable use of part-time labour. There are also advantages of concentrating all returns together in that there can be promotional drives and the like to encourage people to comply with the national date.[58] It has even been alleged that people enjoy these common purgation rites.[59] And despite the disadvantages of the peak load there seem to be even more problems if one goes for a different system whereby the idea of a common tax year for all is abandoned and returns are staggered at different times of the year.

Any system would clearly have to be on the basis of identifying numbers rather than names and the obvious source would be a national insurance number.[60] If it is objected that not everyone has a national insurance number, the reply must be that if Canada and the USA can operate on this basis (i.e. that if someone comes into the income tax completion net without such a number he is allotted one) then there is no reason why the UK cannot do so.

If the vast majority of taxpayers have to complete returns, the next question is how to check them. First of all, one can hope to minimise the problem by intensive publicity at the appropriate time of the year (as in Sweden, for instance) and by warnings of the consequence of misdemeanours (e.g. the tax fraud film shown in Canada). But taking the return as submitted the traditional UK practice has been a manual check of all returns to establish that the allowances granted were correct and to compute any tax payable in excess of that already deducted at source. But if the number of annual returns were enlarged considerably, the demands on Inland Revenue manpower would rise sharply if this system were maintained. One must therefore be prepared to

[58] Another advantage of a common date is that it increases the range of choice of local income taxes, as set out in the *Layfield Report* (Cmnd. 6453, *op. cit*) Cf. Chapter II, p. 50.

[59] 'Finally, the fact that everyone has to file his return by the same date seems to make the tax-paying season a sort of rueful national festival and collective penitential experience justified by the subsequent sense of relief and accomplishment' H. G. Johnson 'Self-Assessment to Personal Income Tax: The American Experience' *British Tax Review*, 1971, No. 2 p. 79.

[60] Cf. C. T. Sandford, J. R. M. Willis and D. J. Ironside *An Accessions Tax,* Institute for Fiscal Studies, London, 1973 p. 108, for the points that such numbers are already in use for some Inland Revenue purposes and that special arrangements can be made for people without national insurance numbers. See also ChapterV, pp. 170–1 and Chapter VI, pp. 197–8.

accept a system where the only universal check is a routine one, preferably by computer, of the arithmetical accuracy and consistency of the return. The really serious checking would then be confined to a sample of returns. The precise way in which samples should be drawn and monitored is a matter for later chapters but we may note here that it can be done with a great degree of sophistication, if so desired. The extent to which it is necessary for the authorities to have far-reaching powers to collect data (e.g. bank account statements and correspondence between an accountant and his client) relevant for an audit is also a subject we discuss later.[61] Clearly, there may be a choice of evils here: the present system may involve a certain amount of official intervention for a large number of people whilst self-assessment may involve very much more for a small number of people.

If it is known that only a certain proportion of returns are audited each year in any depth there must be severe penalties to deter people from making fraudulent returns on the assumptions that there is only a low probability of detection. This comes out very clearly in the US interest charges and penalty rates e.g. interest (non-deductible) at 9 per cent, a negligence penalty of 25 per cent of any tax deficiency together with 9 per cent interest or 50 per cent of the deficiency if civil fraud is proven and the same penalties (plus the possibility of gaol) if criminal fraud is proven. It is true that Part X of the Taxes Management Act, 1970, specified substantial penalties in relation to returns. It is also true that since the 1975 Finance Act interest (at 9 per cent, non-deductible) is much more readily chargeable on late Schedule D taxpayers than in the past,[62] but this is still a much lighter penalty than in the USA bearing in mind the different levels of interest rates in the two countries and the various ameliorative provisions in the UK. And nothing alters the fact that the number of prosecutions and convictions in the UK is incomparably lower than in the USA.[63]

It may well be argued that if a system can be made to work at much lower penalty levels, it is therefore preferable. This argument cannot be accepted as it stands, as all the other differences between the systems must be taken into account. For instance, it may be much more expensive to operate the system with low penalties.

One final point on penalty provisions is that the US system does not depend on them exclusively for its successful operation. Just as, if not more, important is the simple fact that overwithholding took place in the case of 64 million out of 81 million returns in 1973.[64] There is no need to make an enormous effort searching out everyone who fails to make a return if the probability is that

---

[61] For an account of the way in which the IRS used bank account data in bringing Al Capone to book, see J. C. Chommie *The Internal Revenue Service* Praeger, New York, 1970, pp. 98–9.

[62] As a result of the Finance (No. 2) Act 1975 it is necessary not only to appeal against an assessment but also to apply for postponement of tax—and for the Inspector of Taxes to agree—to avoid interest payments from the date stipulated in the assessment.

[63] See Chapter II, p. 40 and Chapter III, p. 107.

[64] See Chapter III, Table III–6.

such people will have overpaid their taxes anyway. However, this clearly does not apply in the case of those not subject to withholding.

If nearly everyone has to file a tax return and repayments have to be made to large numbers of people, the inevitable consequence is a large temporary organisation to cope with refunds quickly and to answer taxpayers' queries.[65] Even though self-assessment and non-cumulative withholding can make substantial contributions to manpower saving,[66] a system which relied largely on manual methods would clearly be under great strain in these circumstances. This in turn points to the inescapable need to speed up computerisation over a very wide range of activities. It is here that the comparison between the UK history in the 1960s and that found elsewhere, especially in the USA,[67] takes on its sharpest edge.

After delays over many years, there are now[68] extensive plans for computerisation by the Inland Revenue in the years ahead. But the melancholy fact remains that the 'productivity' comparison with other tax systems is as follows:

Table IV–1 'Productivity' Comparisons

Country	Year	Number of employees in Revenue ('000)	Population (million)	No. of Revenue employees as % of 000 population	Public Administration costs as % of tax collected
UK	1973	70.7	56	1.3	1.71
USA	1973	71.8	210	0.3	0.48
Canada	1973	14.6	23	0.7	0.91
Sweden	1973	8.0	8	1.0	1.0

NOTES:
(1) The number of employees is not strictly comparable as in each case it refers to total numbers employed in the department responsible for collecting income tax. But in all cases other taxes were collected as well and so there is no obvious bias in the figures.
(2) The approximate number of returns processed was 20 million in UK, 80 million in USA, 11 million in Canada and 5 million in Sweden.
(3) Cf. H.C. 368-iv, 1975/76 *op. cit.*, for further discussion.

The table speaks for itself. Whichever measure of public administration cost is taken, the UK lags far behind other countries, and most especially the USA. It can be said that more extensive computerisation elsewhere is the sole explanation but this argument will not hold water in that productivity at East Kilbride (as measured by the number of tax returns handled per Revenue employee) is twice that of other parts of the UK; but it is still only half that of

[65] Data centre personnel increase from 700 to 7,000 in Canada at the peak of the Revenue's seasonal work-load.

[66] The tax-credit scheme would have led to a net official manpower saving of some 10–15,000 people, with perhaps comparable numbers in the private sector. This was without any elements of self-assessment but also without the need for end-year adjustments in the great majority of cases.

[67] e.g. in 1966 computer expenditure in the USA totalled $155 million, whereas in 1976 it was estimated to be $400 million. It was reckoned that in 1972 an additional 12,000 man-years (i.e. about 16% more) would have been needed to process returns manually in the absence of an automated data processing system. And the cry 'We never closed' seems to be as much a point of honour in IRS computer history as it was with the Windmill Theatre in London in World War II.

[68] See Chapter II, p. 22.

the USA. It can also be argued that on a public cost per taxpayer basis, the Internal Revenue Service came out at $18.7 per head in 1975 whereas the corresponding UK figure for 1974/75 was £11.60. But this argument will not do, either: one would expect that when a 'rich' country is compared with a 'poor' one the costs of services provision will be out of line with costs generally (e.g. haircut prices in New York City compared to London). In other words, it is only the much higher productivity of the IRS which makes the relative costs per head as similar as they are.[69]

Evidence on the total costs of tax administration (public and private) is scant. But such evidence as exists points in the same direction. A US study concluded that total public plus private compliance costs in the USA were of the order of 3.5 per cent.[70] Sandford estimated that in the UK the comparable figure was between 7 per cent and 10 per cent.[71]

The brutal truth is that the UK shows up very badly in this international league table.

3 Fallacious Arguments

We have set out what we think are the valid arguments for and against the introduction of a self-assessment procedure in the UK. It remains now to take note of some other propositions which are frequently raised but are nevertheless invalid.

First, it is sometimes said that there are macro-economic implications in switching from one system to the other in that a self-assessment system would mean larger annual tax payments than the present one. This would be so for tax withheld in that with incomes rising through time (whether due to real increases or price increases) repayments in respect of tax overpaid during the preceding year would be less than tax exacted in the current year. And the switch from preceding year to current year basis for other taxpayers would also lead to a higher annual tax charge in any one year for the same reason. But it would be silly to imagine that any such changes need necessarily have macro-economic implications in that, if such a contingency threatened, income tax rates could readily be adjusted accordingly. It would be more true to say that there would be a different seasonal pattern of net tax payments inside a year (e.g. with repayments soon after the end of the tax year to those over-withheld) but the experience of countries operating non-cumulation with or without self-assessment does not suggest that this cannot be handled easily with the usual fiscal and monetary instruments.

Another fallacy, frequently encountered, is the suggestion that self-assessment would ensure a permanent simplification of the tax system on the grounds

---

[69] See Chapter III, p. 70.

[70] A. F. Ott and D. J. Ott, *Simulation of Revenue and Tax Structure Implications of Broadening the Federal Income Tax Base,* in Studies in Substantive Tax Reform 59(1969), quoted in Commission to Revise the Tax Structure, *Reforming the Federal Tax Structure,* Fund for Public Policy Research, Washington DC 1973, p. 13.

[71] C. T. Sandford, *Hidden Costs of Taxation, op. cit.,* p. 144.

that individual taxpayers cannot be expected to unravel all the intricate sophistries which one finds to-day. It is one thing to say that some simplification is necessary (e.g. children's allowances) preparatory to the introduction of self-assessment. It is quite another to assume that complications would not creep into the system once self-assessment was established. The history of the exemptions and deductions to be found in the American or Canadian tax codes (see Chapter III) is a sufficient illustration.

It can be maintained that increasing complexity has been possible in these countries in recent years because of extensions of computerisation rather than self-assessment *per se*. But that is a rather empty distinction in so far as the satisfactory operation of any self-assessment system is largely dependent on extensive computerisation. Rather than there being a state of affairs where a taxpayer 'strike' over complexity frustrates government plans, it is much more likely that complexity and self-assessment will be made compatible by the growth of relatively unskilled tax advisory services (eg. H & R Block in the USA).[72]

A third fallacy is that there is no need to worry about inequity in the relative income tax treatment of Schedule D and other taxpayers in the UK in so far as special national insurance contributions make up for this. The first point here is that the equality or inequality of national insurance treatment depends on one's views about the incidence of employers' contributions; if one takes the view that these fall largely on employees (whatever the precise manner of shifting) the proposition that Schedule D taxpayers are treated badly for national insurance purposes loses much of its force. But even if such were not the case, it is a highly arbitrary procedure to compensate for favourable treatment in one tax by increasing the level of another. It is obviously far better to correct the inequities at source. And in any event, as we have seen, the introduction of non-cumulation would open the way to the taxation of short-term National Insurance benefits and to the deductibility of contributions, in whole or in part, by employees and self-employed.

Another fallacious argument is that literacy and numeracy standards are so low in the UK that individuals could not possibly cope with their own tax affairs. We have already made the point that quite remarkable proficiency is shown in some other ways such as the completion of betting slips and football pools. More generally, there is no evidence that literacy and numeracy skills are lower than those found in the USA. And in so far as there are individuals who really cannot cope with these problems, one would then expect the tax advisory industry to grow accordingly,[73] not to mention the sales of small electronic calculators.

---

[72] It can be argued that in so far as more tax 'administration' is the responsibility of taxpayers and less that of the government, the constraints on further complications are weakened by self-assessment in that government no longer has to bear the cost.

[73] See C. T. Sandford *Hidden Costs of Taxation* (Institute for Fiscal Studies, London, 1973) for further discussion.

Finally the weakest argument of all is that the UK is different from other countries in that what applies there cannot possibly apply here. This is patently the last defence of these bereft of any intellectual arguments whatever.

4 Conclusions

We must now draw the threads of our arguments together. First of all we have to face the facts that no industrialised country outside the British Isles has a cumulative system of withholding and that other industrialised countries all tend to have some elements of self-assessment in their tax system. This can be shown diagrammatically (though ignoring some fine points) as follows:

Table IV–2 Elements of Self-Assessment in Different Countries

Element	Australia		New Zealand		Canada		Japan		Sweden		USA		UK	
	a	b	a	b	a	b	a	b	a	b	a	b	a	b
1	√	√	√	√	√	√	?	√	√	√	√	√	X	X
2	√	√	√	√	√	√	?	√	√	√	√	√	X	X
3	optional		√	√	√	√	?	?	X	X	√	√	X	X
4	X	X	X	X	√	√	X	√	X	X	√	√	X	X
5	na	√	na	√	na	√	na	√	na	√	na	√	na	X
6	√	√	√	√	√	√	√	√	√	√	√	√	√	X
7	√	√	√	√	√	√	√	√	√	√	√	√	X	X

NOTES:

(1) KEY
- a Wages and Salaries
- b Other incomes
- 1 Taxpayer works out his receipts
- 2 Taxpayer computes and deducts his allowances
- 3 Taxpayer calculates tax payable
- 4 Taxpayer sends cheque for tax due, together with return, soon after year end
- 5 Onus on taxpayer to change his current tax payments, if his income changes significantly
- 6 Tax paid currently (or approximately so)
- 7 Sample checking

(2) This tabulation is only a rough summary; there are many detailed differences between countries

(3) na: not applicable

(4) √=Yes, X=No.

As can be seen from the quickest of glances, the UK has fewer elements of self-assessment in its personal income tax system than any of the other countries in the tabulation.[74] Needless to say, this in no sense proves that the UK system is 'wrong' and the others 'right'; but at least one should pause for thought when one finds oneself very much out of step with other countries.

The precise advantages of any moves towards a greater degree of self-assessment obviously depend on the categories of people covered and the nature of the changes proposed.

For Schedule D taxpayers and the like, the central issue is one of equity i.e. the benefits they derive from the present system of payment in arrears. Although in principle the issue of current versus deferred tax payments can be

[74] It might be noted that 'self-assessment' does not even appear in the index to a standard book on the Inland Revenue (Johnston, *op. cit.*).

divorced from that of self-assessment, one suspects that it would be extremely difficult to introduce a system of current payment on account without some changes in practices which would incorporate elements of self-assessment, whether this was formally acknowledged or not.

For Schedule E taxpayers we have argued that self-assessment is very clearly related to the replacement of cumulative by non-cumulative withholding and that simplification of the structure of allowances would also be highly desirable. The balance of advantage would depend on the precise form of self-assessment and here the crucial question is the introduction of self-coding, with all that it implies for current administrative practices. Foreign experience does suggest that there could be appreciable savings in Inland Revenue administration costs, even after allowing for the greater number of end-year repayments. Although private sector administration costs would increase this would be a matter of greater taxpayer effort as well as an increase in tax advisory activities. So one would expect to find that on balance resources would be freed for other purposes, quite apart from the question whether one prefers private to public administration in this sphere of activity.

This is the first major issue under Schedule E but, as we have seen, there are many others—possibilities of taxing (enhanced) short-term national insurance benefits and so securing a more rational relation to earnings net of tax, greater flexibility in tax rate and/or allowance changes during a fiscal year, the introduction of more progressiveness at the lower end of the income spectrum, a greater range of choice of the form of any local income taxation, a willingness to accept a greater degree of rough justice between individual taxpayers, the introduction of tougher and harsher treatment of offenders and so on.

There is one final point which cuts right across the Schedule D/Schedule E distinction: the possibilities and probabilities of a greater degree of taxpayer understanding under a régime of self-assessment with all that this implies for attitudes towards public spending and indeed the conduct of democratic government.

APPENDIX IV–1

An Experiment in Self-Coding

As is known from at least two sources,[1] the Inland Revenue carried out an experiment in self-coding in 1971. The detailed results have not, however, been publicly released and we must express our gratitude to the authorities for letting us draw on the results of this survey. We shall first of all summarise the survey and the results; then we shall make some comments.

Summary

The survey was conducted by the Social Survey Division of the Office of Population Censuses and Surveys in May 1971. The sample consisted of 728 men and single women living in 26 areas in England and Wales; there were 465 people willing to co-operate, a rather higher response rate than had been expected. As the aim was to test the accuracy with which individuals could code themselves, there had to be a standard of comparison and this was taken to be the details given on an ordinary tax return form (P1) (from which the information is drawn for the official coding by the Inland Revenue). It was thought best to divide the sample into two groups: one was asked to complete a tax return form first and a self-coding form later and in the other group the reverse order was followed. In actual fact there was very little difference in the results derived from each of the sub-samples. In all cases, interviewers called on three separate occasions.

In completing the *tax return form,* the vast majority of respondents did not need any assistance. Nevertheless, people did have various difficulties, most especially with the computation of life assurance relief and the disposal of chargeable assets. More than half the respondents needed less than 15 minutes to complete the tax return form.

In completing the *self-coding form,* the vast majority was once again able to do so without assistance, but rather more experienced difficulties on the way. Life assurance was easily the greatest source of difficulty but the concept of basic coding units (i.e. personal allowances) puzzled a number of people. Although one respondent claimed that he spent four hours completing the return, nearly half were able to do so in less than 15 minutes. However, there were substantial errors when judged by the entries on the tax return forms. These were of different kinds: misunderstandings about life assurance premium relief, mistakes in converting money sums into coding units, errors in calculating basic coding units (e.g. in respect of numbers of children) and failure to translate national insurance retirement pensions correctly into deductible coding units. Nevertheless only 65 per cent of all interviewees expressed doubt about the idea of a self-coding form—even though 14 per cent were dubious about the precise layout of that supplied to them.

1 Select Committee on Tax-Credit, Vol. II, Evidence H.C. 341–II, *op. cit.,* p. 240; and 118th *Report* of Inland Revenue Cmnd. 6302, HMSO, London, January 1976 para. 116; H. W. T. Pepper 'Calculating Your Own Tax' *The Accountant* 17 February 1972.

In comparing the two forms, only one in three of the self-coding forms was consistent with the tax return form and judged to be correctly completed. Those entitled to basic coding units only were the most likely to be correct; and those with deductible coding units were least likely. It was also noticeable that, fortuitously or otherwise, miscalculation of coding units was biased in favour of the taxpayer.

Comments

It is not surprising that the Social Survey report on the experiment concluded as follows:

'Indeed only one in three persons completed the self-coding form correctly. This low proportion argues that, despite the newness of the form, a self-coding system is not a feasible alternative system of assessing coding units. Half the people who have only basic coding units incorrectly completed the forms, as many as 70 per cent of those with basic coding units and further coding units and 84 per cent of people with deductible coding units. These proportions speak for themselves and although undoubtedly the error rate is lower for people with straightforward circumstances than for people with further coding units and deductible coding units, it still is not low enough.'

It is still less surprising that these conclusions have been echoed at other times.[2]

Whether this should be the last word on the subject is another matter. There are several points to make on the other side:

(1) This was an experiment and the interviewees knew this to be so. As a consequence, people may well have been careless. The Social Survey Report itself said in its summary:
'It is impossible to say whether, because this was an experiment, some people were careless about completing the form and thus made arithmetical errors and conversion errors. These errors might not occur quite so frequently in a non-experimental situation.'

(2) A related point is that people are likely to learn by doing in this as in other respects. Confirmation of this general point can be obtained from Japanese experience. Self-assessment for income tax was first introduced in 1947. In 1948 70 per cent of those completing returns had to be 're-assessed'; by 1950, the proportion was down to 4 per cent.[3]

(3) Misunderstanding of the nature of some allowances caused a lot of difficulty. This was especially so in the case of life assurance. But since that time the form of the relief has been changed and may now be simpler to understand; and in any event, the Chancellor proposed in his April 1976 Budget Speech to take this item out of tax allowances altogether by introducing a system of paying premia to insurance companies net of the

[2] *Ibid.*

[3] N. Tanabe 'Blue Return System in Japan' in P. C. Kelly and O. Oldham *Readings in Income Tax Administration,* Foundation Press, Mineola, NY 1973.

tax relief element (another way in which the original Tax-Credit proposals[4] are being introduced piecemeal into the system without saying so). Similarly, the whole operation will be further streamlined when the new non-taxable child allowances come into effect. To the extent that any further simplification or elimination of tax allowances takes place, difficulties with self-coding would be further reduced.[5]

(4) Another major difficulty was the translation of the money value of allowances into the corresponding number of coding units. If the need for this exercise could be avoided, whether by greater standardisation or elimination of existing allowances (or by relegating some of them to an end-year settlement rather than incorporating them in PAYE) a major set of difficulties facing the general public would disappear.

(5) No doubt, a great deal of effort went into the design of the self-coding form. But it is worth remembering that 14 per cent of interviewees did express doubts about its layout and ease of comprehension—doubts which are shared by the authors of this study.

(6) There was no monetary incentive to self-code correctly. One might see a very different response if underestimation of entitlement to allowances led to higher withholding or overestimation resulted in some end-year penalty; and if accuracy in self-coding and in completing one's annual return form carried with it a tax discount.

---

[4] *Proposals for a Tax-Credit System, op. cit.*, para. 51ff.

[5] A possible point on the other side would be if the subjection of short-term national insurance benefits to tax (see above) led to the deductibility of national insurance contributions against tax.

Chapter V

Programming and Phasing of Self-Assessment in the UK

1 Introduction

'In Holland . . . a tax of two per cent, or the fiftieth penny as it was called, was imposed on the whole substance of every citizen. Every citizen assessed himself . . .'[1]

It is a well-known proposition[2] that no economist worth his salt can fail to find a quotation from *The Wealth of Nations* to support his case. So we feel it incumbent to show that we are not below the salt.

In this chapter and the one following we shall set out a detailed programme for the introduction of elements of self-assessment into personal income taxation and capital gains taxation in the UK. We may from time to time make reference to self-assessment in other contexts—most especially value added tax, capital transfer tax and the proposed wealth tax—but in no sense shall we consider any of them in detail; nor do we attempt to cover Corporation Tax in these proposals.

Initially, we shall set out various alternatives for personal income tax and capital gains tax (henceforth now generally referred to as 'income taxes') in the UK in the years ahead, together with a sketch of the background trends affecting the choice between these alternatives. We shall then consider the specific problems arising with self-assessment for Schedule D and similar type income; subsequently capital gains tax; then Schedule E type income. After that, we have some discussion of tax-credits and other related issues. Finally, there are a number of matters more or less common to each of these three taxation areas which we shall explore at length in Chapter VI.

It must be stressed at the beginning that there is an awkward chicken and egg problem here. Some of the difficulties about extending self-assessment to

1 Adam Smith, *The Wealth of Nations,* (Everyman edition), Book V, Chapter 2, p. 333.
2 Cf. J. Viner, 'an economist must have peculiar theories indeed who cannot quote from *The Wealth of Nations* to support his special purposes' in 'Adam Smith and Laissez-Faire', *Journal of Political Economy,* April 1927, p. 207.

Schedule E type income are due to the complexities of the present system; but one cannot envisage simplification in the Schedule E case without also considering it in the context of Schedule D type incomes. But to discuss matters two or three times over would be excessively tedious. We shall therefore adopt the device of postponing discussion of such common threads in the argument to Chapter VI, but referring ahead to them in the individual sections of Chapter V as and when necessary.

2 The Alternatives

UK income taxes might develop in a variety of ways over the next few years. The six main ways, in ascending order of degree of change, seem to be as follows:

(1) SIMPLIFICATION OF ALLOWANCES

By this we mean that the general structure of tax allowances, assessment and withholding procedures now in existence would stay essentially unchanged but that there would be changes on the lines mentioned earlier[3] in respect of children's allowances, life assurance relief, mortgage interest relief, minor personal allowances and so on.

(2) AS IN (1) PLUS MORE EXTENSIVE COMPUTERISATION

This seems to be what is envisaged by the Inland Revenue.[4] However, the precise form which additional computerisation will take is very different from that foreseen a few years ago. At that time, the plan[5] was to have some seven or eight regional centres, on the East Kilbride pattern, which would take over the bulk of PAYE work from local offices, e.g. such routine work as the issue of tax return forms, the calculation and issuing of PAYE codes and the calculation and issuing of assessments. For various reasons these plans were scrapped and the idea now is to have a number of computers connected to local offices by data transmission links. So the staff operating PAYE will stay in local offices even though the record-keeping and routine processing is centralised. A pilot scheme is planned for 1977 and the full scheme is to be in operation 'early in the next decade'.

Until more details are available, it is difficult to gauge the precise outcome of such developments but it is problematical whether computer facilities will be up to North American standards today (e.g. the ease of interchange between social security and income tax data in Canada), let alone what it may be in a few years' time.

(3) AS IN (2) PLUS NON-CUMULATIVE WITHHOLDING

This alternative would mean that we should have something like alternative (2) operating, but with a non-cumulative withholding scheme instead of the

[3] Cf. Chapter IV p. 132.
[4] 118th *Report* (Cmnd. 6302) *op. cit.*, para 118 ff.
[5] Cf. Chapter II p. 22. See also Sir A. Johnston, *The Inland Revenue* (Allen & Unwin, London), 1965, p. 91.

present cumulative system. This would clearly involve somewhat different computer operations (e.g. calling for returns from everyone; and many more payments by the Inland Revenue at the end of the tax year but many fewer during the year, if Inland Revenue and employer repayments are aggregated). If short-term social security benefits were then brought within the tax net, this would be another major change compared to the situation under cumulative withholding. The manpower demands of the Inland Revenue would be much greater than with alternative (2), in that the additional numbers needed for end-year repayments would more than outweigh its manpower saving on repayments during the year.

(4) AS IN (3) PLUS SELF-ASSESSMENT (EXCLUDING SELF-CODING)
For Schedule E type income, the main change from Alternative (3) would be the obligation on a man to compute his tax liability, net of that already withheld, at the end of the year and send a cheque for the balance or make a claim for a refund. For Schedule D type income these changes would be more far-reaching. Tax liability would be likely[6] to be on a current year basis and payments on account would be needed in the course of the year as well as a computation, together with any residual tax payments, at the end of the year. However, coding in some form or other would still be the responsibility of the Inland Revenue and so there would be no scope for manpower savings at official level in that respect.

(5) AS IN (3) PLUS SELF-ASSESSMENT (INCLUDING SELF-CODING)
With this alternative we should approximate towards the US position, with coding being a matter which concerns the individual and his employer (if any) but not the Revenue, together with the necessary restrictions to ensure that a substantial proportion of tax due is paid on account during the year (e.g. the 80 per cent rule in the USA).[7] The role of computerisation is now very different—not at all concerned with coding but very much concerned with comparisons between taxes paid on account and tax due for the year as a whole and with the mechanics of discharging residual tax liabilities, whether negative or positive. Inland Revenue manpower needs would be less than with alternatives (2), (3) and (4), if North American experience is repeated.

(6) TAX-CREDITS
Tax-credits could be considered with any of alternatives (3), (4) and (5), i.e. in association with a non-cumulative withholding system. So this is not so much a separate alternative as a different version of each of these three options. As such it would imply a closer integration with the social security system than would otherwise be the case, in that, for instance, insurance benefits to the

[6] There is no hard and fast reason why moves to self-assessment and to a current year basis must necessarily go together for Schedule D taxpayers. Either change could in principle take place without the other. But it would obviously make good sense in practice for one change to be accompanied by the other.

[7] Cf. Chapter III, p. 68.

sick and unemployed would need to take account of weekly tax-credits. It would also help to diminish the number of repayments which would otherwise be due after the end of the tax year if the long band for basic rate income tax were retained.

3 The Choice of Alternative[8]

Many considerations have to be borne in mind in weighing these various alternatives. Before discussing them, one or two points of methodology need clarifying. First, one must assume that one has to raise the same amount in income taxes in all cases, after allowing for any direct repercussions on social security revenues and expenditures (e.g. making short-term national insurance benefits taxable would presumably mean greater income tax revenue but higher gross benefits). Second, it may well be that one would wish to have some combination of these alternatives, e.g. self-coding for some but not for others in the earlier stages. These two general points must be kept in mind throughout the following discussion.

It is clear that there are a number of changes afoot which will make it harder and harder for a system in the shape of alternatives (1), (2) or (3) to cope. First, even though the total population of the UK may not rise very fast,[9] the proportion of taxpayers to total population is likely to rise. Even if, *mirabile dictu,* personal allowances rise in line with the retail price index increases in real earnings would automatically bring more people into the tax net, more especially if the earnings of low income people rise relatively to those of high income groups.[10] Thus it would seem unlikely that the picture of recent years, during which the number of income taxpayers has continued to rise[11] will be altered in the near future. The planned supersession of income tax children's allowance by child benefit payments to mothers will also mean that more fathers will be liable for income tax than before, simply because they

---

[8] As tax-credits are compatible with a number of alternatives, (6) is not really a choice in its own right and so the discussion in this section is confined to alternatives (1) to (5).

[9] The 1991 projections range from 54,497,000 to 57,618,000 compared with the 1974 figure of 54,522,000 (*Variant Population Projections,* Officer of Population Censuses and Surveys, HMSO, 1975).

[10] As has happened in recent years. Thus it was stated by the Royal Commission on the Distribution of Income & Wealth (*Report* No. 1, Cmnd. 6171, HMSO, 1975 p. 67): 'After 1959 changes were in general less pronounced but the share in pre-tax income of the top 5% continued to decline mainly because of the continued fall in the share of the top 1%. The share of the other quartile groups (including the bottom 30%) increased, with the exception of the two decile groups immediately below the median, whose share did not change'. And there is more casual evidence to suggest a relative rise in earnings for low income groups recently, e.g. the government pay policies for 1975/76 and 1976/77.

[11] Although the number with incomes above deduction card levels fell from 20,995,000 in 1959/60 to 20,319,000 in 1972/73, the latest year for which details are available, it seems highly probable that there has been a further increase since then.

will no longer be kept below the tax threshold by child allowances.[12]

It would also seem likely that the ratio of higher rate payers to all taxpayers will increase over the years, even though higher level incomes may increase more slowly than lower level incomes. Recent years have seen a narrowing of the basic rate level in real terms, e.g. it remained constant in money terms at £5,000 of taxable income between 1973 and 1976, whilst retail prices have increased by 65 per cent between May 1973 and May 1976.[13] So it is not surprising that the number of higher rate taxpayers increased from 370,000 in the earlier year to 1.3 million in 1975/76; or that one of the Chancellor's aims as stated in his Budget Speech in April 1976, was to prevent the number rising from 1.3 million in 1975/76 to 1.9 million in 1976/77.[14] These movements would be reversed by a sufficient extension of the width of the basic rate band but such a development would seem rather less than likely. Given that many higher rate cases need to be looked at in detail, this is clearly a perpetual strain on the system. A small further point is that it can become worthwhile to opt for separate taxation of a wife's earnings when joint incomes reach up into the higher rate bands. So the number of assessments may increase more than the number of taxpayers for this reason alone—quite apart from any impetus to such demands in the name of women's rights.

The number of taxpayers falling within the basic rate band may also be reduced from the other end. It is noteworthy that the restoration of a reduced rate of income tax was one of the proposals in the TUC 1976 *Economic Review*.[15] And according to a Parliamentary reply in March 1976, the UK had easily the highest starting rate for income tax among EEC and other industrialised countries.[16] Although a reduced rate or rates can be incorporated in the present system—this was the position until 1969/70—there are conseqential complications, e.g. with dividend or interest receipts, secondary earnings and wives' earnings.

As we have seen (Chapter IV, p. 133) a demographic change which is clearly in prospect is an increase in the number of people drawing state retirement pension. Such income is subject to income tax but there is no mechanism for withholding at source. Even if personal allowances increase sufficiently to keep

---

[12] Two further points should be made. First, the simultaneous abolition of family allowances will remove an element of taxable income. Second, the number within the purview of the tax authorities, as distinct from the number actually paying tax, is determined by the National Insurance and PAYE thresholds operated by employers. So child benefit will affect the numbers actually paying tax rather than those in the tax net.

[13] Cf. Chapter VI, p. 195 for the 1948–76 comparison.

[14] *Hansard* (Commons) 6 April 1976, Col. 276. More generally, the anxiety of the authorities to keep down the numbers subject to income tax was evident at other points in the same speech, e.g. in relation to widows and pensioners.

[15] A 30% rate on the first £500 of taxable income was suggested (*op. cit.*, p. 84) though it is far from clear that the precise consequences of any such change were fully worked out.

[16] The UK rate was 35% while it was 5% in France and 7.8% in Canada (including Provincial tax). The nearest central government rate was Ireland (26%). *Hansard*, Written Answers, Cols. 247–8, 25 March 1976. See also Chapter III, Appendix III–3, Table III–3.1.

minimum level pensioners without other taxable resources out of the income tax net, this group is likely to form a smaller proportion of total numbers of pensioners as time goes by, given the growth of occupational pensions, own savings and, above all, the new state pension scheme due to start in 1978.[17] This in turn means that a larger proportion of an increasing total of pensioners will have to pay tax. In so far as sufficient tax can be withheld from occupational pensions to cover other income tax liabilities, the difficulties can be minimised. But this is often not so at present, and a number of people each year suddenly become subject to direct collection having been used throughout their working lives to a withholding system by which everything was done for them. If more and more people find themselves in this category, whether because of a greater annual accession to numbers or because of increased longevity, difficulties will clearly multiply.[18]

Another change adverse to the present system would be greater interchange of workers between the UK and the EEC. If, for instance, it becomes a standard feature of our economy for people to work in the UK for a few weeks, and then on the Continent, this may make it marginally more difficult to operate the present system of P45s on leaving employment. Greater numbers of self-employed people[19] will make it harder to justify the present system whereby one section pays income tax as liabilities accrue and another as much as 21 months in arrears. And increasing numbers of people with investment incomes[20] make for further complications, e.g. with capital gains assessments.

Another major issue is the interface between short-term national insurance benefits and wages net of income tax and national insurance contributions. We explored this area at some length earlier[21] and so there is no need to elaborate the argument. It is, quite simply, that we are most unlikely to get out of the morass so long as these benefits are not taxed and it is very hard to see how this can be done under anything like present arrangements.

Finally, one must not forget or neglect the staffing problems of the Inland Revenue. If something like the present system is to continue something like the present manpower strength, if not more, will be needed.[22] To attract the

---

[17] Under the new state scheme anyone with national average earnings, a full contribution record and no other pension would receive a state pension high enough to make him liable for income tax (using 1974 data). This would hold for both single and married people.

[18] Matters are not made easier by the lack of any arrangement for transmitting information from the Department of Health and Social Security to the Revenue when State pensions start to be drawn.

[19] Cf. Chapter IV, p. 134.

[20] Cf. Chapter IV, p. 135.

[21] See Chapter IV, p. 145. The contrast since April 1975 between collecting income tax on a cumulative basis and national insurance contributions non-cumulatively must also be re-emphasised.

[22] It was stated in 1975 that there were staff shortages of 18,000 (*Observer*, 24 April 1975).

necessary skills[23] pay must be competitive with the private sector. In circumstances where productivity is likely to rise less rapidly than in many areas of private activity—the relative price effect again—and when incomes policies are likely to apply more rigidly in the public sector, this may not be easy.

So far we have chronicled a large number of reasons why it may become increasingly difficult to hold the line with anything like the present system and why some major changes may be needed. Are there any arguments to put on the other side? Leaving aside the possibilities of minor, though not insignificant, changes such as devices to avoid issuing new coding notices to everyone when allowances change,[24] there is clearly one argument of some importance: that much more extensive computerisation would so relieve the pressure of routine work that sufficient manpower would be found to cope with the complexities and perplexities we have just outlined. In other words, even if Alternative (1) were not viable on its own the same could not be said of Alternative (2). But this is not really a convincing answer. The fact remains, as we have emphasised repeatedly, that other countries with extensive computerisation have a much smaller official taxation staff relatively to population. So it is not really good enough to argue that more computerisation would enable the present (or even a somewhat reduced) level of staff to cope with the additional burdens ahead. No doubt, increasing numbers of taxpayers in, say, the USA will necessitate staff additions in that country; but even so the case for retaining something very like the present system is not persuasive. It is simply not good enough to use computerisation to shield a system with many well-known drawbacks.

One further point is that the present system, in the form of Alternative (1) or Alternative (2) could operate more easily if less were demanded of it by, for instance, raising tax thresholds substantially. This is no doubt true; but so would all the alternative systems.

Finally, Alternative (3) would undoubtedly call for larger Inland Revenue staffing needs than Alternative (2) and so, on these grounds, is unlikely to commend itself.

We conclude therefore that the underlying trends are on balance unfavourable to the retention of anything like the present system, implying a move to one of the self-assessment arrangements set out in Alternatives (4) and (5).

4 The Phasing of Self-Assessment

From some points of view it would be desirable to make all the changes to a self-assessment system simultaneously; this would avoid awkward problems of

[23] This has always been a source of pride. For instance H. M. Groves wrote as follows ('Income Tax Administration', *National Tax Journal,* March 1959, p. 44): 'The British Inland Revenue staff trades in part on its high morale which is said to rank with that of the famous Canadian Mounted Police and the American FBI'. It should be recorded that the Somerset House library copy of the journal contains a marginal comment which, though partially indecipherable, is nevertheless highly suggestive.

[24] Cf. the proposals announced by the Inland Revenue in connection with the April 1976 Budget changes.

some people paying income taxes under one arrangement and some under another—awkward problems of equity as well as administration. This is, after all, what happened with the introduction of self-assessment in the USA in World War II or in Japan in 1947.[25] But there are plenty of warning signs indicating that such a massive change would be quite unworkable in this country, even if one could assume that the necessary computerisation had already been introduced. Thus it was said when the tax-credit scheme was first revealed in October 1972 that it would take five years to implement fully;[26] and the April 1976 proposal to alter the basis of life assurance premium tax relief is to take three years to come into effect, though this may well reflect the needs of the insurance companies rather than those of the Revenue. If such is the time span for changes which are on a much smaller scale than those for full self-assessment, it would seem inevitable that any moves in this latter direction must be phased with some classes of income being affected before others. This clearly has disadvantages in that existing differences in treatment may be emphasised or new ones introduced. But one simply has to accept this over the interim period, even though the long-run aim is to have uniformity of treatment.

The major distinction must be between income from which tax is currently withheld under PAYE (or closely related arrangements) and the rest. There are reasons of both administration and equity for making such a distinction. As far as equity goes, there is the major distinction between, say, Schedule D Cases I and II where tax is in general paid on a preceding year basis and Schedule E where it is in general deducted as it accrues (and, since 1973, including liability to higher rate as well as basic rate tax). It could therefore be argued that there are strong equity grounds, most especially in an inflationary age, for giving priority to bringing such Schedule D incomes on to a current year basis for tax purposes. This would in fact revive the same relative position as used to be the case, in that Schedule E income tax was also on a preceding year basis before World War II.

From the administrative angle, there is an enormous distinction between Schedule D assessments and Schedule E assessments. The bulk of the latter do not require an annual return, let alone annual assessments, whereas the former require close periodical scrutiny. And the numbers involved are very much less in the former than in the latter case (2.4 million assessments against 25 million employments). It would therefore seem far more sensible to gain experience of the operation of any self-assessment system in relation to a relatively small number of taxpayers used[27] to having detailed negotiations with the tax authorities.

So on both equity and administration grounds, there are arguments for

---

[25] Cf. Chapter III, Appendix III–1.

[26] The analogy here may not hold fully, as it seems to have been envisaged that that set of changes would take place *before*, rather than *after*, extensive computerisation.

[27] At least via their accountants. It is estimated that some three-quarters of Schedule D taxpayers use the services of professional advisers.

making changes in the arrangements for Schedule D Cases I and II well in advance of Schedule E.

This is the main distinction but there are also a number of others to consider. First, there are the remaining types of Schedule D incomes: it seems best to group these along with Cases I and II rather than think of applying self-assessment to them at a later date. This raises one awkwardness which must be faced: at the moment untaxed interest income may be coded out of Schedule E or it may form part of a Schedule D assessment. We have some discussion later about whittling down the area of untaxed interest income but to the extent that it remains it seems to us best not to interfere with existing arrangements. If untaxed interest income is assessed under Schedule D, it would move over to a current year basis along with other Schedule D income; if it is coded out of Schedule E income, that arrangement should stay until Schedule E self-assessment begins to operate, when the need for the difference in treatment would disappear.

Then we have to consider the small number of assessments under Schedules A, B, C and F. As we have seen,[28] delays in tax payment differ somewhat under these headings. But there seems to be no real argument why they should not all be taxed on a current year basis on the same footing as Schedule D. No doubt there could be arguments of detail for slightly differing treatment but they would have to be much more weighty than they seem to carry conviction.

Capital gains raise issues of a somewhat different character whether we look at the equity or administration aspects. In this case, a separate tax from income tax, there does seem to be a case for a separate timetable and our view is that self-assessment should apply in this case after the changeover for Schedule D income and the like but before that for Schedule E. Finally, we should make it explicit that when referring to Schedule E changes we have in mind not just that income currently withheld under PAYE but also other categories such as income earned abroad by UK domiciled people, earnings in the UK or remitted to the UK by people resident but not domiciled here, income taxed by direct collection and so on.

Our conclusion is therefore that it would be totally unrealistic to envisage a switch to self-assessment in one gigantic leap and that the most promising order of procedure would be to start with Schedule D (along with A, B, C and F), then Capital Gains Tax and finally Schedule E. We shall now explore the problems which are more specific to each of these stages in some detail, leaving those which are more or less common to all until Chapter VI.

5 Schedule D

It must be understood throughout this section that we are envisaging changes which would apply to personal tax under Schedules A, B, C and F as well as D. Where there are specific points to note about the differences between these Schedules, we shall endeavour to single them out.

---

[28] Cf. Chapter IV, p. 137.

As we have seen, there is a general equity argument for bringing the taxation of Schedule D, Cases I and II, on to a current year basis but some more detailed points need to be made in this connection. The first is that there can be distinctions between different categories of Schedule D income recipients, even though they may be taxable under the same Case. Thus it was argued not long ago in the columns of *The Financial Times*[29] that partnerships could maximise the tax advantages to be gained from the opening and closing rules for Schedule D assessments[30] by suitable re-formation at appropriate times—opportunities which would not be open to sole traders.

A second question is whether a shift to a current year basis might not introduce greater inequity in other respects than at present. The most important comparison here is with the taxation of companies. Whilst some Corporation Tax will no doubt be paid over in future well after the profits on which it is based have accrued, the proviso that ACT must be paid along with dividends effectively means that a substantial slice (and at the time of writing an overwhelming proportion) of Corporation Tax will be paid more or less concurrently with profits. It would therefore seem that this standard of comparison should not worry us unduly.

Another point in equity is the proposition, sedulously fostered over the last year or two, that the income tax advantages of Schedule D are offset by 'excessive' National Insurance contributions.[31] We do not intend to enter into the details of this charge but simply re-iterate that, if there is any substance in it, the obvious remedy is to change the National Insurance basis rather than try to make amends by perpetuating inequities in the income tax system. Compensation for inequity in one tax by legislating for offsetting inequities in another is a certain way of propagating a luxuriant crop of anomalies.

The general aim in recasting the basis for assessment under Schedule D and the like is to tax people on a current year basis and to collect instalments of tax in the course of the year. At the moment, we have a patchwork system, with Schedule D Cases I and II being taxed in January and July of the calendar year following the fiscal year in which income is earned, with Schedule D Case III being taxed in the January following only, and with Schedule A, for instance, being a payment in January, nominally on a current year basis, but *de facto* on a preceding year basis with any slack being taken up at the end of the tax year.[32]

If provisional instalments of tax are to be paid, one has to decide how

[29] *The Financial Times* 29/3/76. The essence of the argument was that the use of the first year's results for the first three assessments could be a means of deferring substantial tax liabilities. See also *The Financial Times* 21/3/76, 24/5/76 and 1/6/76 for expansion and qualification of the argument. There were 340,000 Schedule D Cases I and II partnerships in 1971 compared with 1.9 million sole traders.

[30] Cf. Chapter II, p. 33.

[31] See Chapter IV, pp. 137 and 152.

[32] The January instalment can be adjusted downwards in special cases such as when current year rents can be shown to be less than the preceding year figure.

frequently and on what dates. Practice abroad differs as the following tabulation shows:

Six times a year	—	Sweden
Four times a year	—	Australia, Canada, USA
Twice a year	—	Japan, New Zealand, South Africa.

One can see readily enough that in collecting provisional tax on account a balance has to be struck between the additional administrative costs of making more frequent payments and the ease and convenience of paying tax in smaller sums.

On balance, it would seem that there is a good deal to be said for quarterly instalments as a compromise between the various possibilities, especially as the UK is accustomed to quarterly payments, e.g. gas, electricity, telephone. Given that we already use 1 January and 1 July[33] as dates for Schedule D it would obviously make sense to stick to these. With 1 April as approximating to the end of the tax year, the only really new date to appear in the tax calendar would be 1 October.

If instalments of tax are to be paid on each of these dates, what should be the basis of the instalment and how should it relate to the final liability at the end of the tax year? Let us clear one minor point out of the way first. In so far as a man has a very small Schedule D assessment, it would obviously not be sensible to insist on quarterly payments. Therefore one needs a *de minimis* provision whereby a man with a taxable income of say, less than £500[34] per annum is not called upon to pay instalments of tax. The precise figure for any such cut-off is a matter for discussion but it might be noted that in 1971 765,000 Schedule D Cases I and II assessments were in respect of incomes of less than £500 p.a. and 1.2 million for incomes of less than £1,000 p.a.[35]

As we have seen,[36] there are considerable differences between countries in formulating the basis for provisional tax. The most sensible course to take would be something like the following. The taxpayer should pay provisional tax on each of 1 July, 1 October, 1 January and 1 April on the basis of one-quarter of the tax due on the *preceding* year's[37] profits *unless* he makes a declaration to the authorities that his position has deteriorated. In that case, he is allowed to pay smaller instalments of provisional tax—and conceivably less in, say, October than in July—but in the foreknowledge that if his provisional payments turn out to be less than, say 80 per cent of his final liability some interest penalty will be exacted.[38] The aim should be for final settlement of a man's tax position for a fiscal year on the first quarterly date after the end

---

33 The date of 6 July for the payment of higher-rate tax on dividends etc. is near enough to 1 July to be classified with it.

34 Grossed up appropriately if tax is deducted at source or if some equivalent procedure is adopted, e.g. as with dividends.

35 *Inland Revenue Statistics* 1975 (HMSO, 1976).

36 See Chapter III, p. 67.

37 It might well be necessary to work towards a situation where accounting years coincided with fiscal years.

38 Subject to a *de minimis* provision, e.g. where the tax shortfall was less than £x.

of that year, i.e. 1 July, assuming that we retain the dates of the present fiscal year.[39] Such an aim brings us face-to-face with a major contrast between the UK and North America. In the USA, it really does seem to be the case that many businesses can prepare their accounts and be in a position to settle their tax liabilities by 15 April, i.e. three-and-a-half months after the end of the tax year. In the UK, the position seems to be that one-half at most of Schedule D accounts are ready by 1 January of the year after the profits are made. It is difficult to know what is cause and effect here—whether an official tradition of not insisting on early completion of accounts has led to this state of affairs, for instance. It would be unrealistic to think that one could move to a North American situation immediately but at the same time it would be highly desirable that some penalty system (perhaps increasing over time) should be introduced for delay in account preparation and rendering.

Where profits etc. increase over time, this system would obviously still confer advantages over other kinds of income in the timing of tax payments and there might be a long run case for somewhat stricter provisions on instalment payments. However, our proposals would represent a set of major changes compared to the present position and would seem to go as far as is desirable for some time to come.

One general consequence of these proposals can be noted now: the need for the special opening and closing provisions on the taxation of profits would disappear and so the long-standing anomaly that the total amount of income brought to tax over the life of an enterprise does not necessarily equal the total amount of income earned over that period would vanish.[40,41] In the case of closures by businesses set up before the new system comes into being, one would have to decide whether the Inland Revenue should continue to have the option to charge tax on a current or preceding year basis in respect of the two years before closing down. The natural course would be to say that the current basis should be the only basis but there may be special reasons why there should be reserve powers.

Many problems would arise in setting up a system of taxation on these lines and it is incumbent on us to face them.

There is a major once-for-all problem: whether or not to have 'forgiveness'.

---

39 We recognise that there are arguments for changing to a calendar year basis (both EEC harmonisation arguments and those relating to the compression of activities, between 6 April and the starting of the main holiday season) but we do not explore the implications here.

40 Cf. P. G. Whiteman and D. G. Milne, *Whiteman and Wheatcroft on Income Tax* (Sweet and Maxwell 1976, p. 317) 'a trader will rarely pay tax on his actual profits and cannot do so if his trade continued for longer than six years of assessment'.

41 Another curious feature of the present system is that the periods taken for the assessment of profits for sole traders and partners do not necessarily correspond to those for the computation for capital allowances. 'There are rules (in Section 72(2) Capital Allowances Act 1968) dealing with these special cases which ensure that for capital allowances purposes every period during which the trade was in existence enters into the basis period for one year of assessment and one year of assessment only'. *Capital Allowances on Machinery and Plant,* (Inland Revenue Leaflet C.A.1., May 1973) para. 39. See also Whiteman and Milne, *op. cit.,* p. 462.

There are precedents here pointing in opposite directions. When PAYE was introduced in 1944, tax outstanding on preceding year income was forgiven, except in the case of civil servants; when surtax was incorporated into the new unified income tax in 1973, outstanding liabilities were not forgiven but some spreading provisions were allowed.[42] However, the Schedule D case is not identical and it is important to be clear about what is at stake. If the level of profits and the tax rate were the same year after year there would be no differences in annual liability between a current year and a preceding year basis.[43] In so far as business profits are higher in the first year of operation of the new system than they were in the year preceding, the Revenue collects more tax in present value terms (assuming the same tax rate) than it would have done.[44] So Revenue difficulties arise only in the case of those businesses with a fall in profits at the time of changeover, in that tax collected on the new current year basis will be less than on the old preceding year basis.

To minimise temptation to manipulate profit levels between years, it might well be necessary in the first year of operation of the new system to stipulate that the level of profits subject to tax would be taken to be not less than that ruling in the preceding year, subject to various *de minimis* and hardship provisions. But this seems to be the maximum degree of restriction which is needed.

We noted earlier that there would have to be an interim period during which the treatment of untaxed interest under Schedule D would be different from that under Schedule E, i.e. the former paying provisional tax on a quarterly basis, the latter being coded out. Ultimately, one would aim at a unified treatment of this source of income but a division on these lines initially would seem to be the best temporary solution.

We now come to those problems of a more permanent nature. The first is the basis on which individuals should pay their various tax instalments. Obviously, the Inland Revenue could issue instructions about the allowances which could be deducted in computing taxable income. In so far as any one individual has both Schedule E income and Schedule D (or similar) income this would in fact be an appropriate method, so long as coding notices incorporating a proportion of the allowances[45] continue to be issued for the former. It would presumably be possible without too much difficulty to give instructions (or at any rate guidance) to the taxpayer about the remainder of the allowances which can be offset against Schedule D income and also about the appropriate

[42] One-third of tax due on earned income or on interest (without tax deduction at source) received in 1972/73 was payable in January 1974, one-third in January 1975 and one-third in January 1976.

[43] There would be a different time-distribution of payments *within* a year. It must also be remembered that tax payments in any one fiscal year are partly in respect of profits of the previous year and partly in respect of the year before that.

[44] Both because the date for final settlement is brought forward and because of the quarterly instalment system. There are consequential cash-flow problems for business which would need to be taken into account.

[45] In essentially the same way as at present.

rates or tables on which self-assessment should be based (including investment income surcharge, if appropriate). In the long run, once Schedule E came on to a self-assessment and self-coding basis this would no longer apply; but, *ipso facto,* there would be no special problem for the Schedule D component of income in that common self-coding principles could then apply to both Schedule D and Schedule E. One could then also allow over-withholding under Schedule E as a means of meeting tax payments on Schedule D income.

This still leaves us with the pure Schedule D type case. There would seem to be no point in introducing a system of official coding when this has not been necessary in the past. It follows that very clear instructions about deductible allowances, the application of higher rate tax and investment income surcharge would be necessary in order to enable people to make the necessary calculations of provisional tax. At the end of the year, even more explicit instructions would be needed with, say, guidance from the Revenue about the implications of the tax provisionally remitted e.g. 'You have claimed £2,000 p.a. in allowances: are you quite sure that your family circumstances justify this, remembering that the personal allowance for a husband and wife is £Y, the retirement annuity relief provisions are so and so etc.': or 'You have calculated so much tax on taxable income at Y per cent and so much at Z per cent; Y per cent applies to the range of annual income up to £a and Z per cent to the range from £a+1 to £b. Does your income really correspond to this?' It is to be hoped that one would be able to dispense with such assistance in the vast majority of cases before very long, but something on these lines might well be necessary in the short run.

Very careful thought will need to be given to a number of other aspects of coding, assessment and collection practices. The most important can be grouped under the following headings:

Use of National Insurance numbers
The layout of tax return forms and the guidance notes to taxpayers
The contacts between taxpayers and tax authorities
Simplification of allowances and tax rate structure
Checking and verification of tax returns
Systems of penalties and direct enforcement
Appeal procedures.

However, these common threads, as we shall call them, are not peculiar to Schedule D and the like and so we propose to leave their detailed discussion until we have looked at self-assessment in relation to capital gains tax and Schedule E. We shall then examine all these matters in considerable detail.[46]

There is one particular point to make at this stage. Whereas Schedule E taxpayers under PAYE have been identified by National Insurance numbers since 1961 when graduated state pension deductions were introduced,[47] this

---

[46] Cf. Chapter VI, *passim.*
[47] See Sir A. Johnston, *op. cit.,* p. 99

has not been so for Schedule D taxpayers. If, as is suggested later,[48] the use of national insurance or analogous numbers would be central to the efficient operation of a self-assessment system, this means that every Schedule D taxpayer would need to be identified by such a number. This would presumably not present any problem for those covered by National Insurance, and especially those paying Class IV contributions. But there would be various other categories, e.g. a widow living on investment income who had never worked in this country or someone who retires to this country after working abroad. It would obviously be necessary for anyone in such a category to apply for a national insurance number. This would, of course, in no way confer national insurance benefits as an automatic result. Similarly, partnerships and trustees would also need to be granted numbers for the same purpose. No doubt these propositions will stimulate some self-appointed defenders of the liberty of the subject to rush to the barricades; but before, or at any rate whilst, doing so, they might reflect that this is standard practice in the USA and Canada.[49]

6 Capital Gains Tax

Capital gains tax raises rather particular problems in that, although a separate tax in law, it is linked to income tax rates.[50] It is paid alongside another tax, capital transfer tax, in the case of *inter-vivos* gifts, with the latter tax being essentially on a self-assessment basis. And it applies to corporations as well as individuals.

At the moment, tax on net capital gains in a given tax year is due to be paid in July of the year following (or 30 days after making the assessment, if that is later) reflecting an average lag of some 9–10 months between the realisation of gains and the payment of tax. In practice, there is some evidence that assessments tend to lag behind the official date. The first question when one contemplates self-assessment is how far tax payments should be brought forward in time. One solution could be to say that individuals should assess themselves at the end of the tax year and send a remittance to the Revenue when transmitting their records of purchases and sales during the year just ended. The more radical alternative would be to insist on quarterly payments of tax in respect of net gains realised in that quarter. On the whole, it may be best to plump for the former alternative—for several reasons. One is that in the short run self-assessment would not apply to Schedule E income; a second is that a contrast between individual and Corporation capital gains might appear to open up if one subjected the former to a quarterly system; a third objection is that there might well be complications with capital losses if one had a system

[48] Cf. Chapter VI, pp. 197–8.

[49] If it is thought inappropriate to label such numbers as national insurance numbers when issued to categories of people such as those mentioned, the term 'income tax numbers' could be used, provided the sequence were the same.

[50] In that half the net gains in a year and, if such gains exceed £5,000, all gains in excess of £5,000 are added to an individual's income, and treated as investment income to determine the appropriate tax rate (subject to the overriding maximum of a 30% rate).

of this sort in that a gain would be taxable more or less as soon as realised whilst a loss would not attract relief until sufficient gains had been made, assuming no carrying back provisions. The longer the period allowed, the less likely is it that one has to carry capital losses forward.

One can readily see that taxpayers would experience difficulties in computing their capital gains tax liabilities. The first source of difficulty might well be the calculation of gains or losses, e.g. because the base was not known with certainty or because of bonus or rights issues between acquisition and sale. The second would be the records needed to carry forward unrelieved losses. The third could be the appropriate tax rate, i.e. (in 1976 figures) 17.5 per cent, 30 per cent or some intervening rate. There are many ways of dealing with such difficulties but perhaps the best one would be to allow people a small refund of tax due if they both complete the return correctly and send in the right amount of tax. This would seem to cater justly for all cases—those who employ accountants for such a purpose, those who are prepared to take the trouble to gather the information and make the necessary computation themselves and those who neither seek expert help nor are capable of doing the exercise correctly themselves.

Clearly capital gains taxation is not an easy nut to crack in the context of self-assessment and one can understand the feelings that it should remain on a Revenue-assessing basis. But various recent developments (the 1972 crediting arrangements for unit trusts and investment trusts, the 1975 increase to £1,000 in the size of exempt proceeds from disposals and the supersession in 1976 of Development Gains Tax by Development Land Tax) have all narrowed the range of transactions attracting capital gains tax. So it is to that extent easier. Finally, it is obviously possible that at some stage there may be a restoration of the short/long distinction, with short-term gains being taxable at the individual's marginal income tax rate. If all other income to which the income tax rate structure applies is being switched to a self-assessment basis, it would be curious, to say the least, not to do the same for such capital gains. On the other hand, if indexation of gains were introduced at any time this would make the task of self-assessment even more difficult.

There are many remaining matters of administrative practice but as these are largely common to all the different types of income, we defer consideration of them for the time being. Just one observation is called for now. Whereas simplification of allowances is extremely important for Schedule E, and only a little less so for Schedule D, it is of no consequence in the capital gains tax case. This section of the common threads discussion is irrelevant to this particular type of income.

7 Schedule E

We must start by reminding ourselves that the case for self-assessment in this general area is very different from that for Schedule D and Capital Gains Tax. We are no longer primarily concerned with matters of broad equity between different classes of tax payers. The arguments now centre on the appropriate amount of public sector administration of income tax; the associated question of the degree of general understanding of the tax system; the possible abandonment of the long basic rate and its replacement by a more smoothly graduated structure, and the closer integration of the income tax and social security systems.

Distinctions can be drawn between different categories of tax payers covered by this general heading and it is a matter for debate whether all of these should come under a self-assessment system or, even if it is agreed that they should all do so, whether some groups should be included earlier than others.

The main categories are as follows:

Those covered by PAYE (25 million employments, about 19 million taxpayers) and those paying by direct collection (thought to be about 200,000). It should be noted that some people may be in both categories.

Those making annual returns under PAYE (about 50 per cent, after allowing for those called on to do so because of job changes etc.) and those not doing so (50 per cent).

Those paying basic rate tax only (about 19 million) and those paying higher rate tax as well (1.3 million).

Those taxpayer units with more than one job (and this group can in turn be divided into cases where one individual has more than one Schedule E type employment and those where husband and wife each work but without separate taxation of earnings).

National Insurance beneficiaries and others.

Directors and others.

Those entitled to Age Allowance and others.

We debated whether there was a case in principle for excluding any of these categories from the scope of self-assessment but came to the conclusion that it was better to include all of them but to modify the application of self-assessment principles in some cases,[51] at any rate in the initial stages. If coverage were less than complete one would have enormous and unacceptable complications if, for instance, a particular individual might be within the scope of self-assessment in one year but not in another.

The application of self-assessment to employees and the like has three main features: *coding, withholding* and *end-year requirements.* We shall discuss each of these in detail.

Coding

As far as *coding* is concerned, there are two main issues: what kinds of allowances (or credits) should be admitted pay period by pay period and what should be left to the end of the year? And what degree of reliance should be placed on self-coding?

[51] e.g. in the case of some types of income, such as that received from employment abroad by people domiciled and resident in the UK, one might well need a quarterly instalment system on Schedule D lines.

On the range of allowances to be given, one has to strike a balance between simplicity of operation and understanding (but involving a certain amount of inaccuracy) and comprehensiveness (but at the sacrifice of simplicity). To some extent, this conflict can be resolved by taking various items out of income tax purview altogether. Thus, child allowances, family allowances and family allowance deductions are to go between 1977 and 1979 and life assurance premium relief in 1979. This process should be pushed further e.g. by changes in the system of paying mortgage interest and by extending the principle of deduction in respect of interest payments.[52] There are also further possibilities of incorporating various types of relief (e.g. professional subscriptions) under a system of standard deduction and of rationalising some of the miscellaneous personal reliefs, such as the dependant relative allowance,[53] though no doubt one would still be left as at present with formidable problems of the appropriate level of expenses allowable e.g. car expenses for salesmen. These changes, actual or potential, would certainly help to resolve this conflict. Nevertheless, a decision still has to be taken on the principle. The answer would seem to turn on the degree of complexity which it is reasonable to expect people to grasp for self-coding purposes. The experience of other countries is relevant here. In the USA the only choice is the number of exemptions claimed, each exemption being of the same value; but it is up to the individual to form his own judgement about the appropriate number to claim, bearing in mind his various sources of income, his deductible expenses and so on. In Canada, withholding exemptions take account of the employee's marital status, the number of dependants and the income of his dependants but retirement savings deductions, for instance, are taken into account only at the end-year settlement. And in Australia, although only some features of self-assessment apply to employee incomes, we find the same general principle of leaving some deductions to the end of the year. On this basis, the right answer in general principle would be to confine the list of allowances for self-coding purposes to purely personal ones (plus standard deduction, if any) coupled with a rather strong expectation that some rationalisation here may be possible.

Now we come to the operation of a self-assessment coding system. For reasons set out earlier[54] we are not convinced that the 1971 experiment showed that this idea is foredoomed to failure in this country; the long-term objective must be to move to something like the US system. Nevertheless, it is emphatically not something which can be introduced for everyone overnight. The following elements would seem to add up to the sort of programme which is

---

[52] As envisaged in the original Tax-Credit Green Paper in 1972 (Cmnd. 5116, *op. cit.*).

[53] It should be remembered that there has already been some movement in this direction in recent years e.g. the abolition of earned income relief and small income relief and some rationalisation of age concessions. The Select Committee on Tax-Credit (*Report, op. cit.*, HC 341–I paras. 112–113) also had observations to make on this subject. Finally the possibilities of some changes (e.g. deduction of tax at source on bank interest) would depend on whether one had something like a universal tax-credit arrangement with everyone paying tax on the whole of his income.

[54] See Chapter IV, Appendix IV–1.

desirable:

(a) *General form of self-coding:* Employers would have a stock of self-coding forms and it would be incumbent on the employee to register the level of allowances (or credits) he wishes to claim. If no such information were given to the employer, the minimum level of allowance would apply.[55] The employer would then continue to operate on this basis until informed otherwise so that, for instance, he would carry the level of allowances prevailing in one fiscal year through to the next one, if there is no information to the contrary. One natural time for a taxpayer to change any such claims would be when he completes his annual tax return, this being the annual opportunity for the Revenue to inform taxpayers of their rightful claims. The precise way in which the taxpayer communicates his claim to this employer is one of some delicacy. Obviously, some employees may not wish to reveal their exact marital status; on the other hand, one of the snags in the 1971 experiment was the inability of the taxpayer to translate the money value of allowances due to him into coding units. What is needed ideally is a translation process which is simpler, whilst avoiding a situation where the employee's family circumstances are only too transparent to his employer. The Canadian system (form TD1) which provides for a simple transformation of total exemptions in dollars into net claim codes, along with very clear instructions may well be helpful in formulating a suitable translation process.[56]

(b) *Existing taxpayers*: We suggest that these should be divided into two groups: those under 55 and those aged 55 or over on the first day of the fiscal year in which the scheme starts. Those aged 55 or over would continue to receive coding notices from the Revenue in the same general way as at present, albeit with a simplified and restricted range of entries. They would not at any stage, however long they lived, be required to code themselves. Those under 55 would be required to start self-coding immediately and would continue to do so even after retirement. Nevertheless, some sort of help would no doubt be required by many in the initial stages.

One way of arranging this might be to say that those who code themselves and also complete their annual returns without recourse to the authorities for help should receive a discount on their tax bill at the end of each of say the first five years e.g. a claim would be made on the tax

---

[55] The employers' organisations expressed opposition to the idea of coding notices coming to them from employees rather than from the Revenue. Cf. HC 341–II and 341 III *op. cit.* pp. 281 and 438; and p. 54. But as we saw in Chapter IV, p. 141 the objection was primarily to a tripartite system involving the Revenue, employees and employers rather than to one involving the latter two parties only. And in any event it still remains to be explained why a system which works for 80 million Americans and 10 million Canadians cannot be applied to 25 million Britons.

[56] e.g. for 1975, the entry would have been for tax deduction under Code 1 if the net total of exemptions claimed was in the range $1,878–$1,981; Code 2 if $1,982–2,201; Code 3 if $2.202–$2,441 and so on, the total number of codes (including that for complete exemption) being 15.

return for a refund of, say, £5–£10 and this would be part of the general settlement after the end of the year. Perhaps one might also consider an initial settling-in year whereby official help was available for all without this disguised element of charge.[57] We select age 55 as being below retirement age for the vast majority of people—sufficiently below for most people to learn the tricks of the self-coding trade before retirement. If people choose to under-declare their age, they would then be caught for self-assessment and so that might be some inducement to veracity. If the tendency were the other way, more people would be in the *status quo* camp for coding purposes, but they would also run into trouble later.[58] One's guess would be that the general bias is more likely to be under- rather than over-declaration. If it is judged impracticable to rely on taxpayer declaration of ages, then one might have to think of allowing everyone ineligible for Age Allowance to opt for Revenue coding and assessment (at the sacrifice of the discount) for a rather longer period than the five years proposed above (ten years perhaps). But this is clearly a less satisfactory alternative.

(c) *New taxpayers*: The Inland Revenue already issues a leaflet to those paying tax for the first time, IR2. We see no reason why such people should not code themselves from the beginning, irrespective of whether they are entering the labour force direct from school or college or whether they are immigrants etc. provided that they have not already reached age 55. Such people are likely to have fairly simple tax affairs for which self-assessment would be entirely appropriate.

Withholding

As we have argued on a number of occasions,[59] a non-cumulative withholding system and self-assessment go hand in hand. This would take some time to bring into operation (e.g. the tax-credit scheme was to have taken some five years and it would appear that the non-cumulative aspect of it was the principal reason) but that is no reason at all for not considering the details and their implications. It would clearly have to be a system (like that in the USA)[60] which allows for withholding at different marginal tax rates, depending on circumstances. Nevertheless, the expectation must be that a large number of taxpayers would receive refunds after the end of the tax year—though not, as at present, during the tax year if unemployed, or sick or on strike. It would also be possible to tax short-term national insurance benefits, at least at some 'standard' rate and so this would have far-reaching implications for social security arrangements. Some of the paraphernalia involved in P.45s could go,

[57] Another variant might be to increase the rate of discount over the years if too many people applied to the Revenue for help.

[58] e.g. a man aged 53 declaring himself to be 57 would be found out eight years later when it became clear that he was not yet entitled to Age Allowance.

[59] Cf. Chapter IV, p. 131.

[60] Cf. Chapter III, p. 63.

there being no need for an employer to have a continuous record of earnings throughout the year for people not continuously in his employment nor for the Revenue to keep track of every movement of every employee throughout the year and to shift files from district to district accordingly.

One or two other consequences of this change in the withholding system need to be noticed. The first point is that the catching-up process inherent in the cumulative system would go. Thus if an individual is slow about telling his employer that he has married, the weeks in which tax continues to be deducted as if he were single will only be compensated for *after* the end of the tax year as distinct from *later* in the tax year. Similarly, suppose the government increases the level of annual allowances in month 2 of the tax year but reduces it to the original amount in month 11. The logic of the cumulative system is that it should in principle (even if in practice this would be very difficult)[61] extract sufficient tax in the remainder of the fiscal year to ensure that the taxpayer's total tax bill over the year would be the same as if the two changes in allowances had never been made. The non-cumulative system could perfectly logically allow the taxpayer to keep the benefits of the increases in allowances for the period they were in being.[62]

End-Year Requirements[63]

When we come to the *end of the tax year,* the major change would be the need for *everyone* to make a tax return, as distinct from only about 50 per cent. This would obviously require a major educational effort and a great deal of propaganda (not to mince words) about the need to meet the filing deadline, as well as the temporary discount for accuracy suggested above. As far as the supply of return forms is concerned the sensible kind of procedure would be for each tax district to supply each taxpayer on its books with the return form thought to be most appropriate[64] but to encourage anyone who wishes to do so to obtain another[65] form from his nearest tax office. We deal later[66] with the whole subject of form design and the layout and format of instructions to be issued to the taxpayer. All we need do here is to echo the title of the original pamphlet issued in 1799 to explain the new Act[67]

> 'A Plain, Short, and Easy Description of the Different Clauses in the Income Tax, so as to Render it familiar to the Meanest Capacity.'

We also deal later with the subject of penalties for inadequate withholding (whether the fault of the employee or employer), late filing, late payment of

---

61 This difficulty is recognised in the normal Revenue practice of switching from a cumulative to a non-cumulative system of deduction when it becomes known in the course of a year that a man has been paying too little tax (e.g. because the allowances to which he is entitled are reduced).

62 The same benefits would have to be given to Schedule D taxpayers too.

63 This subject will be explored more intensively in Chapter VI.

64 Cf. Chapter VI, p. 185 for further discussion.

65 More generally, there might well be a case for a form which allows the taxpayer to keep an exact duplicate record of his return. See Chapter III, Appendix III–2.

66 Cf. Chapter VI, p. 183 *et. seq.*

67 As quoted in Johnston, *op. cit.,* p. 54.

residual tax[68] and so on.

As far as non-official help to the taxpayer goes, there are two points to make. One is that there would have to be a great improvement in the speed of employer performance in telling employees of total pay and total tax deducted whilst in their employment. In the case of people who stay with one employer throughout the year this is fairly straightforward. In the case of those who change jobs, it would obviously be necessary for them to have as many pieces of information as the number of jobs held (except in so far as there were consolidation if more than one spell were spent with the same employer).

Finally, there would no doubt be a boom in the tax-preparer and tax-assistance industry. This too is considered further below.[69]

8 Tax-Credits and Other Matters

Such are the main features of self-assessment for the employee. There are various other ancillary points to note.

The first and most important is: what additional problems arise if one wanted to introduce a system of tax-credits? As we have emphasised earlier, this is logically an entirely separate issue in that one could have self-assessment without tax-credits and tax-credits without self-assessment (though not without non-cumulative withholding).[70] However, let us assume (as we believe to be the case, though we are not concerned to argue it in full here) that there is a strong case for the further integration of the twin combinations of positive and negative taxation, known as the income tax and the social security systems. How would the arguments differ from those which raged in 1972 and 1973 if a self-assessment system were in being?

It may be convenient before proceeding to remind ourselves of the main outlines of the tax-credit proposals as presented some 3–4 years ago.[71] The general principle was that for some 90 per cent of the adult population and their dependants (the principal exclusions being self-employed and very low income earners together with special arrangements for higher rate taxpayers) the main annual personal allowances were to be replaced by a system of weekly tax-credits.

With withholding on a non-cumulative basis, a man would then pay tax at the basic rate on the whole of his income but receive credits against his tax, the amount depending on family circumstances. Normally, tax would exceed credit but in those weeks when it did not (e.g. if sick and away from work)

[68] It would no longer be simple to collect under-payment of tax in one year by coding adjustment in the year following, once coding ceased to be official, unless there were special provision for this in the case of delinquent taxpayers. This leads to the question whether it should be possible to override self-coding by official coding when large sums are underpaid. Cf. Chapter VI, p. 201.

[69] Cf. Chapter VI, p. 191.

[70] Essentially because in the cumulative case the amount of negative tax in any one pay period is a function of total income and total allowances (or credits) since the beginning of the tax year and not just of income and allowances (or credits) in a single pay period.

[71] Cf. Chapter II, p. 47 for details, and Chapter VI, p. 195 for further discussion.

the credit would then be paid out for the relevant amount. It was expressly provided that national insurance beneficiaries, both long, and short-term, would be within the scheme and it was proposed to resuscitate the original intention of taxing short-term as well as long-term benefits in such cases.

There are several important respects in which the scenario would differ if self-assessment were in being. The first is that the constraint on the earlier proposals was that the full application of the system would in effect have been confined to people in the basic rate income tax band and this in turn meant that there was a high premium on maintaining the width of this band in real and not just in nominal terms. The essence of the proposals was that the major advantage of the cumulative system of withholding (i.e. that total tax withheld over the year is exactly right for most people) would not be lost by transferring to a non-cumulative system which allowed negative taxes to be paid in periods when income fell substantially. Provided that there was only one tax rate which was relevant for most people, the number of end-year adjustments could be kept to a minimum. This constraint would no longer apply to anything like the same extent with self-coding and self-assessment, in that end-year repayments would be a normal state of affairs. The administrative necessity to retain a broad basic rate band would no longer be there in that Revenue manpower savings at other points should more than suffice to take on any additional work of repayments; so the original necessity to exclude low and high income earners from the scheme would no longer remain. Moreover, the possibility of a different graduation of the rate structure would immediately open up opportunities[72] for many different patterns of re-distribution (e.g. whether to concentrate relief at the bottom end of the scale or not) and so cut the ground from under the feet of those who so vociferously claimed that the tax-credit scheme was a middle-class ramp.[73]

The second proposition is in a sense the reverse side of the first: in the same way as it can be argued that self-assessment would facilitate the introduction of tax-credits, so would the latter help the former. This would be so in that negative tax payments during the year when sick or unemployed etc. would obviously cut down the amounts needed in end-year repayments. This would have advantages in equity, in that sick people would get the benefits when off-work and not just at the end of the year; but at the same time the amounts paid would be related to the man's circumstances in that week and not as now,

[72] Subject to contraints on the total revenue needed from income tax. If, for instance, one takes the line that the present revenue total is sacrosanct and that neither basic rate nor higher rates should be increased, it follows automatically that there is no possibility of introducing lower than basic rates for lower paid people. Even small reduced rate concessions can be costly in revenue terms given the configuration of income distribution in this country. These points were very clearly made in the Inland Revenue evidence to the Layfield Committee.

[73] There would also be great advantages in having a system of tax-credits which was near-universal in its coverage. From an equity viewpoint, every one would have some income as of right; from an efficiency viewpoint, poverty surtax problems would be less. Poverty identification would also be easier in the long run (e.g. N. Barr and J. Roper 'Tax-Credits: An Optimistic Appraisal', *Three Banks Review,* March 1974).

to the irrelevant circumstances of his position in previous weeks or to coding items which do not reflect purely personal allowances. It would also have administrative advantages in that the number and amount of end-year repayments would be reduced.

A third point is that the original scheme excluded self-employed people, on the grounds that they paid tax half-yearly in arrears and so, it was argued,[74] it would be inappropriate to pay out weekly credits as income was earned. Our self-assessment proposals would, however, put taxation of such people on to something much more nearly approaching a current basis and would also involve quarterly tax instalments. This would therefore remove this obstacle to their incorporation into such a scheme, although obviously the details of its application to them might need to differ from those relating to employees.[75] It is worth noting that there was a hint about self-assessment for self-employed people in the Green Paper itself.[76]

Some of the controversies surrounding the Green Paper will sort themselves out in the not too distant future, e.g. treatment of children and life assurance premia. However, there were plenty of others which are still to be resolved such as the treatment of married women's earnings, the extension of the principle of deduction of income tax at source from interest income and so on. And no doubt, the developments in the social security field such as the proliferation of different types of benefits for industrial injury in recent years have added to the complications of integration with the income tax system whilst at the same time making integration even more necessary. However, these would be there whether or not there were a move to self-assessment and so are not of the same prime concern to us here as those which are intertwined with self-assessment principles.

As with Schedule D and Capital Gains Tax, there are a number of general matters which we postpone for later discussion but we should refer now to those which are of the most relevance in the Schedule E case. One is the very great importance of the simplification of allowances so that they can be 'familiar to the meanest capacity', to use eighteenth century language again. If this cannot go very far, one would have to opt for the second-best alternative of admitting only a restricted range of allowances into the self-coding procedure. A second is to emphasise the positive role of the over-deductions likely to occur under the non-cumulative system of withholding. This is the great sanction on people to submit their returns quickly at the end of the year; it is invaluable in the case of people who for one reason or another are leaving the country after working here;[77] and it is immensely useful as an indirect, if rough and ready, means of compensating for the non-collection of tax on certain

74 *Proposals for a Tax-Credit System* (Cmnd. 5116, *op. cit.*) para. 93.
75 A further difficulty is that the incentive to understate income would be increased if the whole of it, and not just the excess over personal allowances, were the basis for tax.
76 Cmnd. 5116, *op. cit.*, para. 71.
77 This subject is considered further below, Cf. Chapter VI, p. 201.

forms of interest income and the like. So although the role of tax-credits in minimising the number and amount of end-year repayments is to be welcomed in 'straightforward' cases, it is indispensable that tax should be over-withheld in others.

A final question is the implications of self-assessment for local (or, for that matter, Scottish or Welsh) income tax. As this subject is dealt with in other chapters[78] we need do no more here than make the point that self-assessment opens up a possibility of a scheme based on year-end income totals,[79] which cannot be contemplated under our present arrangements. There would be many problems to overcome in any such system, e.g. the notion of lump sum payments to local authorities at the end of the year would be strange to people cocooned in the PAYE tradition.[80] But if anyone throws up his hands in horror at the idea there is a very simple reply; this is common practice in North America where State (or Provincial) income taxes are common and indeed there may, as in New York City, be *three* layers of income tax, Federal, State and Local. The fact that British people were beaten by Americans in one respect in 1776 is no reason whatever why they should be beaten by them in an entirely different respect in 1976.

[78] Chapter II, p. 50 and Chapter VI, p. 195.
[79] *Local Government Finance,* Cmnd. 6453, HMSO, May 1976, p. 196 ff.
[80] It would, of course, be possible to withhold local income taxes on an approximate basis during the tax year.

Chapter VI

Further Aspects of a Self-Assessment System

1 Taxpayer Assistance

Forms

The previous chapter discussed self-assessment as it would apply to specific categories of income. Here we are concerned with broader aspects such as assistance to the taxpayer and enforcement that are much less related to the type of income and the complexity of a man's affairs. The first part of this chapter deals with taxpayer assistance, while enforcement is discussed in section two. The concluding section discusses some administrative implications.

Taxpayer assistance is discussed conveniently under four heads—tax returns and other forms, instructions and explanatory literature issued by the tax authorities, other types of tax advice and simplification of the tax structure. These are discussed in turn.

There are two approaches to the design of tax returns. In the UK currently the P1 return is fairly all-purpose and is completed by the majority of those taxpayers who file a return. This approach may have had its advantages when the great majority of incomes were wages taxed under Schedule E so that relatively few returns were filed. But the number of people with affairs sufficiently complex to require an annual return is increasing steadily; however, many of these cases do not require a return with as wide a coverage as the P1.

The alternative approach[1] used in the USA, Canada and elsewhere, is the 'looseleaf' approach. In this system only those items which virtually *everyone* has to complete are dealt with in their entirety in the basic return. Other more complex matters like business profits or capital gains are calculated on separate attachments and the final figure is then entered as a single item on the main return. The entire return thus consists of the main return form which everyone completes, plus a series of supplementary attachments for those whose affairs

[1] Cf. Chapter III, Appendix III–2.

warrant them. Henceforth we use the word 'return' to refer to the main return, and 'attachment' to refer to the supporting pages (if any) submitted with it.

We favour such a system for the UK, both because of its flexibility, and because it minimises complications for those with simple tax affairs. It should prove possible to design a system under which nearly all those who are currently dealt with entirely by PAYE would have to complete only the main return containing space for the calculation of (1) total income (net of the expenses of earning it) and (2) total income free of tax. From these it is then easy to calculate (3) taxable income and (4) tax due.

A specimen of this type of return is given in Appendix VI–1. The first main section deals with total income, and contains space to enter the various components of income of both husband and wife. It is tempting to consider a breakdown of income into the minimum number of logical categories consistent with adequate documentation of the return. But to aid the transition to self-assessment there is a clear advantage in retaining existing categories. We therefore suggest (somewhat tentatively) ten types of income; these could be revised later, if necessary:

(1) Employment income (Schedule E, Cases I, II and III),
(2) Self-employment income (Schedule D, Cases I and II),
(3) State retirement pension and occupational pensions (Schedule E, general charge),
(4) Dividend income (Schedule F for liability to higher rates of tax),
(5) Interest from government securities (Schedule C),
(6) Interest, annuities (Schedule D, Case III),
(7) Income from property (e.g. furnished lettings), (Schedule D, Case VI),
(8) Income from land and woodlands (Schedules A and B),
(9) Income from abroad (Schedule D, Cases IV and V),
(10) Miscellaneous income (Schedule D, Case VI).

For all sources of income other than earnings under Schedule E and small amounts of interest from banks and building societies, supplementary attachments would have to be filed. For instance, someone with self-employment income would have to complete an additional attachment relating to small businesses, which would itself contain sections for (1) gross business revenue and (2) business expenses (including such matters as the depreciation of capital equipment).[2] The net profit resulting from this calculation would be entered on the main return.

The next section of the new return deals with the calculation of total tax-free income. It contains spaces in which to enter amounts tax-free by virtue of personal allowances (i.e. for self, wife, children, wife's earned income allowance) plus other allowances such as the additional personal allowance and claims for a dependant relative. There would also be provision to enter non-

---

[2] As in Schedule C of the US tax return which is attached to the main (1040) return; a working example is given on pages 36 and 37 of *Tax Guide for Small Business, 1976 Edition,* Publication 334, US Department of the Treasury, Internal Revenue Service.

business deductions such as mortgage interest payments, and superannuation contributions if these were not paid net of tax.

Documentary evidence would have to be supplied of most types of income. Employment earnings would be covered by the equivalent of the current P60 (or several P60s in the case of someone employed by more than one employer during the year). Equivalent documents would have to be issued by payers of interest and dividends. Payers of pensions, too, would be required to issue recipients with an information return giving details of gross pension paid, type of income (e.g. what proportion was capital), tax withheld and social security number. All these would be submitted with the return.

Subtracting total tax-free income from total income calculated earlier yields taxable income; tax due can then simply be read off a table supplied with the return and compared with tax already withheld at source to obtain a figure for net tax liability.

In addition, the main return would include a section to cover the calculation of national insurance contributions due on Schedule E income. This section would be used mainly by those who wished to claim a refund of overpaid National Insurance contributions (e.g. someone with several jobs or paying contributions on both Schedule D and Schedule E income). Contributions on earnings taxed under Schedule D would be calculated on the separate Schedule D attachment. Separate attachments would be submitted also for capital gains, capital transfer tax, and, if appropriate, wealth tax.

Consideration should be given also to the possibility of a very simple, short return for those with simple tax affairs. Such a return exists in the USA where it is used by some 30 per cent of taxpayers, who have only employment earnings plus small amounts of unearned income and who claim the standard deduction. In Canada it has not been found possible to design a short form of sufficient generality to be useful to a large proportion of taxpayers. The main use of such an option in the UK is to those who are currently covered by PAYE and are not assessed annually; it would be usual for those with mainly Schedule E income to file a short return or possibly a standard return with no attachments, while those currently receiving Schedule D assessments would file the standard return with at least one attachment.

A considerable amount of thought has to be devoted to the distribution of such tax packages. Assuming it is possible to design a short form there will be a need for at least two types of package—the short and the standard. Additionally there is a requirement for two entirely separate types of distribution. First, there should be a centralised distribution by mail to each taxpayer of the same type of return and to the same address as was applicable in the previous year. Second, all tax returns and attachments have to be available in tax offices and possibly also in post offices for people who have moved from their previous address and whose return has not been forwarded to them; for those who require a different type of return from the previous year (e.g. someone who filed a short return the previous year, but has since become self-employed and therefore has to file a standard return with a Schedule D (Case I and II) attachment); or simply for those who have lost or spoilt the return they received by post.

Written Instructions

Though largely anecdotal there is plenty of evidence to suggest that many taxpayers find the written guides currently issued by the Inland Revenue complex and hard to follow. Admittedly, no tax structure will be simple but there are many ways in which Inland Revenue literature could be made simpler and clearer than it is. A study by Sandford[3] of individual taxpayers found that an appreciable proportion (39 out of 235) of these who employed a tax adviser gave the complexity of the tax returns as one of their reasons for doing so.

It is clear that self-assessment requires an entirely different attitude by the tax administration towards the taxpayer. When the onus of assessment is on the Inland Revenue, as currently, there is no particular incentive for them to explain to the taxpayer how the tax system operates, beyond giving minimal instructions about the completion of the return. A system of self-assessment will clearly be more successful the greater the degree of taxpayer understanding.

It is far beyond the scope of this study to dream of re-writing the Inland Revenue's instruction and explanatory leaflets. But it is possible to discuss a variety of general improvements which should be made as part of the introduction of self-assessment. The most general point is the question of presentation. Most leaflets currently in use contain rather densely packed small print—even if the words were identical they would be far more effective at conveying information if the spacing were more generous (though this would of necessity increase printing and postal costs). But there is also considerable room for improvement in the wording of the material. The present authors are acutely aware of the difference between the mastery of a given body of material (an intellectual attribute) and the ability to convey that material to others (a teaching attribute). It is one thing to understand something oneself—but to transfer this knowledge to others requires an entirely different skill. It is rare that one person does well on both counts, and Inland Revenue publications might well benefit from the attention of expert *writers,* rather than the highly trained tax experts who have dealt with such matters hitherto.

The 'Tax Return Guide 1976–77' (Form 11P (Ins)) sent out by the Inland Revenue with all related returns is illustrative of the point. One of its main faults is compactness. In writing technical prose such as the drafting of legislation, one of the aims is always to be as concise as possible. But the tax return guide is not and should not be a technical document, but an information or teaching device. To assert that redundancy of words is the essence of good

[3] C. T. Sandford, *The Hidden Costs of Taxation,* Institute for Fiscal Studies, 1973, p. 138. See Chapter III, Appendix III–2.

teaching is probably stretching the point—but it is fair to observe that teaching normally benefits from calculated repetition and less concise formulation.[4]

In paragraph 20 on page 3 we read:

> 'If your pension is from the Irish Republic tax is chargeable on the full amount after deducting annual interest, etc. payable out of it before 6 April 1980 on a debt incurred before 27 March 1974 to a person not resident in the United Kingdom.'

The same information would be conveyed far more clearly thus:

> If your pension is from the Irish Republic you will normally be liable for tax on the full amount. However until 6 April 1980 you may deduct interest payments made out of this income *provided that*
>
> (a) the debt was incurred before 27 March 1974, *and*
>
> (b) the recipient of the interest is not resident in the UK.

In paragraph 33 on page 4:

> 'If you are liable to tax only at the basic rate you will not have to pay any tax on your building society interest. If you are liable at the higher rates or to the investment income surcharge the liability on your building society interest will be calculated on the actual interest "grossed up" at the basic rate e.g.—

Interest received	£65
Plus notional basic rate tax	£35
Higher rate or surcharge calculated on liability	£100

> The notional basic rate tax is however, allowed as a credit against any higher rate tax payable.'

Our suggested version would be as follows:

Building societies have to pay tax on their income, and this tax is regarded as paying in full your liability for tax at the basic (35 per cent) rate on your interest receipts from the building society. So if you pay tax only at the basic rate you will not have to pay any tax on your building society interest. But if you pay tax at one of the higher rates or are liable for the investment income surcharge you will have to pay additional tax calculated in the following way:

Interest received from building society	£65
Basic rate tax paid on your behalf by building society	£35
Gross interest received	£100
Gross tax liability at (say) 50 per cent	£50
Less basic rate tax paid on your behalf by building society	£35
Net additional tax liability	£15

[4] We are not denying that in choosing the wording of such leaflets one treads a delicate balance between being simple and being accurate. We merely question whether current Inland Revenue literature gives the most useful balance.

Thus if your tax rate is 50 per cent the additional tax you pay is £15.

Another example of the benefits of similar treatment can be found in paragraph 69 on page 8 relating to charges to capital gains tax. Giving attention to the wording of tax literature is very much part of US practice, considerable effort being devoted to translating (almost literally) literature used by the general public from the language of tax experts to that of an *average* layman.[5]

In addition to such general points a number of specific techniques have been found to be useful teaching devices in a number of countries (e.g. North America and Sweden).[6] The most important of these is the use of examples. Tax return guides should take a step-by-step approach, starting by listing the documents needed for the preparation of a tax return, and then proceeding methodically through the return with plenty of examples of how to complete each section. At some stage an example of a fully completed return should be given. Features such as 'What's New in 1976?' and a list of the most frequently asked questions (together with answers) have also been found to be useful elsewhere. Sweden goes as far as to publish a cartoon strip about completing a tax return.

It was mentioned earlier that most people who are currently covered entirely by PAYE would file a short return or the standard return with no extra attachments. Particular attention should be devoted to the instructions and examples relating to these returns—for instance, detailed explanations should be given of the various personal allowances and of the rules for deducting expenditure on mortgage interest and superannuation. Separate instructions should be given for the various attachments—in other words the instructions as well as the return should be of the 'looseleaf' sort, so that those with simple tax affairs could concentrate on the carefully designed main instructions and could ignore the more complex and technical instructions dealing with, for instance, depreciation or capital gains.

Other Forms of Tax Advice

ASSISTANCE FROM THE INLAND REVENUE

Quite apart from well designed forms and clearly written instructions all evidence from other countries indicates that taxpayer assistance is one of the major claims on the manpower of the tax administration under a system of self-assessment. In any switch to self-assessment such assistance is of vital importance not only during the transition, but also in the long-run. In the USA in particular, there is admiration for the automaticity of PAYE from the viewpoint of the taxpayer, and some attempts have been made there to devise an 'automatic' short return. Though a case may be made for switching to self-assessment on the grounds that the cost of PAYE is higher than its

[5] We are not advocating the use of slang—simply the use of words in their everyday rather than their technical sense.

[6] See Chapter III, Appendix III–2.

undoubted benefits it is imperative that any system of self-assessment incorporates as many as possible of the advantages of PAYE. Thus considerable effort must be devoted to the ease of the system for the ordinary taxpayer and the amount of help accorded him.

The system of decentralised Inland Revenue offices originated in the idea of local independence; it was also to make it easy for taxpayers to contact their Inspector of Taxes. But this strategy was partially vitiated by the fact that the individual's Tax District is that of his employer and hence the system of easy consultation breaks down for those who are employed by firms with many branches who have only one Tax District. In addition in recent years much London PAYE work has been moved out to the London Provincial offices, in most cases hundreds of miles away. Partly to counteract the consequences, there are now a number of PAYE Enquiry Offices[7] which minimise the problems of dealing with tax returns at a distance. The effectiveness of these offices rests on the fact that some 50 per cent of enquiries can be answered without reference to the taxpayer's file.

Ease of contact with the Inland Revenue is a *sine qua non* for a self-assessment system to operate smoothly. Provision has to be made for taxpayers to contact their Inspector of Taxes easily (a) by telephone, (b) in person and (c) in writing. In the USA the first two are far more important than the third.[8] One might speculate that taxpayers with simple and complicated cases are equally likely to seek advice in person, but in the simple cases currently dealt with by PAYE the use of the telephone is more likely while in more difficult cases, such as Schedule D assessments or capital gains information is more likely to be sought in writing.

Regardless of whether this speculation is accurate it is hard to imagine a system of self-assessment running smoothly without an efficient and cheap (to the taxpayer) telephone enquiry service, as exists in the USA and Canada. Both countries have free services even if the taxpayer has to telephone long-distance. The need for long-distance telephone facilities for taxpayers in the UK would depend in part on whether the tax authorities had a computer system as in the USA which enabled a tax office in London to gain access via computer to a tax return normally handled in one of the provincial districts. If this facility were available then the taxpayer would have to make only a local call to make an enquiry. Otherwise, it would be essential for taxpayers to be able to make telephone enquiries either free or for the cost of a local call. It has always been in the tradition of the Inland Revenue to have tax advice readily available locally to the taxpayer—hence the decentralisation of its offices—and the

[7] There are 31 such offices in London (because such PAYE work has been moved to the London Provincial Offices), and 30 in Scotland (where all PAYE files are at East Kilbride). There are also two offices in Manchester and one each in Reading, Redhill, Slough, Watford and Woking.

[8] As cited in Chapter III the US Internal Revenue Service in 1975 received approximately 29 million telephone calls, 11 million visits in person, and 190,000 written enquiries—*Annual Report 1975* Commissioner of Inland Revenue, *op. cit.*, pages 6 and 13. See also Chapter II, Table II–6.

continuation and improvement of this tradition would be essential with self-assessment. Since telephone enquiries may not be useful in complex cases, the Inland Revenue should have the right to request that the enquiry be made in writing.

There are those who would argue against such an arrangement on the grounds of its cost. We leave aside the question of whether or not current charges for long-distance calls in the UK are in any way a true measure of their economic costs, and content ourselves with observing that it is not sufficient simply to say that such a facility would 'cost a lot'. The appropriate measure is to compare the cost of free (or cheap) long-distance telephone enquiry services with the cost of other methods of helping the taxpayer, such as the cost of writing a letter (i.e. the cost both to the taxpayer and to the administration); or the cost incurred by the Inland Revenue (and hence by society) if the return is completed wrongly for lack of advice and has to be corrected; or the arbitrary income transfer that results if the return is incorrectly completed, but the error is not discovered.

If local offices were able to obtain easily by computer the taxpayer's return from whichever office normally handled it, enquiries, not only by telephone, but also in person would be greatly facilitated. Such an arrangement would be ideal. As a second-best it would be necessary for local offices to be empowered to telephone whichever tax office had the return in order to discover its details. This is predicated on the fact that the return would be computer-accessible which, for reasons to be discussed below, is essential to the operation of a self-assessment system. If current experience were to carry over to self-assessment some 50 per cent of enquiries would necessitate access to the taxpayer's return.

As we have suggested (Chapter II Table II–6) the Inland Revenue already has to deal with a large number of enquiries, and almost certainly more enquiries per taxpayer than in the USA. Thus while each request for information and assistance might be more complex under self-assessment it is not obvious that there will be a dramatic increase in their sheer volume.

Whether enquiries are made in person or by telephone it is crucial that answers be forthcoming rapidly. One reason for this stands out above all others: for a self-assessment system to work there have to be rigidly enforced deadlines for the filing of returns and the remittance of tax due. Such matters cannot wait until the Inland Revenue has the time to deal with them (as at present), and hence enquiries have to be dealt with quickly, otherwise, the taxpayer would be able to claim (with justification) that his return would have arrived punctually had his queries been dealt with promptly.

As well as the roles already mentioned, self-assessment imposes two additional duties on the tax administration. First, efficiency can be increased by publicity/propaganda campaigns around filing time to remind taxpayers of relevant information and to warn of the consequences of evasion. To this end television programmes, newspaper articles, and possibly cartoons and films are helpful. Second, if the taxpayer is to assess himself it is useful (though not essential) for him to be able to find out in advance from the tax authorities how they propose to treat a particular transaction for tax purposes.[9] Such facilities exist in the USA, Canada, and Sweden, where they work well. The resources that would be required are likely to be small since this is not a service patronised by large numbers of taxpayers.

Entirely separate from Inland Revenue assistance, but still within the domain of the public sector is the role in tax affairs of state education. In the USA many schools now include simple tax affairs in their curriculum. Teaching in this area has proved highly successful (including stories of teenage children helping their parents to complete the family tax return). The scope for similar education of future taxpayers in the UK should not be overlooked.

ASSISTANCE WITHIN THE PRIVATE SECTOR

Under present arrangements tax help in the private sector is usually given by fully qualified accountants to those with more complicated tax affairs (mainly Schedule D income and capital gains). Under a system of self-assessment one would not expect this sector to change a great deal—complications under the present system will, by and large, remain complications under self-assessment. But with self-assessment an altogether different sort of tax help is likely to spring up for those with relatively simple tax affairs.

Turning first to a discussion of low cost tax help for those with relatively simple returns, foreign experience suggests that such an operation is both necessary and in the main beneficial. In North America it was repeatedly stressed in interviews that if the low cost tax preparers were suddenly to disappear the entire system would seize up. While this might be a slightly exaggerated view it is clear that no serious problems arise out of the operations of companies such as H & R Block, and the fears expressed in this country about the dangers of 'unqualified tax help', if not groundless, are at least overstated.

In any case, low cost tax help is inevitable if self-assessment is introduced, so that the real issue is not whether such an operation is good or bad, but of what controls, if any, might be necessary. It is possible to make out a case for licensing tax preparers, on the grounds that effective control weeds out sloppy and unskilled work, and so enhances the efficiency with which the tax system operates and reduces the resources that need to be devoted to tax administration.

Like all discussions of quality control, however, the issue is less one of desirability than of effectiveness. One of the reasons why there is no licensing

[9] These facilities are useful not only for resolving potential controversy in advance, but also for informing the tax authorities about what taxpayers are up to and hence giving early warning of any loopholes that need to be plugged. See *Annual Report 1975*, Commissioner of Internal Revenue, *op. cit.*, page 36. This service is not given in the USA for schemes that are pure tax avoidance devices.

in the USA and Canada is that no one can devise a workable system.[10] It would not be impossible for the Inland Revenue to lay down minimum standards for tax preparers, but it is asking a lot of them to administer tests or examinations to hundreds of would-be tax preparers each year. Possibly this task could be left to the accountancy profession, but it is still highly questionable whether it is worthwhile to devote resources to such a task. There is then a question of whether such an examination would have to be taken annually to take account of changes in the law. But if so, why should only tax preparers be subject to annual examination—why not also accountants, or at least those people who work in accountants' offices who have not yet qualified?

But even leaving aside such demarcation disputes there is still the problem of how to enforce such standards. London cannot enforce the hygiene laws against fly-by-night hotdog stands. How much more likely is it that with existing resources it would be impossible to police tax preparers adequately. And even if it were possible would it be worthwhile to devote resources to such an activity when it might be performed much better by the public voting with their feet, and simply avoiding those preparers with a bad reputation? A minimum safeguard would probably suffice; we suggest that it would be sufficient if those people who prepared someone else's return for money were obliged to enter their name and addresses on the return. Giving a false name or address could be made a criminal offence. Thus an inadequate preparer could be prosecuted under criminal law if he falsified his identity, and sued under civil law otherwise.

The changes in the sector of tax preparation currently dealt with by accountants are likely to be much smaller, though self-assessment would cause short-term difficulties for them in a number of ways. Accountants would have to get used to a single filing date, and various other aspects of the new system would have to be learned and accommodated. But such evidence as exists indicates that the frequent changes in tax administration in Britain have been dealt with relatively easily—for instance no real problems arose over the integration of surtax into the unified tax structure.

We interviewed a number of accountants, who considered that long-run aspects of self-assessment such as payments of estimated tax on a current basis would not cause much additional work provided that estimated payments were simply based on the preceding year's actual payments, with the right to reduce payments should income fall. However it is difficult to make accurate predictions of the effects of introducing a new system without a detailed knowledge of what the system would be; so such conclusions must be regarded as somewhat speculative.

It was felt that the calculation of final tax liability at the end of the tax year would undoubtedly involve accountants in more work, since these calculations would have to be more accurate than the estimates of tax liability which

[10] However, the Japanese tax administration sets examinations for unqualified tax practitioners who may operate only if they pass the examinations.

accountants normally furnish to their clients under the current system. Additionally, all returns would have to be ready by a single filing deadline.

As an offset, however, accountants would probably save work because self-assessment would involve them with fewer communications with the Inland Revenue. Under self-assessment the Inland Revenue would accept most returns after an arithmetical check only and so correspondence would arise in the main only for incorrect returns and for those returns selected for further investigation. This would contrast with present practice under which a considerable number of returns are queried.

It thus seems unlikely that the amount of work per return would increase substantially for accountants. There remains, though, the question of how many additional taxpayers would use the services of an accountant. There are various reasons for thinking that the number is likely to be small. First, the costs of staff are such that although there is a price at which accountants can profitably provide a tax preparation service for individuals, that price is high and not likely to attract a large number of new clients. Second, if self-assessment really does make it reasonably easy for taxpayers to complete their own return—particularly if the return itself and related literature are laid out clearly—then some people who currently employ an accountant may find that they have no need to do so under self-assessment. Casual evidence from North America lends support to the view that self-assessment does not dramatically increase the demand for accountants.

Whether tax assistance comes from accountants or from unqualified tax preparers it is essential to make explicit the responsibilities of tax advisers. For instance, should tax advisers be liable to prosecution if the return contains incorrect information? We suggest that the taxpayer should be solely responsible for the factual basis of the return and his adviser should be liable for prosecution only if he knowingly participates in fraudulent activities. Accountants would thus not be expected to audit the taxpayer's affairs and would be able to enter on the return a disclaimer such as: 'Prepared on the basis of information supplied by J. Doe'.

Simplification of the Tax Structure

ALLOWANCES AND DEDUCTIONS

The preceding discussion was concerned with changes that are an essential accompaniment of self-assessment. Simplification of the entire structure of income tax may not prevail in the long run (as US experience shows), but if of very great importance at the time the new system is introduced. Since simplification would be of far more assistance to, say, wage-earners whose only income is from one job than to those whose affairs are already complicated, simplification would be most useful at the time that self-assessment was extended to taxpayers currently covered by PAYE.

The whole issue of simplicity should be thought of in the context of equity and resource costs. In general, increased equity requires increased complexity, which in turn means that the tax system costs more to administer. There is thus a trade-off between equity and cost, and the optimal degree of simplicity should, at least in principle, reflect society's view on the costs it is prepared to pay for a given degree of equity.

At a more practical level the tax-credit proposals[11] offered a useful blueprint for the sort of simplification that is feasible for personal allowances and deductions. From the point of view of self-assessment there were two main simplifications: first, the tax relief granted in respect of children was not age related, and, second, a standard deduction of £30, which could be claimed by anyone regardless of actual expenditure, was included in the tax structure. At the time of writing it is planned to phase in the first of these in the late 1970s in the guise of child benefits. The second is rather more complicated. Under present arrangements deductions for the expenses of employment (e.g. uniforms, tools, etc.) are negotiated on a plant-by-plant basis, so that no-one receives more than his entitlement. If a standard deduction is given and is equal to the average of deductions currently granted it will be very small and will simplify very little since many people will have to claim expenses in excess of the standard amount. If a large sum is chosen the standard deduction becomes a rather expensive method of simplification. It might be useful to consider an earnings-related standard deduction of the sort used in Canada, where taxpayers may claim an employment expense deduction of 3 per cent of employment income up to a maximum deduction of $150.

A further simplification embodied in the tax-credit scheme was that mortgage interest payments and life assurance premia were to be paid net of tax by the taxpayer, with building societies and insurance companies receiving the remainder directly from the Inland Revenue. It was announced in the Budget of April 1976 that from 1979 life assurance premia would be paid net of tax. While such an arrangement was essential to the operation of the tax-credit system, which was designed to require few end-year adjustments despite non-cumulative withholding, these characteristics are much less crucial to a system of self-assessment under which end-year adjustments would normally arise for other reasons. In fact, the taxpayer will have to go through the necessary calculations on his tax return anyway, so that the issue of whether or not he pays mortgage interest and life assurance premia net or gross of tax is much less important than the formula under which such items are deductible.

Other simplifications of allowances, which were not included in the tax-credit proposals, concern the various allowances for the blind, the old, dependant relatives, etc. Clearly, these could be simplified in any of a large number of ways and the more extensive the simplification the greater the assistance to Schedule E taxpayers. Since most forms of simplification are compatible with self-assessment we make no specific proposals about these secondary personal allowances.

[11] *Proposals for a Tax-Credit System, op. cit.* See also Chapter V, p. 179 for further discussion.

THE STRUCTURE OF TAX RATES

Under present arrangements end-year adjustments are kept to a minimum both because of cumulative withholding and because of the long basic rate band. The tax-credit proposals were designed to keep end-year adjustments at a minimum despite non-cumulative withholding, but this was only achieved by having a constant rate of tax on all income from £0 to £5,000. The long basic rate band is the *sine qua non* for the avoidance of end-year adjustments. Once this constraint is relaxed (as it would be with self-assessment) the administrative need for a long basic rate band is far less.

With self-assessment it would, for instance, be possible to have a scheme along the lines of the tax-credit proposals, but with steadily rising marginal tax rates. Whether such a development is essential to notions of progressivity is debatable—but nevertheless one of the main ostensible reasons why the tax-credit proposals foundered was because they were not able to incorporate a reduced marginal rate of tax for those with low incomes.[12]

With or without tax-credits self-assessment would enable the Inland Revenue to give up their long struggle against erosion of the top end of the basic rate band, whose real value in 1976 is a little over half its value in 1948, despite the fact that real income has doubled over the period.[13,14]

Indexing of the personal allowances and rate bands, though possible under present arrangements, would be easier with self-assessment, if only because there would be no need for the Inland Revenue to recalculate many code numbers hastily after each budget. In Canada the nominal value of the personal allowances is increased each year and the relevant figure is included as part of the tax return. Similarly the tax tables are recalculated annually and included with the return. The whole process requires very little extra effort by either the taxpayer or the tax administration. While observing that this is perfectly possible under self-assessment we are not concerned here to comment about its desirability.

For the same reason self-assessment makes easier the administration of the sort of local income tax advocated by the Layfield Committee.[15] The present system is designed to ensure that most people are accurately withheld during the year, thus avoiding end-year adjustments. The Layfield proposals therefore

---

[12] See the evidence by Kaldor in *Select Committee on Tax Credit, Vol. II,* pp. 211–232, and counter-arguments in Barr and Roper: 'Tax Credits: An Optimistic Appraisal', *Three Banks Review,* No. 101, March 1974.

[13] The size of the standard/basic rate band for a family of four was £1,625 in 1948 and £5,000 from April 1976. Over the same period retail prices rose from 42 to 200 (1970=100). The value in 1976 terms of the 1948 figure is thus approximately £8,000.

[14] We have already made the point (Chapter V, p. 180) that charging lower marginal rates on lower levels of income would require higher rates elsewhere to obtain the same revenue yield. With the average burden of taxation at its present level there are those who argue that this is not possible. We are simply making the administrative point that self-assessment, unlike the present system, is compatible with any structure of rising marginal tax rates.

[15] *Report of the Committee of Enquiry into Local Government Finance, op. cit.*

had to advocate the inclusion of the employee's area of residence in his code number so that local as well as national income tax could be withheld accurately. This would not be necessary under self-assessment, since the employer would simply calculate how much income tax to withhold and then add (say) 5 per cent to cover approximately the employee's liability for local income tax. Any discrepancy of tax due would be dealt with by an end-year adjustment which would in most cases be necessary anyway for other reasons.

This is a point of some weight given the Inland Revenue's estimate that the local income tax proposed by the Layfield Committee would cost some £100 million to administer and would require some 12,000 additional Inland Revenue staff.[16] Under a system of self-assessment a local income tax would require many fewer additional staff since a local income tax (like provincial income tax in Canada) would necessitate only the use of different withholding tables and the addition of one or two lines to the tax return. Under the present system local income tax would require about 12,000 extra Revenue staff, under self-assessment only an extra 1,000 at the most. Thus if a local income tax were introduced self-assessment would save some 11,000 Revenue staff on that account alone, quite apart from savings in other areas. The cost-saving argument for self-assessment is thus vastly strengthened by the potential introduction of a local income tax.

A final issue is the relative treatment of single people and married couples Self-assessment is compatible with any treatment of married couples from complete aggregation (as used to exist in the UK), to a completely separate treatment of husband and wife (as is virtually the case in Canada), or income splitting, as exists in the USA. It is noteworthy that in 1969 the USA changed the tax treatment of married couples without changing their system of self-assessment. This demonstrates the point that decisions on this question of equity can be made independently of the method of administering income tax.

2 Enforcement

Checking

It is useful to distinguish the activity of checking from that of verification. Checking is concerned simply with the completeness and internal consistency of a return, and so ensures that all the necessary parts have been completed and that the arithmetic is correct. For instance, if the taxpayer states that he has three children a check will be made to ensure that he has claimed the allowance appropriate for three children. In contrast, verification concerns itself with the accuracy of the information on which the return is based—for instance, whether the taxpayer really has three children. Thus checking may reveal that the taxpayer owes extra tax, but is unlikely to reveal evasion.

With self-assessment it is necessary to check all returns—all the more so with a newly introduced system. As a matter of historical record, although the

[16] *Ibid.*, Chapter 11, paragraph 25, page 198.

USA and Canada today have a 100 per cent check they did not do so when self-assessment first became a mass phenomenon in the early 1940s. Such a job was beyond the manpower of the tax administration before computers did the bulk of the work. But it is wrong to conclude that because the USA and Canada managed with less than 100 per cent checking it would be possible for the UK to do so—what happened in North America occurred many years ago when the structure of their income tax was much simpler than ours today. And even then there was evidence that many mistakes went unnoticed. It would therefore be necessary to check all tax returns, whether simple Schedule E cases or more complicated cases of self-employment—and both the main return and all supplementary attachments.

The first step in any checking procedure would be to check manually that all necessary documentation was complete, e.g. that (in contrast to the present) the employee's P60 was included, along with any supplementary attachment and a cheque if any additional tax was due. At this stage the return would be checked also for completeness, e.g. the signature of the taxpayer, the names of all dependants, etc.

If complete, the next stage would be to feed the return into the computer, including the details contained on any supplementary attachments. As was mentioned in Chapter III in the discussion of tax administration in North America this process is one of the most labour-intensive of the entire operation. Once fed into the computer the return would automatically be checked for the accuracy of its arithmetic and internal consistency (e.g. if the item for business profits on the main return was not zero the computer would automaticaly look for and check the data from the supplementary attachment dealing with business income). The role of computers in this operation is discussed further below.

If the computer found no errors in the return an interim settlement would take place, in which the Inland Revenue accepted payment of additional tax enclosed with the return, or issued a refund if one was claimed. Such a settlement would end matters for most taxpayers, but would in no way prejudice the Inland Revenue's right to conduct further checks on and verification of the taxpayer at a later date.

Such a procedure is likely to result in manpower savings not only because the system is automated, but also because checking (as defined above) would apply to all returns but verification to only a small percentage. This is in contrast to the present British system under which almost all returns are subject to at least some verification activity.

Before turning to a discussion of verification it is necessary to mention one change from current procedure. If computers are used it is essential that each taxpayer must have a unique identification. While there are various ways of doing this, the easiest and most widespread method in other countries is the use of the taxpayer's social security number. This means that it is necessary for all income recipients, whether working or not, to have one (and only one) social security number; thus some people currently without (e.g. a widow receiving investment income but without an earnings record would have to be issued with one. It would need to be emphasised to people that the possession of such a number in itself gave no entitlement to national insurance benefits, but would in such cases be used only for identification purposes. Publicity would be necessary also to make people aware of the fact that they would need to know their social security numbers in order to file their tax returns.

This, broadly, is the system in operation in both the USA and Canada. Although there have been occasional prosecutions for tax fraud which revealed, for instance, that a taxpayer had 12 social security numbers the system works well in the vast bulk of cases, and there is no obvious reason why an appropriately modified version would not work in the UK.[17,18]

Verification

Checking is concerned only with the completeness of the return and the accuracy of its arithmetic, and accepts the truthfulness of the basic information. Verification accepts the accuracy of the arithmetic and concerns itself with the accuracy of the facts supplied by the taxpayer. Unlike checking, verification is not applied to everyone, nor is everyone who receives some sort of audit subject to the same procedure. It is necessary to have at least two types of verification procedure (henceforth called 'audits'), one for simple cases (basically those currently dealt with by PAYE, plus simple Schedule D cases), and one for more complicated returns.

The simple audit would normally be a routine affair whose sole function was to verify information supplied by the taxpayer in his return. Items covered would be those documents which today have almost automatically to be submitted to the Inspector of Taxes, such as details of marriage and children, and details of mortgage interest payments. In addition the taxpayer might be asked to give details of bank deposit interest or information about a dependant. In the main such investigations would simply require the taxpayer to produce documents for inspection by the Inland Revenue. If documentation could not be produced the taxpayer would be assessed for additional tax, plus any penalties (discussed below). It would be rare for any investigative work to be done in such cases.

More thorough audits would be reserved for complicated cases such as partnerships. In such cases the Inland Revenue would need the power to examine company books and bank records, and would frequently conduct a considerable amount of investigative work. This immediately raises the more general question of the appropriate powers of the tax authorities and the

[17] At East Kilbride taxpayers are filed by their National Insurance number, which is, in any case, already shown on all P60s. More generally links between the Inland Revenue and the Department of Health and Social Security are increasing albeit slowly—e.g. Class 4 National Insurance contributions are currently collected as part of the taxpayer's Schedule D assessment.

[18] One of the authors mistakenly applied for a second social security number in the USA and was automatically re-issued with his old one!

circumstances in which they would be permitted to examine taxpayer records.[19] This in turn raises more detailed questions about the circumstances in which Court authority would be needed and when administrative power would suffice. Issues are also raised of powers of seizure over both financial assets such as bank accounts and over fixed assets, and of the relative treatment of the taxpayer's home and his place of work. These points are discussed further below.

We do not propose to lay out a detailed blueprint of what powers the Inland Revenue should have. But in our opinion any discussion should start from the proposition that tax returns are an area to which notions of gentlemanly conduct frequently do not apply. Evidence of this is seen abroad in the number of otherwise impeccably respectable people (judges, ministers, lawyers) who end up in prison for tax fraud. Some people will comply willingly with tax law—but many others will do so only out of fear of the consequences of doing otherwise. It is imperative under a system of self-assessment for the Inland Revenue to have (and to use) powers sufficient to act as a deterrent.[20]

Two further points are the size of the sample to be audited and the method of its selection. Clearly, simple PAYE cases should be sampled less intensively than more complicated cases, not only because the latter are more likely to contain errors, but also because they offer more opportunity for evasion. The simple case of income from employment only is typically overwithheld under a non-cumulative system, so there is virtually no opportunity for evasion. The size of the sample to be subjected to the various types of verification activity would have to depend both on the depth of the audit and on the manpower which the Inland Revenue was able to devote to such activities. In North America the overall sample is of the order of 2–5 per cent of total returns, disproportionately concentrated on the more complex returns and those involving higher incomes (see Chapter III). In the early days of self-assessment the minimum sample should be closer to 5 per cent than to 2 per cent, possibly falling slightly as experience is gained of the new régime.

There are two broad ways of selecting returns for audit. In the USA the selection is almost entirely computerised, as outlined in Chapter III. In Canada the computer merely sorts out the returns into broad audit classes (e.g. by business and non-business income and by income level) and selection is then done manually within each audit class. Sampling rates differ drastically between audit classes. At least initially, it would be much easier to select returns for audit using the Canadian method, leaving open the possibility of switching to more sophisticated methods of selection at a later date. Thus once the returns had been checked by the computer they could be divided

---

[19] This question was recently under discussion in the context of the extension of Inland Revenue powers proposed in the April 1976 Finance Bill.

[20] 'Professor Oldman seriously questioned the results of what is known as voluntary compliance as a decisive element of tax collection. He instead tended to highlight the psychological pressure originating in enforced action.' *CIAT Newsletter: Inter-American Center of Tax Administrators,* Vol. 8, No. 9, May 1976, page 4.

into (say) three classes: (a) those currently dealt with entirely by PAYE, (b) those currently receiving an annual assessment of some sort, and (c) those with capital gains, each class split up by income level. If the income groups are below £5,000, £5,000 to £10,000, and over £10,000 there will be nine audit classes, and the sampling rates will be highest for those with high incomes and/or with Schedule D type income or capital gains.

Other Issues in Enforcement

PENALTIES

In order of their application the Inland Revenue require three strategic types of power:

(a) power such as subpoena and summons to obtain taxpayer records. Such powers are needed for the verification activities discussed above,

(b) power to enforce interest and other penalties for late filing and non-filing of returns and late payment of tax due (discussed in this section), and

(c) power to obtain taxpayer assets, if a taxpayer refuses to comply with an assessment (discussed in the next section).

Clearly the Inland Revenue requires the power to impose fines of various sorts both to encourage compliance with the tax system and to punish those who do not comply. Penalties are required for at least three different orders of offence:

(i) Simple cases of returns being late, or tax being late, because the return contained an error. An interest penalty some 2 per cent in excess of the rate of inflation[21] should suffice for this purpose.

(ii) Relatively minor cases of evasion, such as overstating expenses or claiming a non-existent dependant relative. For this purpose an interest penalty of some 25 per cent of unpaid tax, with possibly a floor of £50 would probably suffice.

(iii) More serious cases of evasion where evidence is not sufficient for a criminal conviction, or where a criminal conviction has failed. In this case an interest penalty of 100 per cent of unpaid tax, with a minimum of, say, £500 might be an appropriate order of magnitude.

In addition to these there would also be criminal penalties where convictions were obtained. Ideally, all these penalties (other than criminal ones) should be imposed automatically. Such a procedure has various advantages. First of all, it removes the Inspector of Taxes from odium, since he has little control over the penalty; second, such penalties can be issued automatically by computer, saving the time of skilled manpower for more difficult tasks; and third, the taxpayer will know much more clearly the penalties he will face if caught evading. There should be no discretion in the imposition of penalties at the *assessment* stage. Flexibility should exist, but the correct place for this

[21] As measured, for instance, by the percentage change in the General Index of Retail Prices in the year ending shortly before the start of the tax year in which tax was underpaid.

is at the enforcement stage, discussed below.

Finally, the penalties have to be high enough to be a deterrent. This is particularly true of the interest penalty applied to simple late payment. If this is allowed to lag behind the rate of inflation it will pay people deliberately to pay late since it will be cheaper to borrow from the government than from commercial sources.

DIRECT ENFORCEMENT

It is one thing to issue an assessment for additional tax together with penalties and quite another actually to collect the outstanding amount. It is for this purpose that the Inland Revenue requires powers over taxpayer assets. The process of collecting additional tax revenue should start with the issue of a series of demand notices. The number of notices sent, and their timing, should depend (a) on the type of case and (b) on the amount outstanding. In the USA it is customary to issue four notices at weekly intervals for underpayments of personal income tax before any additional action is taken. In the vast majority of cases payment is forthcoming in response to such written demands, so that additional powers are required relatively infrequently.

If such demands are not met it is necessary to consider both Inland Revenue policy and its enforcement powers. Policy concerns the flexibility, if any, to be granted over enforcement. This raises questions of what tolerances will exist (i.e. how small assessed amounts have to be if enforcement action is not to be taken), and of the treatment of people who have genuine difficulties in paying immediately. These are both matters primarily for the Inland Revenue itself to decide.

As a background to enforcement powers the Inland Revenue should have certain powers also to try to prevent the under-payment of tax in the first place or the continuation of under-payment once it has started. Thus for those who are in arrears with their payments the tax authorities should retain their current power to fix the taxpayer's code. Thus taxpayers would normally code themselves, but this could be over-ridden for those in arrears with tax payments. In such circumstances it would be illegal for the taxpayer to use any code except that supplied by the authorities. Similarly, the Inland Revenue may need powers to require people to settle their tax affairs before leaving the country—though with over-withholding, self-assessment would not need to differ substantially from the present system.

There are four broad types of power over taxpayer assets that the Inland Revenue could have:

(a) the power (with or without court sanction) to issue earnings attachment orders,[22]

---

[22] Since these powers are rather weak in the UK new legislation would be required Failing that, reliance would have to be placed on the Inland Revenue's power to over-ride the code supplied by the taxpayer.

(b) the power (with or without Court permission) to seize financial assets of the taxpayer such as money in bank accounts,

(c) the power to prevent the sale of real assets before tax liabilities have been paid, and

(d) the power to seize real property.

The last two powers would, presumably, not be available to the Inland Revenue without Court permission.

Again we offer no view as to the powers the Inland Revenue would require. It is not obvious that greater powers would be required than at present since there is no reason why people would be less likely to pay self-assessed liability than liability established by the Inland Revenue. Self-assessment crucially requires powers to obtain taxpayer records, as discussed earlier—but quite possibly enforcement powers would not need to be substantially greater than those presently operating.

APPEALS

The present system of appeals (described in Chapter II) is not likely to require any substantial change. The only major reform currently under discussion is the introduction of legal aid for tax cases. This can be justified on the grounds that the taxpayer is usually at a disadvantage *vis-à-vis* the Revenue since he stands to gain only the tax in dispute in his own case, while the tax authorities stand to gain the disputed tax from all taxpayers similarly placed.

3 Administrative Implications

Computerisation

We start from the standpoint that a high degree of computerisation is essential to self-assessment, both for routine tasks (printing labels, pre-addressing returns, sending out assessments and demand notices) and for checking completely the arithmetical and internal consistency of all returns and supplementary attachments along the lines discussed above.

There are two broad ways of tackling such a problem. To discuss these it is necessary briefly to recapitulate some of the technical discussion of Chapter III. The simplest and most reliable way of storing returns in the computer and for recalling them later is through magnetic tape and microfilm. If a particular return is needed then, analogous to searching for a particular piece of music on a domestic tape recorder, the tape is searched until the right return has been found. This, broadly, is the system used in the USA and Canada, and works best when the structure of tax administration is centralised. The USA has only ten computer centres for the whole country, with one central installation to co-ordinate their activities; Canada now has two data centres for processing returns, but only a single computer installation. If the UK were to use such a system then local tax offices would require time to obtain access to returns because the correct tape would have to be located and linked to the computers;

in addition the local offices would only be able to read the return, and not to enter additional information on the taxpayer's file. It would therefore not be possible to correct errors via the computer as is possible with IDRS in the USA (see Chapter III).

A second, and much more sophisticated way of handling the problems of storage and retrieval is via the use of random access devices such as disc storage. As suggested in Chapter III, the analogy here is with a juke box—once the taxpayer's social security number is entered his return can be located within seconds. Such an 'on line' system is much faster at retrieving returns than the system using magnetic tape and/or microfilm, and since it enables local offices not only to read the return, but also to enter information it is much more suitable to a decentralised organisation. With such a system returns could be entered into the computer in local offices; the return would then be processed by a computer anywhere in the country, and could then be read and any necessary corrections made by any local tax office.

The Inland Revenue's first approach to computerisation was with the Centre 1 installation at East Kilbride, discussed in Chapter III. The original idea, since abandoned, was to have nine such centres covering the entire country. The philosophy of this scheme was very much that of the more centralised approach discussed above. The difficulties with Centre 1 have been in part the result of trying to operate a computer system side by side with the old manual system, thus forcing the computer system more or less to mimic the manual procedure. Clearly this is far from satisfactory, since were one to design from scratch a system of tax administration by computer it would be very different from one designed to be operated manually. Such problems would presumably not arise if self-assessment were fully computerised from the first, and *a fortiori* if computerisation were introduced before any decision on self-assessment was taken.

But difficulties arise also out of centralisation itself. The disadvantages of large centres have included in practice difficulties in recruiting and keeping a large staff, and vulnerability to industrial disputes. Small local districts are thought to be more convenient for taxpayers, to involve fewer unpopular staff transfers, and to be more compatible with the Inland Revenue's tradition of the independence of Inspectors. For these reasons, as we saw in Chapter II, a pilot study is currently being undertaken by the Inland Revenue along the lines of the second broad approach to computerisation—namely an on-line system based on the present pattern of local districts. Such a system, based on decentralised offices with centralised computers is being tested and would deal automatically not only with all PAYE work, but also with the assessment and collection of tax assessed under Schedule D, Capital Gains Tax and Corporation Tax.

While timetables for ambitious schemes of this sort have to be regarded as only approximate, the Inland Revenue anticipated in 1976 that a fully automatic on-line data processing system would be in operation by the mid-1980s.

To this extent the computerisation necessary for self-assessment is already being put in train.

The blueprints for any such scheme are highly complex and technical and considerably beyond the bounds of this study, not to mention the capacity of the authors. But two general comments are worth making. First of all, for obvious reasons, it is imperative that a computer system once installed should never break down. Both in the USA and Canada there is justifiable pride that while there have been short-run panics within the ranks of the tax administration the computer system as a whole has never broken down. The primary aim of the system should be simply to do the job. The sophistication of the system should be very much a secondary consideration—it is generally much easier to instal and run in a system that is fairly simple and reliable and then to improve it later. At all costs the Inland Revenue should avoid the temptation of the best becoming the enemy of the good. Rather than developing the 'most highly developed computer system in the world' it would be much wiser to take over tried and tested techniques that work well elsewhere, even if that means using US equipment.

A second strategic comment is that computers have their own strengths and weaknesses and these are different from those of people. While this point is so obvious as to be trite it can easily be overlooked in the design of computer systems; these should be constructed from scratch taking explicit account of the characteristics of the computer

The Peak Load Problem

One could avoid a large peak in Inland Revenue activity around filing time if people had different tax years. This could be done either by having staggered filing on an alphabetical or social security number basis, or by using the taxpayer's birthday as a filing date, or simply by allowing people, like companies, to choose their tax year.

There are obvious practical difficulties with all of these methods of staggered filing, but additionally there are more serious problems. First of all, there is that of inequity between early and late filers, though this is minimised if withholding is extensive so that late filers do not in fact pay tax later, but merely file a return later. A second difficulty arises if the nominal value of personal allowances changes from year to year to take account of inflation. If the single person's tax-free allowance is £700 for one April–April tax year and £800 for the next, then a taxpayer with a tax year starting in October will have to prorate to obtain a tax-free allowance of £750. This complicates the system both for the taxpayer and the tax administration, and makes it impossible to enter on the tax return the nominal amount of the various allowances.

A more general loss with staggered filing is the possibility of conducting an intensive publicity campaign around filing time, and generally enforcement becomes more difficult if there is no longer one universal deadline for filing to which everyone has to adhere. For these sorts of reasons staggered filing, though seriously considered, has been rejected in North America. While one should not minimise the problem of a peak load of activity it would appear that the problems associated with it are less serious than those associated with staggered filing. It is worth mentioning that the peak applies strictly only to the checking and taxpayer assistance activities of the Inland Revenue—verification would be a more leisurely year-round activity.

The intensity of the peak is obviously related to the speed with which returns are processed and end-year adjustments completed. In the USA and Canada most additional tax payments have been made within four months and most refunds within six months of the end of the tax year, whereas in Sweden the same cycle takes 18 months. Self-assessment is thus compatible with both a long and a short cycle after the end of the year, and so the following proposals are rather tentative.

We suggest that following the end of the tax year on 5 April (or, possibly, 1 April), the latest date for filing should be 1 July. This is a slightly shorter time than is allowed in the USA and Canada but has the advantage that 1 July is a day on which payments of estimated tax would be made and hence one that would readily be fixed in the mind of the taxpayer.

Administrative convenience demands that no interest be paid to the taxpayer on a refund of overpaid tax if the refund is issued promptly. But equity requires that the Inland Revenue should pay interest if a refund on a return which is filed on time is delayed by more than some specified length of time (say two months) from the latest date for filing. Such a deadline is less onerous on the authorities than it sounds since foreign experience suggests that most returns on which refunds are due are filed well before the latest filing date. In practice, therefore, the Inland Revenue would normally have considerably longer than two months in which to issue refunds.

To make filing by early July possible it would be necessary to require all information returns such as P60s to be issued by 1 May (or at the latest by 14 May). This would involve the issuing of information returns not only by employers as currently, but also by all payers of interest and dividends and all payers of miscellaneous incomes such as fees. Whilst this would involve a substantial change from current practice for income payers other than employers this sort of system works well in the USA and Canada.

If a deadline of 14 May or earlier were either impossible or unenforceable it might be necessary to delay by one month both the latest filing date and the date on which refunds attract interest. The timing of end-year adjustments is clearly a matter for the mutual convenience of taxpayers, employers, and the Inland Revenue—but it would certainly enhance the acceptability of the scheme if refunds on returns filed sufficiently early could be issued in time for the summer holidays. As already mentioned, the fact that taxpayers received a tax refund in July 1976 was regarded as one of the main selling points of the incomes policy of which it was a part.

A separate question is whether or not the Inland Revenue would continue to issue assessments. In Canada returns are processed by computer and an assessment automatically generated for each return that is arithmetically correct. Thus a taxpayer who correctly submits with his return a cheque for his net tax liability will be issued with an assessment for $0. In the USA, by contrast, no assessments are issued. Since self-assessment is compatible with either method we make no recommendation on this point.

Finally, once the rush of end-year adjustments is over the authorities could start auditing activities, which would then proceed throughout the year.

The peak that results from these end-year arrangements has several implications for Inland Revenue staffing. First of all, some permanent Inland Revenue staff will have to move from their 'regular' job to a 'filing period' job around filing time. For instance, a Tax Inspector who dealt with verification activities out of the peak period could move into supervision of checking or into taxpayer assistance for three months or so of the year. Second, there would, of course, be a need for part-time staff for three to four months of the year. These would be used especially for key-punching, but also for other routine checking operations such as ensuring that all necessary documentation had been submitted, opening letters, etc. This would merely be an extension of current practice since the Inland Revenue already employs over 5,000 part-time staff.[23]

[23] In the year ending March 1975 the Inland Revenue employed casual staff equivalent to 5,128 full-time staff. See *Report of the Commissioners of Her Majesty's Inland Revenue*, year ended 31 March 1975, *op. cit.*, p. 29.

APPENDIX VI–1

Tentative Design of a New Tax Return (Form SA1)

In presenting a draft return appropriate to a system of self-assessment it is in no way intended to exhaust the possibilities but merely to provide a very tentative suggestion illustrating some of the points involved. We are extremely grateful to J. Walter Thompson & Co. for their assistance in designing the return Form SA1 (Fig. V1–1.1).[1]

The main principle is that taxpayers with straight-forward financial circumstances, e.g. wage and salary earners with perhaps a little investment income and no complicated deductions, could be catered for by a simple return along the lines of Form SA1. Taxpayers with more complicated finances would be required to provide a fuller account on appropriate forms (S1, S2 etc.) which would be attached as supplements to the main return. If, for instance, an individual had dividend or interest income exceeding some minimum amount, he would be obliged to list the details on the appropriate supplementary form and enter the total on lines 6 or 7 of Form SA1. In the case of trading and professional incomes the current practice in the United Kingdom is for accounts to be submitted in addition to the return. This could fit in conveniently with a system of self-assessment provided that the total income from such a source were entered on the main return. It might well be possible to design a simpler form than SA1 for use only by taxpayers with simple circumstances like the returns employed in the USA and Ireland (see Chapter III, Appendix III–2), but the return presented here is itself one that could be sent to all taxpayers together with the supplementary forms for use where necessary.

As suggested earlier the main return and additional forms should be sent in duplicate. The taxpayer would then have a spare in case he spoiled the first one, and more important, he would be able to keep a copy for future reference. The Inland Revenue currently check each return with a taxpayer's previous return and it seems quite reasonable to make it easy for the taxpayer to be able to do the same.

One feature of Form SA1 is that many of the allowances etc. have been removed from the main return. This has certain advantages such as taxpayers having less need to worry about questions of no relevance to their particular circumstances, but it may have a disadvantage in that some taxpayers might fail to claim all the allowances to which they are entitled. However, given that taxpayers have a financial interest in claiming in full, that taxpayers would normally have a copy of the allowances they claimed on their previous return and that it should prove possible to provide an effective tax return guide, the numbers put at a disadvantage are likely to be small. The main reason for the detailed questions on personal allowances to be found on the tax returns

[1] The particular tax district listed is one dealing with the affairs of people working in central London; there is no other significance in selecting this particular district.

Figure VI–1.1 Form SA1 (Front)

District

H.M. Inspector of Taxes
London Provincial 10 District
Tyne Bridge Tower,
GATESHEAD
Tyne and Wear, NE8 2DT

Date of issue ____________

In any inquiry please quote
000 / 000 000

TAX RETURN FORM SA1
Income tax year 1986-87

WHAT YOU HAVE TO DO.

FIRST:
Read Part A of the accompanying notes.

THEN:

1. Complete the return using Forms S1 to S6 if necessary.
2. Calculate your tax bill or refund.
3. Check your arithmetic.
4. Sign the declaration.
5. Send the return back to me by ____________

W.M. BLOGGS *H.M. Inspector of Taxes*

FULL NAME ____________

ADDRESS ____________

NATIONAL INSURANCE NUMBER

YOURS							
SPOUSE'S							

OCCUPATION
YOURS ____________

	SELF	WIFE
A. Total income (see line 9 overleaf).	**A.** £	£
B. Allowances and deductions (see line 19 overleaf).	**B.** £	£
C. Taxable income (subtract B from A).	**C.** £	£
D. Total tax due (use enclosed tax table).	**D.** £	£
E. **Tax withheld at source (line 23 overleaf).**	**E.** £	£
F. If *line D* is greater than E enter BALANCE DUE INLAND REVENUE.	**F.** £	£
OR		
G. IF *line E* is greater than D enter REFUND DUE TO YOU.	**G.** £	£

Declaration

False statements can result in prosecution.

To the best of my knowledge and belief the particulars given on this form are correct and complete.

SIGNATURE (*taxpayer*) ______________________

DATE ______________________

SIGNATURE (*tax preparer*) ______________________

DATE ______________________

Form SA1 (Back)

Income

Code Number

1. Wages, salaries, tips and other income from employment.
2. National Insurance pension.
2a. Other pension(s) (specify on Form S5).
3. Other benefits.
4. Trading and professional income (attach Form S1).
5. Interest from United Kingdom building societies.
6. Dividends, interest and annuities taxed before receipt.
7. Interest not taxed before receipt. (If either items 6 or 7 exceed £00 attach Form S2).
8. Any other income (give details on Form S6).
9. **TOTAL INCOME** (add lines 1 to 8).

PLEASE READ THE NOTES

SELF	WIFE
1. £	£
2. £	£
2a. £	£
3. £	£
4. £	£
5. £	£
6. £	£
7. £	£
8. £	£
9. £	£

Deductions

10. Expenses against earnings. (attach Form S3)
11. Interest paid. (attach Form S3)
12. Other deductions. (attach Form S3)
13. **TOTAL DEDUCTIONS** (add lines 10 to 12).

PLEASE READ THE NOTES

SELF	WIFE
10. £	£
11. £	£
12. £	£
13. £	£

Allowances

14. Self (claim £735).
15. Married allowance (if appropriate claim £350).
16. Wife's earned income allowance.
17. Dependent relative's allowance.
18. Other allowances (attach Form S4).
19. **TOTAL ALLOWANCES AND DEDUCTIONS** (add lines 13 to 18).

PLEASE READ THE NOTES

	SELF	WIFE
14.	£	£
15.	£	£
16.	£	£
17.	£	£
18.	£	£
19.	£	£

Tax withheld at source

20. Tax withheld from wages salaries and other employment income.
21. Tax withheld from building society interest.
22. Tax withheld from dividends and other investment income (attach forms P.60 and S5.
23. **TOTAL TAX ALREADY WITHHELD AT SOURCE**

PLEASE READ THE NOTES

	SELF	WIFE
20.	£	£
21.	£	£
22.	£	£
23.	£	£

currently used in the United Kingdom is that the Inland Revenue and not the taxpayer has the responsibility for calculating the reliefs. The need to provide so much detailed information would disappear if the calculations were performed by the taxpayer. Form SA1 takes into account the proposed reforms regarding children's allowances and life assurance relief.

A possible addition to the suggested return is an option for taxpayers to have any refunds due to them credited against future estimated tax liability. Such a feature appears on tax returns used in the USA and would require only a single additional line on the first page. Should National Insurance contributions become deductible against tax this could be catered for on the return with an extra line under the section dealing with deductions.

One or two other points may also be made. As the taxpayer may be entitled to a rebate, it would be necessary for him to provide evidence that tax had been withheld from his income. At present employers issue a P60 to each employee on the payroll at the end of the tax year. This form shows not only the pay and tax withheld by that employer, but, because PAYE is cumulative, also the pay and the tax withheld by any previous employer during the tax year. If cumulation were to be abolished it would be necessary, as we have seen, for employers to issue a P60 or equivalent for every person employed by them at any time during the tax year, and not just for those employed at the end of the year. Individuals would then be able to attach to their returns documentary evidence of tax withheld from their earnings. Similarly, vouchers specifying the amounts of tax withheld from other forms of income such as interest, dividends and pensions would also be attached to the return. In addition, with a system of self-assessment it would be necessary for the building societies to inform their investors of the gross value of their interest payments and the amount of tax deemed to have been withheld, as well as the net amount of interest.

Index

fn indicates footnote reference
g indicates glossary reference